George Michael

The Biography

1963 – 2016

Also by Rob Jovanovic:

Kate Bush: The Biography

Michael Stipe: The Biography

Big Star: Rock's Forgotten Band

Nirvana: The Complete Recording Sessions

Perfect Sound Forever: The Story of Pavement

Adventures in Hi-Fi: The Complete REM

Beck! On a Backwards River

George Michael

The Biography

1963 – 2016

Rob Jovanovic

piatkus

PIATKUS

First published in Great Britain in 2007 by Piatkus Books
This paperback edition published in 2017 by Piatkus Books

1 2 3 4 5 6 7 8 9 10

A CIP catalogue record for this book
is available from the British Library

ISBN 978-0-3494-1732-5

Designed and typeset in Dante by Paul Saunders
Printed and bound in Great Britain by
Clays Ltd, St Ives plc

Papers used by Piatkus are from well-managed forests
and other responsible sources.

Piatkus
An imprint of
Little, Brown Book Group
50 Victoria Embankment
London EC4Y 0DZ

An Hachette UK Company
www.hachette.co.uk

www.littlebrown.co.uk

CONTENTS

PROLOGUE

FINAL

fi·nal

1 pertaining to or coming at the end; last in place, order, or time: the final meeting of the year.

2 ultimate: The final goal is world peace.

3 conclusive or decisive: a final decision.

4 constituting the end or purpose: a final result.

5 pertaining to or expressing the end or purpose: a final clause.

'I'm constantly reading people's opinions of me and they're not that good in general. I've never really been able to work from a position where people are very sympathetic with me simply because I've always been successful in this country; you're constantly defending yourself. And when you're defending yourself you do find that you're analysing your motives for this, your reasons for that. I have to be careful not to absorb too much of the aggression I get towards me in the press. But I've always been pretty self-analytical and my songs have always been like that. But then I'm probably a lot of things I wouldn't have been had I not become famous.'

George Michael

'After Wham! split everyone expected better things from me. But I don't regret the break-up. I had prepared myself for the fact that Wham! was going to end. For the last couple of years, Wham! was very much my venture, anyway, so it wasn't so frightening. The pressure is on Andrew now. He is working on an album and I've advised him. It's only natural that the public is going to be sceptical about his work. He's going to surprise them, though, because his music is a lot better than people think.'

George Michael

On 28 April 1923 Wembley Stadium hosted its first ever event. The FA Cup final between West Ham United and Bolton Wanderers was a game everyone wanted to see. The official crowd figure is listed at 126,947, though it's commonly accepted that well over 200,000 were actually crammed inside that afternoon.

Almost fifty years later, in 1972, Wembley hosted its first concert. But it was in the 1980s that it put on its most famous musical events. Queen recorded a live album there, while Genesis, U2, Madonna, Bruce Springsteen and Michael Jackson all sold out the 72,000 tickets, sometimes for many consecutive nights. In a decade when bigger was best and money ruled, success meant playing to the biggest, most profitable crowds. And for musicians, playing at Wembley meant you'd made it.

Growing up in Bushey, just a few miles from the shadow of the stadium's twin towers, was a young boy who on a good day could almost hear the football chants of 'Wem-ber-ley, Wem-ber-ley' drifting over north London. As an adult he would play his music at Wembley Stadium on many occasions. He played there for AIDS charities; he was there for perhaps the grand old stadium's most famous concert of all – Live Aid; he stole the show at the Freddie Mercury tribute concert; and he performed for Nelson Mandela. It was there too that he performed the swan song for his band Wham!. That boy, of course, was George Michael.

As Wham!, George and his friend Andrew Ridgeley were to become the most successful pop duo of the 1980s. The two boys, both sons of immigrant fathers, burst on to the scene in 1982. Projecting an image of healthy tanned bodies, big hair and unbelievably white teeth, they *were* the 1980s to many. They set numerous records, becoming the first group since the Beatles to have back-to-back number one singles in both the USA and the UK. They created a hysteria not witnessed since the Bay City Rollers ten years earlier, tapping into a hormone-charged demographic most people thought had died out with punk and disco. Along with Duran Duran they spawned a new wave of hysteria-driven boy bands: before you knew it Bros, New Kids on the Block et al were driving young girls crazy across the globe, their appearances at record stores bringing city centres to a standstill.

But by 1986, Wham! had done everything they could together. The pop icons of the decade decided to call it quits. They'd sold millions of records, they'd toured the world, including China, and they had more money than they could spend. So where better to play their final show than at Wembley Stadium? And, at a venue renowned for hosting sporting finals for the last 63 years, what better name to give that last show than The Final?

A year earlier Wham! had also played to a sold-out Wembley Stadium, on that occasion as just one of a host of big-name acts brought together by Bob Geldof and Midge Ure under the umbrella of Live Aid. George Michael had privately announced his plans to go solo at the end of 1985, and events leading up to Wham!'s last appearance had been carefully planned ever since. Six months later, just as Michael turned 23, the band were sitting at the top of the charts with 'The Edge Of Heaven' and were about to unleash a compilation album. The press had been filled with Wham! stories for weeks, set against harrowing tales of the fall-out from the Chernobyl nuclear disaster. The last ever Wham! show had sold out in a couple of hours. There had been talk of a 'Semi-Final' show on the Friday night, though even that would not have been enough – they could easily have sold out a week of shows. But money wasn't the issue: after two massive video screens had been paid for, the concert cost around £750,000 to stage (the same as the original cost of building the stadium), and at the end of it they only broke even. And most important, the band wanted a single show to add an emphatic full stop to the ride.

As a boy, Andrew Ridgeley had dreamt of becoming a professional footballer; now he was going to play at Wembley. It wasn't what he'd originally had in mind, but it wasn't a bad second best. On that hot summer's Saturday afternoon in June 1986 the scene outside the stadium looked like the build-up to a cup final. Flags fluttered in the gentle breeze and Wembley Way, the approach to the twin towers, was packed solid with fans, many bedecked in Wham! T-shirts, scarves and hats. The organisers had kept back thousands of tickets to sell on the day in order to scupper the dealings of ticket touts. Queues had been building up at the turnstiles for hours and as soon as they opened, a sea of humanity flooded into the stadium looking for the best vantage points.

No one at the front would be going anywhere for the next few hours, and security men were soon passing bottles of water to the crowd – bottles which would be replaced by hosepipes as the night wore on. Meanwhile, around the world, millions of fans who hadn't been able to get tickets held vigils or played Wham! singles over and over all day long. Many teenage tears were shed. It was as if someone or something had died. For many, the end of Wham! signalled the end of youth. It was time to grow up, a frightening prospect for some. Why couldn't things just stay as they were?

Backstage there was a mix of sadness and excitement, but for the principal actors in the drama it all passed in a blur. Members of the UK pop elite mingled with friends and family. Elton John set up a paddling pool in the 90-degree heat and served champagne from his trailer. Video game machines were set up to keep people occupied while they waited and waited.

Asked shortly before going on stage if he had any regrets about the end of the band, George Michael emphatically said no, while Andrew Ridgeley jokingly pretended to strangle his partner. There was a hint of truth behind this gesture, though Ridgeley didn't tell his partner of his true feelings until a film documentary in 2004. 'I didn't enjoy it as much as other shows,' said the guitarist. 'The entire period leading up to that was a difficult one for me. I just kept thinking: once the encore's done, that's it. That was a difficult concept to get to grips with; we just didn't know how to take the concept of Wham! into adulthood.'

An out of touch Gary Glitter opened the show at four in the afternoon while the sun still beat down. He was followed by Nick Heyward, ex of Haircut 100, who ended with crowd favourite 'Fantastic Day', but who was elsewhere to exemplify what George Michael would have to avoid, a solo career gone bad. Other delights to keep the crowd amused included the first showing of *Foreign Skies*, the re-edited version of a film about Wham!'s 1985 trip to China. This was projected on the two giant video screens flanking the stage, which was hung with a massive curtain that read 'THE FINAL'.

The real drama started at 7.30 pm. The opening notes of 'Everything She Wants' rang out over the 72,000 heads and were greeted with mass screaming. Moments later, to even higher-pitched screaming, the curtains were pulled back to reveal the band. To the loudest screams yet, George Michael entered stage right with two male dancers. Dressed in tight black jeans, leather boots and jacket, and the inevitable shades, he and the dancers made their moves, Michael himself taking solo trips down the long catwalks that reached out into the crowd from either side of the stage. When Michael returned to centre stage some three minutes later, Andrew Ridgeley appeared, along with backing singers/dancers Pepsi and

Shirlie. He too went on a lengthy walkabout before theatrically removing his long black coat. The near seven-minute introduction over, the song proper kicked in, the whole audience singing along to every word. Every shake of the hips, every glance at the crowd, every nuance was greeted by ear-shattering approval. It was going to be a long night.

An emotional George Michael made several speeches during the show, saying that he had 'four years of thank yous to make'. All the hits were played, hits that defined the pop world of the mid-1980s: 'Wake Me Up Before You Go-Go', 'I'm Your Man', 'Last Christmas', 'Club Tropicana' . . . the list went on and on. Pepsi and Shirlie underwent several costume changes through the show, appearing for 'Bad Boys' in oversized wigs. 'The whole day was just sparkling,' recalled Shirlie Holliman. 'It stopped at a good time, on a high. Everyone was in a great mood and Pepsi and I had these huge beehive wigs to wear; they were very heavy and very funny.'

Ronald McDonald, who was actually Elton John in fancy dress costume, appeared at a grand piano while George Michael conducted the crowd through 'yeah, yeah, yeahs' for 'The Edge Of Heaven'. The clown stayed around to perform 'Candle in the Wind' with George Michael, the pair of them blissfully unaware of the connection the song was to have with Michael's future friend, Princess Diana.

As the sun set and the stadium was cloaked in darkness the band cranked up the excitement further with 'Wham Rap!' and an emotional 'A Different Corner', dedicated to a mystery 'special friend'. An energetic 'Freedom' ended the main set. Encores included 'Careless Whisper', 'Young Guns (Go For It)' and 'I'm Your Man' with Simon Le Bon, a finale for which all the performers took the stage. George and Andrew performed a lap of honour along the catwalks before Ridgeley seized the mic to say 'Thank you George'.

And then they were gone. A spectacular end to a spectacular, if short, pop life. After the show the cast and crew decamped to the Hippodrome where the party lasted long into the night. But while millions of fans mourned the end of Wham!, it was just the beginning for George Michael.

After the end of Wham! in 1986 George Michael set off on an even more wondrous solo career. Stopping off during his first solo world tour, he appeared again at Wembley as part of the Nelson Mandela 70th birthday tribute concert. And, having performed at charity events held at Wembley Arena next door, Michael returned to the stadium in 1992. After enigmatic Queen front man Freddie Mercury passed away in November 1991, the rest of his band arranged an AIDS awareness show in which various guest vocalists took the lead in performing Queen's back catalogue. And it was Michael who stole the show, giving one of the most impressive and impassioned vocal performances of his career. It wasn't until years later that the public found out why.

In the late 1990s it was announced that Wembley would be demolished and a new national stadium would replace it on the same site. Debate raged about incorporating the famous twin towers in the new design but eventually, in 2002, they felt the wrecking ball. Chelsea won the last FA Cup final at the 'old' Wembley in 2000, England lost their last game there to Germany, and American rockers Bon Jovi played the last concert.

As Wembley decayed during the 1990s, so did George Michael's personal life. After suffering the loss of the two people closest to him, he was beset by grief which he would finally overcome only in the twenty-first century. He was involved in a series of public scandals, though many of these were overplayed by the press. Professionally he was involved with a lengthy court case with his record label, and lost much of his American audience. But after a break of 18 years, during his 25th year in the music business, he felt the time was right to tour again. In the midst of further tabloid stories, Michael returned to touring in 2006, playing a string of European arena shows.

The keys to the new improved Wembley Stadium were handed over by the contractors to the Football Association in March 2007. The completed stadium was marvellous, with a 300-metre tall arch visible for miles around and a seating capacity of 90,000. Rock band Muse announced that they would be appearing at the rebuilt stadium on 16 June 2007 but afterwards it was announced that George Michael would have the honour of playing the first show, on 9 June. The first show sold out so quickly that a second was added for the following day. Alex Horne, managing director of Wembley Stadium, called it 'fantastic news' when the shows were announced, adding: '[George Michael is] no stranger to this great stage, having performed at the old stadium with both Wham! at Live Aid and as a solo artist. This is a fitting first gig in the new stadium. We are looking forward to putting the stadium back on the world map as a major music destination.'

When he walked triumphantly out at Wembley, George Michael also put himself back on the musical stage. Like the famous old stadium, he was an English icon that had been resurrected and he could now look forward in his career to a bright new future.

George Michael was a driven man. He was hardworking and proud, afraid of money and insecure but incredibly rich and famous. He was very private but spoke openly about his personal life. Michael often said in interviews that celebrities he had met nearly always had one thing in common, something that had enabled them to reach the peak of their respective professions. It wasn't some special quality, or a gift that had been bestowed upon them; it was that they all had something missing. They'd all had to overcome something or prove something or plug a gap in their lives, and that had given them the sense of purpose that enabled them to achieve their goals.

It was exactly the same for George Michael. Ask different people about him and you get different answers. But take enough angles and snapshots and you get more than just a pile of fragments, a million unconnected facts. You can see the whole picture of George Michael. Here is his story.

PART ONE

•

1963–1986

ONE

IMMIGRANT

1963–1975

im·mi·grant

1 a person who migrates to another country, usually for permanent residence.

2 an organism found in a new habitat.

'My name is Georgios Kyriacos Panayiotou. To the outside world I am, and always will be, known as something else. But it's not my name.'

George Michael

George Michael is an English pop icon. He could not have been born in a better place or at a better time to achieve his future goals, though for much of his early life he probably didn't realise this fact. Ten years later and Wham! would never have been given the chance to develop and build their success; ten years earlier and he would have been swamped by prog rock or punk. As it was, the drab negativity of the late 1970s meant that a bright young group with a positive attitude would be likely to find a massive following, especially if they had the looks, and the tunes, to match.

It's been said before that the past is a foreign country. When looking back at the England of 1963 you see a place almost totally unrecognisable from the England of today. The ethnic make-up, social and political causes and international relations were all very different, and yet in some ways strangely familiar. Liverpool dominated the pop charts: in mid-June the Beatles were number one with 'From Me To You', closely followed by Gerry and the Pacemakers ('I Like It') at number two, Billy J. Kramer and the Dakotas ('Do You Want To Know A Secret') at number three and Billy Fury ('When Will You Say I Love You') at number four. American president John F. Kennedy was in West Berlin, where on 26 June he made his famous 'Ich bin ein Berliner' speech. Back in the UK Harold Macmillan's government was trying to contain the Profumo scandal.

It was into this 'foreign' world that on 25 June 1963 Georgios Kyriacos was born in north London, the third child and first son to the Panayiotou family. The head of the young family was Kyriacos Panayiotou, a Greek-Cypriot immigrant who had arrived in England a decade earlier in 1953. Kyriacos had been born in 1935 in a traditional Greek homestead on the island of Cyprus. The family had lived for decades in the village of Patriki, about 18 miles north-east of the city of Famagusta along the 'tail' of land that juts out from the Bay of Famagusta and into the Mediterranean. Home for many centuries to a small Greek population of a few hundred, the village was located in a region which, when the land was partitioned in the 1970s to avert perennial conflict, would become the Turkish part of Cyprus.

Kyriacos was one of seven children, having three brothers and three sisters. Like the vast majority of the island's populace, the Panayiotou family were farm workers. In the north of the island the small dusty farms were home to olive and citrus groves, while in the south grapes and root vegetables were harvested. In many ways life was lived as it had been for centuries, with all working together for the good of the family unit. Several generations of one family often lived under the same roof in the rural villages, and the Panayiotous, like most traditional Mediterranean families, were extremely close.

But trouble was on the horizon. For hundreds of years Cyprus had been strategically important for various regimes and ideologies. In the 1950s the island was largely populated by Greeks with a minority population of Turks, while the British occupying forces added a third dimension. Early in the decade, Greek Cypriots began a movement to form a permanent union with their Greek homeland. As the decade progressed, this campaign was to escalate, with riots taking place outside the British embassy in Athens, until in 1959 the dispute was settled and the island was ceded from Britain to Greece. Before this, while the Turks and Greeks of Cyprus readied themselves to do battle, Kyriacos Panayiotou was finishing school and finding work as a waiter. Then, as he reached the age of 18, came Great Britain's call to the Commonwealth for immigrant workers. In 1953, two years before the riots reached Cyprus, he decided to try his luck and head for the UK.

For Kyriacos himself, the timing was perfect, but he also had his family to consider and his exit was tinged with remorse. One less worker meant one less salary to add money to the family pot. With civil war looming, a conflict into which all the island's young men would undoubtedly be dragged, it was a good time to go, but on the other hand he would be the first member of his family to leave. However, he did have a travelling partner, his cousin Dimitrios. The pair arranged to work their passage on a ship bound for England and in the summer of 1953 they set sail. Legend has it that they arrived with less than £1 between them.

London in 1953 was still abuzz from the coronation of Elizabeth II on 2 June, after Edmund Hillary had brought glory to the Commonwealth by conquering Mount Everest for the first time on 29 May. Panayiotou was greeted in England by the sounds of Frankie Laine and Mantovani purring from radios on the dockside as he weaved his way through the bustling quay where goods from around the world were unloaded. On arrival he and Dimitrios immediately headed for the group of Greek Cypriots they knew were living in north London, and through family connections they were able to secure room and board while they looked for work. As a teenager in a foreign land, a land where a language was spoken of which he knew little, Kyriacos decided to simplify things by changing his first name to the more easily pronounceable Jack and shortening his surname to Panos. He soon found employment as a waiter, while Dimitrios set about working as a tailor.

The newly named Jack Panos, like others of his generation, social standing and background, regarded hard work as the key to future success. Appreciating that he was at the bottom of the ladder, he began the long hard slog of pulling himself up. With little room and board to pay from his wages, he found that he had enough money left over to maintain a healthy social life while sending some back to his family in Cyprus.

Panos worked hard, putting in long shifts at the restaurant, but as a fit and agile young man he always found the energy to go out dancing when he wasn't at work. He would patrol the north London dance halls with Dimitrios and could dance a mean routine to the sounds of Tommy Steele and Elvis Presley as he grew to love both English and American rock and roll. He also attended various Greek events, dancing the night away at more than one wedding while managing to balance a full glass on his head. But it was rock and roll that he really loved – as well as, being quite good looking, the attention he received from the girls. He was certainly enjoying life in England.

At a dance in 1957 Jack met a young girl named Lesley Angold Harrison. (The 'Angold' part of her name dated back to her ancestors, who had fled Paris at the time of the French Revolution.)

Lesley enjoyed rock and roll dancing as much as Jack and the pair soon became an item, displaying energetic dance routines on Friday nights at the clubs and dance halls. They made a great couple, Lesley's working-class background fitting in nicely with Jack's own hardworking ethos. She lived with her parents and brother in one of a row of Victorian houses on Lulot Street near Highgate Hill. Around this time a local newspaper was running an item called 'Search for a Star' and Lesley sent in a photo of Jack. It was published above a caption that said, with slight exaggeration, 'Jack Panos is chased down the street by girls wherever he goes.' Before long, Jack proposed and Lesley accepted. Despite some reservations on the part of Lesley's father, they were married soon afterwards.

Jack and Lesley didn't have the most salubrious of starts to married life. Their first abode was a small flat above a laundry in Finchley, where house-proud Lesley fought a constant battle to maintain her standards of cleanliness and tidiness. She also had to deal with her father's disapproval of the marriage. As George Michael explained: 'Most people wouldn't realise but the Cypriots as one of the countries in the Commonwealth were kind of invited to come to the mother country to rebuild the place after the Second World War. There were places that would say, "No blacks, No Irish, No Greeks." So my father was part of that. My mother's father didn't attend their wedding because he was Greek, in those times he saw it as absolutely the same thing as marrying someone of a completely different colour. And so I'm only a little way away from that experience.'

In 1959 the young couple were blessed with a daughter, Yioda. But children cost money, so Jack upped his work rate and was soon spending seven nights a week waiting tables, taking on lunchtime work as well to bring in more cash. Two years later a second daughter, Melanie, was born. By now Jack's hard work was beginning to pay off and he'd been promoted to the post of assistant manager at the restaurant. A year later the final child, a son, arrived and was named Georgios Kyriacos.

The day of the birth was one which would resonate throughout the family for ever more, for conflicting reasons: their joy at the birth of a son was tragically mixed with the news that Lesley's brother had committed suicide. After rumours that he'd been found to be, or was at least suspected to be, homosexual, he was discovered dead with his head in a gas oven. Gay rights in Britain during the 1950s were unheard of; in fact gay men had no rights. After several high-profile court cases it wasn't until 1957 that Lord Wolfenden published a report recommending that 'Homosexual behaviour between consenting adults in private should no longer be a criminal offence.'

'I didn't know of the existence of my mother's closest sibling until I was 16 or 17, because he had killed himself,' George Michael later explained. 'The idea of so wanting to leave this world and at the same time not wanting to because it would spoil the pregnancy of your sister; it's just horrible, beyond horrible. And my mother told me that she thought he was gay. They had a very difficult childhood, and for some reason she didn't think it was appropriate to talk to us about it until we got to a certain age. It's a tragic story of how much more difficult it must have been as a gay man in the 1950s. If he'd held on and beaten his depression for long enough, he would have seen the changes in life that would have made him at least a happy middle-aged man.'

As it turned out, depression and suicidal tendencies ran in the family. Lesley was again devastated when she found her father's body after he had taken his own life. Once more, young Georgios was not told of this tragedy until much later in his life. George Michael would write about the events in the song 'My Mother Had A Brother', which appeared on the album *Patience*.

Though they had been a culture-conscious couple at the end

of the 1950s, the Swinging Sixties largely managed to pass Lesley and Jack by. Their flat was way too small for two adults and three children, so the family moved into its first house. Exemplifying the immigrant making his way in capitalist society through hard work, before the end of the 1960s Jack Panos took the plunge and opened a restaurant of his own, the Angus Pride in Edgware.

While this move meant his family would potentially be much better off financially, it entailed a further increase in Panos' working hours. He couldn't yet afford a very large staff or trust certain aspects of the business to others, so he spent ever more time out at work. It also put an extra strain on Lesley. She was always working a day job, coming home to look after the children after school and then working in the restaurant to help out at night as well. For a while Lesley worked in Hyde House, a local high-rise office block, another time she was employed in a local fish and chip shop for the lunchtime shift. For the super-clean housewife this was awful: she detested the smell of the fish and the cooking fat that pervaded her clothes and hair. Still, she would do her shift, go home, scrub up and be ready for the children to come home from school. But the constant toil began to take its toll. Though the home would be spotless, Lesley was often on the edge of anger and exhaustion.

George Michael could later recall this tired woman because he spent most of his home time with her. He remembered that as a young child he and his sisters would often be warned to keep quiet when their father was at home because he was asleep between shifts at the restaurant. Georgios consequently built a much stronger bond with his mother than with his father. Jack wasn't a completely absent father – he did manage to spend some time with his son – but the youngster found this time was never long enough. Spending most of his time with his mother and two sisters, the young Georgios quickly became used to having females as his constant companions. The male influence on his early years was minimal, while his feminine side was allowed to flourish.

Georgios received an early feeling of stability through his mother and a hardworking attitude from his father, although George Michael later admitted that he could never work as hard as his father did. Jack's upbringing in Cyprus had been strict, with corporal punishment included, but he was determined not to treat his own children in the same way. In his 1990 autobiography *Bare*, Michael says his father physically punished him only twice as a child, and that on both occasions he deserved it. But the hard work left scars on Georgios. He recalls never being praised at home; his parents always seemed too busy for things like that.

Fifteen years after arriving in England with nothing, Panos was the owner of a restaurant, while the family were in the midst both of moving house and rising very quickly from working to middle class. While Jack provided Georgios with ever more material comfort, Lesley had the greater influence on her son's development. His English mother was almost 'classless', in the sense that it was difficult to know which class she belonged to. Her own mother had worried that she would turn into a tomboy and so sent her to convent school, which put her off religion for life and dissuaded her from imposing religious beliefs on her own children. Despite her working-class background she spoke with a middle-class accent. Her approach to money was very different from that of her husband. While Jack constantly sought to improve his family's standing by earning as much as he could, Lesley was almost afraid of money. This feeling filtered through to her son, who would have the same attitude to money well after he'd become a multi-millionaire.

George Michael later said that he thought his mother always knew he was gay. 'How could she not have been worried by my sexuality if her brother's sexuality killed him?' he said. 'When you put your family tree together you understand so much more about who you are. Sometimes I felt that my mum made me feel that I wasn't man enough, or boy enough, when I was growing up, which was so out of character for her, because she was such a great mum, and so liberal in her attitudes.'

In 1968 Georgios started at the local Roe Green Primary School on Princes Avenue. One of his earliest friends there was David Mortimer, who lived on the same street. Georgios' other male pal was his cousin Andros, Dimitrios' son. While Jack had settled in north London, his travelling companion had eventually landed in south London, but once they had started their own families, they would take turns on a Sunday to travel across town for the day.

In 1968, Jack took his family for a holiday in Cyprus for the first time and was joined by Dimitrios and his family. Not long after Jack left Cyprus, his father had died, so Georgios never had the chance to meet his Cypriot grandfather. And other things had changed dramatically on the island since Jack's departure. The Panayiotou family had been forced to move home after the partitioning of the Greek and Turkish communities, and one of Georgios' earliest memories of Cyprus was being told not to pass through a certain set of gates. It was carefully explained to the five-year-old that the Turks patrolled on the other side and he could be shot there just for being Greek.

Georgios was usually a quiet boy who didn't stand out from the crowd, but on the Cyprus trip he displayed his first hint of a wild streak. One day during the trip, Georgios and cousin Andros decided to steal some sweets from the local shop. They achieved this easily and scoffed the proceeds of their crime. The next day they went back and repeated the feat. Day after day this continued, the pair becoming ever more daring until they managed to make off with a whole box of toy cars. Georgios wasn't really interested in toy cars, but he was excited by the fact that he could get away with it. When Jack Panos found out about the thefts he was outraged and slapped his son around the legs for good measure.

The Panos family would take several holidays on Cyprus as Georgios was growing up – in other years the family vacation would be a visit to members of Lesley's family on the Kent coast – and over time Jack helped five of his six brothers and sisters follow in his footsteps to England.

The family moved in 1969 to a semi-detached suburban house in Burnt Oak, Edgware, near the restaurant. Here the Panos family had neighbours, including an elderly lady on one side and a large Irish Catholic family on the other. For the first time Georgios, now six, had a garden of his own and he was fascinated by it. He would spend many hours amusing himself deep in the plants, collecting insects as many young boys once did. He would also wander off to the nearby fields to explore, which sometimes alarmed his mother. He often woke up early and sat at his bedroom window waiting for the sun to rise so he could go outside to play.

Before the age of seven Georgios took his first musical steps when he started violin lessons. He would continue these for six years, more at the behest of his parents than because of any burning desire to be a musician. But on his seventh birthday, in 1970, he was given a portable cassette recorder, and his imagination ran wild. Aided by anyone he could rope in, be it his sisters or David Mortimer, he would record himself singing the popular tunes of the day, using the original songs as backing tracks, as well as rudimentary ditties that he dreamt up himself. He and his accomplices would also script spoof radio shows, jingles and adverts.

Georgios wasn't keen on the violin lessons and soon began to sense that he wanted to be a singer, though he didn't know if he could really sing or not. And despite Jack's earlier love of rock and roll, any music heard around the house by the early 1970s would invariably be Greek, which Georgios grew to hate. Then one day he found an old wind-up record player that his mother had discarded in the garage. With it he unearthed a trio of seven-inch singles, two by the Supremes and one by Tom Jones. It was a combination that would later tint his own musical output. As soon as he arrived home from school Georgios would either head to his bedroom to record the latest tune he had dreamt up or dash into the garage to play the three singles over and over again.

As well as supplying Georgios with his earliest singles (in 1973, at the age of ten, he bought his first single, Carly Simon's 'The Right Thing To Do', which grazed the Top 30), Lesley kept a close eye on what TV shows her son watched. One programme that he was allowed to stay up past his normal bedtime to watch was Michael Parkinson's chat show, which Lesley felt was good wholesome family viewing. Little did she know that years later a whole hour of the show would be dedicated to her son.

Jack kept discipline around the house on a tight rein. Mel and Yioda were allowed absolutely no boyfriends and when they went out Georgios often had to act as a chaperone. When the girls started regular ice-skating trips, Georgios had to go along as well. On these Saturday afternoons he found himself attracted to a girl called Jane, but she was pretty and he was chubby and wore glasses. At the time he thought he had no chance, though he would later meet up with Jane again.

Georgios also sang at boy scouts' gang shows but his father was less than supportive, always telling his son that he couldn't sing and had no talent for music. Being a quiet boy, Georgios just took his father's words in, though he didn't believe a word of it.

Georgios was a little too young to be fully immersed in the make-up and transvestite look of the glam rock explosion but he watched the movement from afar. The artist that he really latched on to was Elton John (a snippet of his home recording of John's 'Crocodile Rock' was used in a documentary about the singer years later). In 1974 Georgios was to see his biggest musical hero live for the first time, when Elton played at Vicarage Road, the home of Watford Football Club, to raise funds for the ailing side.

The autumn of 1974 saw Georgios step up to Kingsbury High School on Princes Avenue. The school has a reputation for producing talented and successful musicians and singers: Rolling Stones drummer Charlie Watts, jazz saxophonist Courtney Pine and Sugababes Keisha and Mutya all attended Kingsbury at one time or another. But Georgios' brief tenure at Kingsbury didn't allow much time for the shaping of his musical future. Friends recall that he would often be asked to leave class for being 'smart mouthed' to the teachers. He also managed to get himself thrown out of the school choir for talking too much. And at the end of the academic year his father, who was about to open a second restaurant, decided that the family should move house again.

Georgios needed to register for a new school before the 1975–76 academic year. Perhaps mindful of his son's minor misdemeanours at Kingsbury, Jack wanted to send him to a private school. But Georgios was dead against the idea. Worried that his friends would call him a sissy and that the other pupils would intimidate him, he steadfastly refused even to sit the entrance exam. Jack tried to change his son's mind, but knew he was fighting a losing battle.

He did, however, manage to convince his son, and his daughters, to take Greek lessons. A scruffy minibus would collect the students via a circuitous route and drop them off at the Saturday morning classes. No Greek was spoken in the Panos household, so Georgios and his sisters were already at a disadvantage when they started the lessons. Most of the other students had a grounding in the language already, but the Panos children were left bemused; the teacher refused to speak any English, so they sat scratching their heads for most of the morning. Once again Georgios did not exactly embrace his father's culture; at best he seemed indifferent to it. After two years of Greek lessons Jack finally gave up, sparing Georgios and his sisters further Saturday tedium.

With the threat of private school averted, Georgios had six weeks of summer holidays ahead of him before starting at a new state school. The family also moved to Radlett – at least, they bought a house there. The large detached property required a complete facelift, and so they briefly moved into the flat above

Jack's restaurant while the work was carried out. During this time they mainly ate the same food served at the restaurant and Georgios soon found himself piling on the pounds with a diet of steak and chips. He would continue to be self-conscious about his weight all through his adolescence and into adulthood. But the transformation of Kyriacos Panayiotou into Jack Panos was now almost complete; the penniless city-dwelling immigrant was now a relatively affluent inhabitant of middle England's leafy Hertfordshire suburbs. Mr Jacks restaurant, as it is now called, on Station Road, Edgware, was to become a local institution.

On 9 September 1975 Georgios Panos donned his green blazer and set off for his first day at Bushey Meads comprehensive school in Bushey, Hertfordshire. As a new second-year student, he arrived at the tree-lined front lawn in its pretty suburban setting knowing no one. Wandering down the halls clutching a scrap of paper that told him where to go, he eventually found his new class. His new form teacher asked the sea of pre-pubescent indifference in front of him if anyone would volunteer to take the new boy under their wing and show him around until he became acquainted with his new surroundings. Most of the pupils avoided eye contact with the teacher. But one boy's face lit up and his hand shot into the air. 'I will, Miss!' said the eager pupil. His name was Andrew Ridgeley.

Georgios took his seat next to Ridgeley, afterwards following his new friend religiously from class to class. At the first break, the pair headed to a corner of the playground where a game of 'King of the Wall' was taking place. This entailed one child standing atop the brick wall, whereupon everyone else had to try and knock the current 'king' from his perch and claim his place for themselves. Ridgeley ran enthusiastically into the heart of the melee and soon found himself as the 'king'. Georgios, who had never been one for physical sports or games, stood to one side while Ridgeley taunted those at the bottom of the wall, including his new companion. Eventually the new boy had had enough of the jibes and joined in. He was big for his age and managed to battle his way through the crowd and topple his new friend. It was the birth of a lasting friendship.

From day one of their meeting Ridgeley made it clear that he had two aims in life. He was determined to be a professional footballer, and if he didn't succeed he was going to be a pop star. With Georgios' vague ambition to be a singer they were an ideal fit. Ridgeley was the perfect friend at the perfect time: Georgios was starting to feel a little inhibited about his looks and size, while Ridgeley was supremely confident and outgoing. 'I saw him and the way that he was talking about things and I felt that here was someone I wanted to know and be friends with,' said George Michael. 'From the moment we met we really hit it off and all we seemed to talk about was music.' Little did they know that this meeting would be the turning point in both their lives. The effect that each would have on the other, in vastly different ways, would set them both up for life.

TWO

AMBITION

1975–1981

am·bi·tion

1 an earnest desire for some type of achievement or distinction, as power, honour, fame, or wealth, and the willingness to strive for its attainment: too much ambition caused him to be disliked by his colleagues.

2 the object, state, or result desired or sought after: the crown was his ambition.

3 desire for work or activity; energy: I awoke feeling tired and utterly lacking in ambition.

'As a boy my biggest fear was that my huge ambitions would stay just out of reach of the child I saw in the mirror.'

George Michael

Georgios Panos never wanted to be rich and famous. He just wanted to be famous. The money side of fame wasn't what appealed to him, it was just a by-product of his major goal. Fame would make him the centre of attention, which wasn't always the case at home, especially as far as his father was concerned. Fame would banish his low self-esteem and his growing self-consciousness about his looks. Fame would give him everything he craved and solve his adolescent problems. All he had to do was become famous and he'd be happy. Or so he thought. He was still an average student and often melted away into a crowd, so the attainment of fame wasn't going to be easy. But it was made easier by co-opting Andrew Ridgeley into the scheme. Ridgeley was outgoing and confident to the point of cockiness. No new situation seemed to faze him and he seemed super-cool to the relatively shy Georgios.

Even though the Panos family was doing well financially, Georgios was never just given pocket money, he had to earn it by doing chores around the house. Jack Panos was still cautious even though his business was prospering, and never forgot his humble beginnings. He was equally cautious about his son's education. Having accepted defeat in the bid for a private education, he kept a close eye on how Georgios was adapting to his new school in Bushey. Jack and Lesley were especially wary when Georgios introduced his new friend Andrew Ridgeley.

The Ridgeley and Panos families had quite a lot in common. Albert Mario Ridgeley, Andrew's father, was raised in Cairo by an Egyptian father and an Italian mother. When his mother died in 1953, at the time of the Suez crisis, Albert jumped on a ship bound for England, just as Jack Panos was doing across the Mediterranean. Like Jack, Albert arrived in England penniless. What he did possess was an aptitude for languages. He left Egypt already fluent in Egyptian, English, French and Italian and managed to secure a place at the University of St Andrews, where he studied German and Russian. On graduation he signed up with the Royal Air Force, serving time in Berlin before returning to a job with Canon cameras in the UK, which is when he met Andrew's mother Jennifer. They married and had their first son, Andrew, in Windlesham, Surrey on 26 January 1963, six months before Georgios Panos was born. A second son, Paul, followed soon afterwards. When Andrew was five years old the family relocated to Egham in Surrey, not far from Heathrow Airport, and later they moved the 20 or so miles to Bushey where Jennifer worked as a teacher at Bushey Meads school.

Andrew's exotic good looks came from his father. He seemed to be permanently suntanned, to the point where he was sometimes bullied and called a 'Paki'. 'Andy didn't spend time looking in mirrors because he was absolutely convinced he was gorgeous,' said George Michael years later. And it was true, Ridgeley walked around as if he was God's gift. The impressionable Georgios rode on his coat-tails. Though they were only six months apart in age the gap often seemed much wider. The correct pronunciation of 'Georgios' is 'Your-gos', so Ridgeley called his friend 'Yog'. Much to Georgios' dismay, this mutated into 'Yoghurt' around the school yard. Georgios was equally dismayed by the teachers' attempts at his name, which usually got no further than 'Georg-ee-os'.

Despite having (or perhaps because he had) a teacher for a mother, Andrew was never very interested in school. He was an idle student and could be disruptive in class. Once he realised he wouldn't make it as a professional footballer he set his sights on being a pop star, and what good was school to a pop star? Aside from the occasional dark-skin jibe, his sartorial elegance and outgoing demeanour made him very popular among his classmates and he displayed a juvenile sense of humour that meshed perfectly with that of Georgios. 'Neither of us was interested in school beyond the social sense, as a meeting place,' said Ridgeley. 'A forum, that's what school was. That's when it was really good.' This attitude endeared him neither to his teachers nor to Jack and Lesley Panos. Georgios' parents took an instant dislike to Ridgeley when he swanned into their house exuding his most confident aura. Lesley forbade Georgios to be in the house with Ridgeley when she wasn't home.

The pair spent much of their spare time in the park. 'I know that one of the places I always went to was the park,' says Ridgeley.

'It was a kind of central meeting area for me and all of my friends, and all the girls would go there too. I'd play football there as well at every opportunity that I could. It's funny to walk around there now and enjoy those memories. I liked the people in the town too, because they weren't – and still aren't – pretentious at all. In a way, I'm pleased that I grew up there and not in a huge city.'

For his twelfth birthday in June 1975 Georgios had been given a set of drums by his parents. At the end of his first year at Bushey Meads, he spent the summer holidays with Ridgeley in one or other of their bedrooms, banging away on the drum kit, composing simple ditties and recording them on his little cassette deck. Though at first they were just messing about, Georgios was fast coming around to Ridgeley's idea of *really* wanting to be a pop star. David Mortimer was learning how to play guitar and he sometimes joined in. They shared a love of the music of Elton John and Queen. Georgios had long been a fan of Elton John, but Queen were fast becoming his favourites. He was especially taken with the dramatic showmanship of Queen's front man Freddie Mercury. In 1974 Queen had released their classic album *Sheer Heart Attack*, which included 'Killer Queen' and 'Stone Cold Crazy'. The following year they toured the world in the costumes of Zandra Rhodes, taking the rock concert spectacle to new highs. The vocal gymnastics of 'Bohemian Rhapsody' cemented the band's position as one of the most innovative and exciting of the 1970s and secured Georgios Panos as a lifelong fan. Ridgeley and Panos would go into Watford on a Saturday and spend time perusing the record shops for the latest additions to their collections.

Compared with some schools in the suburbs between north London and Watford, Bushey Meads was quite liberal. Though some of their classmates later joined the marines, Andrew

Ridgeley described it as 'a bit of a poof's school', which explained why his sometimes over-loud dress sense – years before the New Romantics made dressing up the hip thing to do – didn't get him a kicking once in a while. On one occasion Ridgeley went out wearing a blue shirt, pink tie and cerise satin trousers, creating quite a stir among his peers. Another time he arrived unannounced at a Panos family New Year's party dressed in a kilt. But Jack and Lesley had eventually grown to accept Ridgeley. They knew that they had to let their son choose his own friends.

Ridgeley had grown up with a brother and loved hanging around with girls. School discos were his forte. Georgios, on the other hand, felt intimidated by them. With his mother and sisters constantly around him he'd grown comfortable with being around women in a very non-sexual way. The thought of encountering females in any other scenario scared him half to death. By the age of 13 or 14 Georgios would see all his friends making out with each other at house parties and disappearing into bedrooms and bathrooms, while he was left alone feeling depressed and ugly.

After the almost unbearably long, hot, dry summer of 1976 the boys returned to school in September with thoughts of being pop stars etched indelibly into their brains. As usual school offered a stage on which they could have fun; for the most part, lessons passed them by. With the help of his sisters, Georgios was undergoing something of a makeover. His hair was growing into a kind of bushy perm, his sisters plucked and shaved away at his unibrow to give two distinct eyebrows for the first time and he managed to convince his parents to let him wear contact lenses instead of his clunky-looking glasses. He'd already had hopes of being an airline pilot dashed when it was found that he was colour blind. 'I was fat and ugly and I had glasses,' he told the *Daily Mail* in 1990. 'I also had one big bushy eyebrow. I have now had it treated to make two eyebrows. For years I would try and grow my hair long to cover it.'

Having been a staple of men's fashion throughout the decade, long hair was on the way out. The Queen's Silver Jubilee year of 1977 arrived, and so did punk. But Georgios and Andrew had little to rebel against and so the movement passed them by, although Ridgeley did quite like The Jam. The other musical explosion of 1977, however, was disco. This was something that the boys latched on to in a big way, especially the phenomenon of *Saturday Night Fever*. After its New York debut late in 1977, the film would dominate music for the next year and beyond. Its soundtrack included 17 songs, 11 of which were released as singles and seven of which became number one. Sales of the album eventually topped 40 million worldwide, keeping it at the top of the charts for 18 weeks while John Travolta was catapulted to superstardom. Most boys wanted to be able to dance like Travolta's character Tony Manero, and Ridgeley and Panos were no different. They also saw depicted in the film other concerns that they could relate to in their everyday lives: unsupportive parents (at least as far as music went), racial tension, unemployment. No wonder the film and soundtrack were so well received in England.

As well as recording spoof songs and jingles in their bedrooms they would work on ever more elaborate dance routines that they would later try out at the school disco. Georgios was a less natural dancer than Andrew but Ridgeley took the time to teach Travolta's moves to his friend step by step until he had them nailed down. Sometimes Georgios would babysit for a family across the road: inevitably Andrew would call round and they'd work on their dance routines. As well as the Bee Gees they'd put on records like Quincy Jones' 'Stuff Like That', and as Georgios later admitted 'we would walk rather stupidly across the room.' Georgios also started to express his musical leanings at school, where at the end of the 1978 school year he performed a 'Drum solo: own composition' before his fellow students.

As Georgios gained in confidence the pair started expanding their horizons. As well as school discos they strayed as far as

Bogart's Club in Harrow where future BBC Radio 1 DJ Gary Crowley hosted disco nights. Around this time Georgios met his first girlfriend, Lesley Bywaters. She told him that she liked his eyes. But Georgios still had a great underlying insecurity and thought she was making fun of him, as he'd only recently given up his glasses. He kept his distance until he realised she really meant it and the two became an item for a while. Georgios would buy her disco records, including Chic's 'Dance, Dance, Dance'.

In the 1978–79 academic year Georgios would be sitting his O level exams. A battle of wills was already developing: his father wanted him to progress to A levels and then go to university. He knew how hard he'd had to work for everything and thought that if his son took a degree it would give him a head start up the ladder. Georgios was bright enough to follow this route but he didn't see it as a way of becoming a star in the music business. In fact he saw another way of making a tentative step on the ladder to success. He started busking.

In what became a regular ritual, Georgios and David Mortimer would skip school on a Friday and head into London armed with a guitar and a small arsenal of songs. By now they'd written a couple of songs of their own and worked out their own versions of songs by Elton John, David Bowie and the Beatles. The best pitches were usually long gone by the time the pair arrived in the morning, but they would nevertheless set up in a tube station for the best part of a day, often Green Park station at the busy intersection of the Victoria, Jubilee and Piccadilly lines. By their own account the pair were actually quite good and even made a little money. Sometimes their hard-earned takings would be stolen before the day was over, but they enjoyed performing anyway. Georgios was especially taken with the way that his voice and the acoustic guitar reverberated through the station.

Spending whole days at a time in a tube station, they came across some interesting characters. One afternoon they heard a commotion and looked up the entrance escalator to see a large skinhead in a red jumper running down towards them. As he arrived at the bottom he ran towards Georgios screaming, 'Give us yer fucking jumper!' Despite a half-hearted defence of, 'But this is my best jumper,' Georgios swapped with the skinhead who ran off, presumably in order to avoid being spotted by the police. The bemused busker was left with an oversized Fred Perry jersey to wear on the train home.

The Friday routine would usually continue with Georgios and David rushing home with the day's takings then getting changed and going out for the night to spend their earnings as quickly as they could. The nightclubs opened a whole new world for Georgios. Disco was just making its way on to the radio but in the clubs his ears were opened to different genres of music.

The Friday bunk-offs didn't greatly harm Georgios's academic results. He cruised to five O-level passes without really trying. The non-busking Andrew Ridgeley made even less effort and passed fewer exams. In accordance with his father's wishes, Georgios stayed on at Bushey Meads to take A levels in Music Theory, Art and English Literature. 'It's only when the kids are in their late twenties that families really face up to what they are,' said George Michael. 'You've gone out into the world, you've probably got a family of your own, and you're finally in a position to look back and see if your own family was normal. I suppose enough of the damage your parents have done to you has left you by then too. It was at that age I realised how dysfunctional my childhood was.' Despite his parents' pressure, Georgios was happy enough to go along with them while he worked out a way into the music business.

Deciding that he needed the 'adult' environment of college for his A levels, Andrew Ridgeley enrolled in September 1979 at Cassio Sixth Form College on Langley Road in Watford. Spice Girl Geri Halliwell would also attend a few years later. He managed to stay for the whole two years but admitted that he only ever completed about a week's worth of work. Ridgeley had the time of his life at college, drinking and trying a few more serious vices. George Michael later told *Q* magazine that Ridgeley had tried LSD. '[Andrew] took acid and had the most awful, awful time. A really bad trip. He never took it again for years and years and years. Just his description of what happened to him really put me off. I'm just too much of a control freak and really couldn't handle the idea of things coming at me and not being able to stop it. I still hear horrible stories about things happening to people on stuff like acid. It's just too extreme for me.'

In the autumn of 1979 Ridgeley said he wanted to form a band of his own right away, but Georgios told him he would have to wait until he'd finished his A levels, which were way ahead in the future, in July 1981. Ridgeley simply couldn't wait that long and badgered his friend until he relented, agreeing to have a band practice that night – at his own parents' house. Lesley and Jack were not impressed at the racket made in their living room by a gaggle of noisy teenagers. It was decided that in future they would alternate the practice venue between the various parents' houses to minimise the disruption.

By now punk had run its course in the UK and a wave of ska bands were starting out. Ridgeley and Panos initially aspired to join them. At the very first practice the ad-hoc band put together a song to use as their theme tune, calling it 'Rude Boy'. They also attempted their own ska version of Beethoven's 'Fur Elise'. The 'band' had something of a revolving cast of characters. Initially it was a five-piece: Andrew's brother, Paul Ridgeley, played drums, David Mortimer (who changed his name to David Austin) and school friend Andrew Leaver were on guitars, while Georgios and Andrew sang. They didn't have a bass player until Tony Bywaters (brother of Georgios' ex-girlfriend Lesley) arrived. He had shoulder-length ginger hair and was immediately christened

'Dill the Dog' after a character from kids' TV show *The Herbs*. Georgios recalled that while Bywaters was a nice guy and had some good equipment, he didn't really fit in and his stay was short-lived. Another friend, Jamie Gould, also had a short tenure with the band.

Having decided to call themselves The Executive – perfect in a country that had voted Margaret Thatcher and an upwardly mobile Tory government into power during May 1979 – the band started practising regularly. Georgios, however, almost made his live debut elsewhere. 'I had nearly made my stage debut with The Quiffs,' he told the *Daily Mail* in 1990. 'They were some of the people Andrew knew from college. And one night their drummer dropped out. I could play the drums and they knew I could, but they took one look at me and said I couldn't do it. I didn't look the part. I just looked too bad. I remember being crushed by that.'

Georgios rebounded from the disappointment by concentrating on his own band. The Executive borrowed heavily from ska's leading lights. Madness had achieved Top 20 placings with 'The Prince' in September and 'One Step Beyond' in November, while The Specials had also broken into the scene with Top 10 hits 'Gangsters' and 'A Message To You Rudy' during the year. Although rooted in the hardcore Jamaican beats dating back to the 1950s, the ska music played by these bands was a UK version. Known as 'two tone', it fused elements of punk into the equation while pushing the envelope of racial harmony in the face of tensions that were to culminate in riots in major cities up and down the country during 1981, in Toxteth, Liverpool and Handsworth, Birmingham, and closer to home in Brixton, south London.

The Executive managed to swing their first public performance on Bonfire Night 1979 at Bushey Methodist Hall as part of the local cub scouts' fireworks show. With their next show pencilled in for December, the band had some promo photos taken to go along with a demo tape they were preparing. Georgios features in the pictures as a tousle-haired youth with an almost Amish beard, dressed in a cream-coloured cotton suit and slip-on shoes. Andrew is snapped lounging in a chair, wearing a stripy top and white waistcoat.

The Executive's eight-track demo tape included 'Rude Boy' and their fast version of the Doc Pomus and Mort Shuman tune 'Can't Get Used To Losing You', made famous by Andy Williams back in 1963. They tried hawking it around a few record labels but had no luck. The tape wasn't as bad as George Michael and David Austin now make out: the labels thought it was too derivative but at least they were on to something. 'Rude Boy' was dismissed as sounding like Bad Manners' 'Special Brew', while four years later The Beat released their own ska version of 'Can't Get Used To Losing You', reaching number three in the charts with it.

Tension was once again developing between Jack Panos and his son. Georgios dropped out of his Music Theory course and was now pursuing only two A levels. As far as Jack could see, Georgios had little talent for music and he thought his son was wasting his time. One day Georgios put on a copy of The Executive's demo tape in his father's car. Jack started giving him another lecture about how this wasn't going to lead anywhere and the normally placid Georgios finally snapped. He told his father in no uncertain terms that he was going to have a career in music, that he was sick of being told he wasn't good enough, that the least his father could do was give him moral support. On another occasion his mother tried to get him to give up the band: Georgios threatened to quit school if she made him.

Andrew Ridgeley thought he might have found a way in for the band when he heard that his neighbour from down the street, Mark Dean, was working in the record industry. Dean, a couple of years older than Ridgeley, had signed Secret Affair, who had a minor hit with 'Time For Action'. But he wasn't interested in this kids' band from down the road. He refused to even listen to the tape. Ridgeley persevered and passed a copy to Dean's mother. She made sure her son listened to it, but his feedback was that they were rubbish.

In the summer of 1980, between years one and two of their A level courses, Georgios and Andrew were in danger of drifting apart. Ridgeley was spending more and more time with his new college pals at Cassio and the only time he and Georgios really got together was at band practice. Even that was falling apart. During the autumn more and more members dropped out until only Panos and Ridgeley remained. After a failed demo tape and about ten live shows, including at least one at Cassio College, The Executive was no more.

The remaining duo faced a music industry twisting and turning from the departing punk and disco scenes, while increasingly keen to take on the so-called new wave and new pop bands. The way was opening for the New Romantics, Adam and the Ants et al, artists who embraced a culture in which dressing up to have a good time was no longer frowned on. They wanted to create their own audience rather than try and fit in with an existing one, and they would succeed. But could Ridgeley and Panos find their own niche in this ever-changing musical climate?

In January 1981 Andrew Ridgeley met Shirlie Holliman at a local pub. Like Ridgeley and Panos, Holliman had attended Bushey Meads school but the two had never spoken. They started going out together and she soon became a close friend of both Georgios and Andrew. Though they were now 18 they still worked out dance routines in their bedrooms and Holliman was eager to join in. She thought the boys made a good pair because Ridgeley was so flashy and Panos so sensible: 'Andrew was the funny charming one and George would be, "You go first, I'll be right behind you".'

In the summer of 1981 the country had been captivated by the royal wedding of Prince Charles and Lady Diana Spencer, the defeat of Björn Borg by John McEnroe at Wimbledon after five straight titles, and the courage of Bob Champion, who beat cancer to win the Grand National at Aintree. In the USA, President Ronald Reagan appointed the first female Supreme Court Justice, Sandra Day O'Connor, and the baseball season resumed on 9 August after a players' strike. The news was not all positive, though. Later, just down the road from the Peckham flat into which Ridgeley and Holliman had lived in, riots left Brixton burning. Unemployment was rising and the youth of the country were growing dissatisfied. One young man went so far as to fire blank shots from a pistol at the Queen as she rode down the Mall on a horse during the Trooping of the Colour.

That summer, despite by his own admission only attending about one lesson out of every seven, Georgios passed his A levels. But he had no wish to go to university, and a summit meeting with his parents followed. They insisted that he find a job and gave him six months to get a record deal; otherwise he'd have to give music up for good or he'd be out on his ear. So he took on a series of low-paid jobs to keep his parents happy. He washed pots and served drinks at his father's restaurant, but one drinks order after another was mismeasured and he moved on. He worked as a building site labourer, but he was never cut out for manual labour and that didn't last even for a week. He worked in the stock room of a branch of British Home Stores, but was fired when his boss found him working without wearing the company shirt and tie. Longer periods of employment included a job as a cinema usher at the now defunct Empire cinema on Merton Road, Watford. This was fine apart from the tedium of seeing the same films over and over.

David Austin worked through the summer as a local swimming pool attendant and the trio of Panos, Ridgeley and Holliman would visit him at the pool, go swimming and then troop off for ice cream and drinks. Shirlie had a car, so she could drive them all around.

Ridgeley had worked briefly as a cleaner and then in a warehouse but he'd packed it in and signed on the dole instead. 'It was OK for Andrew to be on the dole because he was still living at home and he was a lazy bastard who just didn't want to go out to work,' said Georgios. 'I worked on a building site, I was a DJ in a restaurant, I was a cinema usher.'

Finally he landed a job as a DJ at the Bel Air dinner-dance restaurant in Bushey. For someone who had been in a ska band and before that had been a hardcore disco fan it was heartbreaking work. The customers would come and eat their meal to a background of suitably relaxing lounge music; then, as the tables were being cleared, Georgios, who was stationed out of sight behind a pillar, would announce that he hoped the diners would partake of some dancing. It was usually the first time they actually knew a DJ was present; he would get sweaty palms just thinking about having to make the announcement, as everyone would instantly turn and look to see who was talking into the microphone. But he was taking home £70 a week. Though he gave some to his mum for board, he had plenty of spending money left over.

Georgios travelled to work each night at the Bel Air by bus. On these journeys his mind could wander away from the drudgery and he started dreaming up tunes in his head. This started a lifelong ability to compose songs in his head while travelling, at first on public transport but later in cars and eventually in planes. One night he was hit by a flash of inspiration as he stepped on board the bus. By the time he arrived at the restaurant he'd come up with the basis of a song called 'Careless Whisper'.

Meanwhile, Ridgeley and Holliman were living in a rundown flat in Peckham, south London. The south London flat was a long journey for Panos to make when he wanted to visit his friends or work on songs, but on one such trip he told Ridgeley about his new song. Ridgeley added some guitar chords to Panos' melody and they were off and running. The words had come to him when thinking back to Jane, the girl he'd met at the ice rink years earlier. He'd met her again since and they'd gone out for a while, but at the same time he'd also been seeing another girl called Helen. Though neither of the two girls had known about the other, he imagined the situation if they had and wrote the lyric accordingly.

Even though Georgios' sister Melanie memorably called it 'Tuneless Whisper', he knew he had a good song on his hands. He and Ridgeley recorded a demo version and Panos carried around a tape of it. After finishing his stint at the Bel Air, Georgios briefly worked as a DJ at a health club. On his last night there he played the demo tape of 'Careless Whisper', not caring what happened or if he got into trouble. To his amazement the dance floor filled, even though no one had ever heard the song before. This success filled Panos with the confidence that he could make it as a songwriter. He wasn't sure whether he was a strong enough singer or whether he'd spend his life writing songs for others to perform, but buoyed by this little triumph he set to work on more new songs.

The practice space at the south London flat didn't last long. Fed up with poor heating and having to use an outside toilet, Ridgeley and Holliman decided that the romance of living together didn't overcome the need for basic necessities and went back to live with their respective parents, though they remained a couple. Panos and Ridgeley knew that time was running out. If they were going to make a go of it they would need to get some record label interest. To do this they needed more tunes of the quality of 'Careless Whisper'. So Georgios Panos set to work.

THREE

FANTASTIC

1982–1983

fan·tas·tic

1 conceived or appearing as if conceived by an unrestrained imagination; odd and remarkable; bizarre; grotesque: fantastic rock formations; fantastic designs.

2 imaginary or groundless in not being based on reality; foolish or irrational: fantastic fears.

3 extravagantly fanciful; marvellous.

4 incredibly great or extreme; exorbitant: to spend fantastic sums of money.

5 highly unrealistic or impractical; outlandish: a fantastic scheme to make a million dollars betting on horse races.

'So I created a man that the world could love if they chose to, someone who could realise my dreams and make me a star.'

George Michael

'When I was 19 or 20 there were any number of fairly ordinary up to quite good-looking people I could take home. Now, if I chose to, I could walk into a room and leave with people who are much better looking or think a lot more of themselves. It's ironic really, now that I don't choose to, a lot of people are available to me. I find the idea of being that much of a catch for someone a very masculine and very castrating position to be in. There's no chase, you don't have to do anything.'

George Michael

When 1982 opened, unemployment was still at the centre of the political and social agenda, hitting the three million mark for the first time since the 1930s. Sheffield's Human League topped the first chart of the year with 'Don't You Want Me', which held the number one spot for five weeks. Synth pop and pure guitar pop were making waves in the UK. Haircut 100 had started the swing towards guitar pop with their hit single 'Favourite Shirts (Boy Meets Girl)', which wasn't a million miles away from what was being brewed up in Bushey.

So for Georgios Panos and Andrew Ridgeley the year started with a sense of optimism and excitement. They were working on new songs and enjoying the nightlife of an expanding London club scene. These new movements were the antithesis of punk: while in the 1970s credibility had been gained by making serious music, the 1980s already seemed to take the selling of records and making money as the measure of success. Andrew and Georgios became a reflection of the times that they were living in. Middle-class kids were on the dole for the first time ever, but rather than worry about it, they still wanted to have fun.

By 1982 the London club scene was beginning to take off as the likes of Grandmaster Flash brought hip-hop to UK dancers. At Le Beat Route club on Greek Street Ridgeley and Panos would mix with Steve Strange and members of Spandau Ballet while displaying their sometimes sexy, sometimes camp routines on the dance floor. They started messing around with simple raps and catchphrases that they'd utter while parading their moves. One such phrase was 'Wham! Bam! I'm the man!' Initially this was little more than the latest in their long history of in-jokes, but it seemed to stick. Changing it to 'Wham! Bam! I am a man!' they had the basis of a rap. They added lyrics about what they knew, having fun and being unemployed, themes captured in the line 'I'm a soul boy/I'm a dole boy' and the final refrain 'D-H-S-S' (aka the Department of Health and Social Security, where the unemployed had to go each week to sign on in order to receive their dole money). They decided that the 'Wham!' part of the rap sounded so good they'd take it as the name of their band. The new tune became 'Wham Rap!', their very own theme tune. 'We didn't sit down and consciously write the song the way that it was,' says Ridgeley. 'It just came out that way. The rapping style wasn't current then, as a lot of people seem to think. It had been going in America for ages. Besides, to try and cash in on a craze is a bit ridiculous because no matter how much you plan something to coincide with a fashion, you've probably missed the boat by the time the record is released. So we never tried to manipulate the market in that sense.'

Their musical inspiration came from records and clubs rather than from seeing live bands. Going to see bands didn't always appeal to the boys and anyway, they couldn't afford it. 'The only thing we really had to go on was the records we'd been collecting for years,' explained George Michael. 'In a way, we were quite untainted by any performing bands because we didn't go to watch many. The fact that we were later on the dole for quite a time meant that we didn't have the necessary cash to be able to finance any expensive equipment for ourselves either in the way of instruments or recording gear.'

'We were also fortunate in having a few friends who had some better recording gear than us and we occasionally went there or borrowed it,' adds Ridgeley. 'Most of the day was spent writing and trying to rehearse our own compositions. We knew that if we were to stand any chance of landing a recording contract with one of the major companies then it would have to be on demos of our own compositions and not cover versions. You need to be able to show them that you are capable of sustaining some kind of creative output.'

In February they took the plunge and paid the princely sum of £20 to hire a Portastudio (a small, portable recording set-up). The owner came included in the price, and that morning he arrived at the Ridgeley house and set up his equipment in the living room. The boys had planned to record demos of three songs during the day, using a Doctor Rhythm drum box as their electronic backing band. Paul Ridgeley joined them to sing backing vocals on the first track, 'Wham Rap!'. Compared to the released version this demo was much harsher and included a fair amount of swearing. Singing into a microphone strapped to a broom handle, things took longer than anticipated and they'd barely finished 'Wham Rap!' when Jennifer Ridgeley arrived home from school. This brought a break in proceedings. No sooner had they started on the second song, 'Careless Whisper', than Albert Ridgeley came home from work and things ground to a halt once again. But by the end of the day the £20 had managed to buy them one complete song, even if it was just a rough demo, and about a minute of another.

Copies of the tape were quickly run off so Georgios and Andrew could start touting it around every record label they could think of. With no manager or agent they did all the leg work themselves, usually turning up at label offices unannounced. On their arrival the duo would act businesslike and professional, telling the receptionist that they had an appointment booked. She would invariably look at her notes; not seeing their names, she would say that they didn't. The boys would slowly start to lose their patience, insisting that they did have an appointment and that it wasn't their fault *she* had made a mistake. On most occasions the ruse worked and someone would come out and see them.

They would then sit in a room while the label representative listened to the tape. Time after time the tape would play for less than 30 seconds before it was stopped and they were told, thanks but no thanks. 'I had been trying to get a deal with either a publisher or a record company for roughly two years,' George Michael told the Chancery High Court in 1993. 'I went to many record companies, but the only ones I remember are the major ones. I went to Chrysalis, A&M, EMI, Virgin. I don't actually recall all the names of the various companies I went to. Basically the A&R departments showed no interest and I played tapes of demos and they weren't interested.' Virgin's response was, 'Oh no, not another synthesiser band!' Other labels were equally unimpressed. The hopefuls skulked back to Watford.

In later years George Michael was asked why he hadn't formed Wham! with David Mortimer. The simple answer was that they'd have killed each other if they had been working together constantly. They would both have tried to take control. Andrew Ridgeley, on the other hand, was a perfect fit for Georgios. And Mortimer had less faith than Ridgeley in his friend's writing ability. About to set off on a trip to Thailand, he told Georgios that if his songs were any good they would have been signed up already. Georgios ignored him and went back to work on two more new songs, 'Club Tropicana', which he wrote with Ridgeley, and 'Come On!'. By the time Mortimer got back from his trip a record deal was in place.

The duo had finally managed, through a slightly circuitous route, to catch the ear of Mark Dean with the new songs. A friend of Andrew Ridgeley's was playing in The Quiffs, the band which had earlier rejected Georgios as a drummer on account of his looks. The band knew Dean, and persuaded him to listen to the tape. It was a big improvement on the demo by The Executive that he'd previously rejected. Agreeing with Georgios that they needed to spend £200 on re-recording the two songs plus some new ones in a real studio, he offered to sign Wham! on the spot.

Dean's stock in the record industry was on the rise. He'd

signed Soft Cell and ABC, achieving great success with both. Soft Cell's 'Tainted Love' had reached number one in August 1981 and was followed up with a number four hit, 'Bedsitter'. Along with the Human League, ABC led the New Romantics coming out of Sheffield and had chart success of their own, culminating with three Top 10 hits in 1982, 'The Look Of Love', 'Poison Arrow' and 'All Of My Heart'. On the back of these successes Dean had a growing reputation and with it some bargaining power. He managed to broker a deal with American giants CBS to launch his own label, called Innervision. Wham! would be his opening gambit.

Dean had held his initial meetings with Wham! in borrowed offices on South Molton Street, and the band were unaware of the tightrope he was walking in order to start his own company. To facilitate a speedy launch Dean had borrowed £150,000 from CBS to use as artist advances. CBS would handle the new label's distribution and put up another £75,000 to enable Innervision to pay for professional studio time. But all this would have to be paid back to the corporation from any future earnings that the label might make. The small print on the contract between the labels showed that CBS would certainly be protecting its investment. Innervision would be paid a royalty of 15 per cent, based on sales, but out of this figure Dean would have to pay royalties to the artists, usually in the region of 8 per cent. CBS also said that if they advertised any Innervision product on TV they would only pay half the agreed fees to help cover the cost of the commercials.

By March 1982, with his father's words of ultimatum – 'Get a label, get a job or get out' – echoing in his head, Georgios was willing to sign with almost anyone who showed an interest in the band. Innervision's offer was the only one on the table, even if it did say they'd get no royalties on sales of 12-inch singles. On 24 March Wham! were at the Halligan Band Centre in Holloway recording professional demos of their best songs with a backing band. Georgios was blown away by the version of 'Careless Whisper', with a full band and saxophone, that was played back to him along with 'Club Tropicana' and the brand new 'Young Guns (Go For It!)'. He felt that they had the makings of something big. But later that day he effectively signed it all away.

Mark Dean met them at the studio and, obviously aware of how good these songs were, insisted that they sign the contracts right away. They went to a café round the corner where Dean explained that due to upcoming CBS release schedules they had to sign that very afternoon, there was no time to get the contracts checked out properly. He offered them £500 each, set against future earnings, and they signed on the dotted line.

'Mark Dean was just as green as we were,' George Michael said later. 'I think he got turned over by CBS to a certain extent. Obviously he wanted to get his company off the ground via us, and he had a good track record.' The contract tied them in for a series of five albums in five years, or if they split, a further ten solo albums each. But Georgios didn't care about the money or the details, he just wanted to be famous. There was no big party or celebration after signing the deal. Georgios celebrated his £500 windfall by going out and getting his ear pierced.

Back in 1982 there was no internet to get a buzz going about a new band. No MySpace. No YouTube. So CBS came up with the idea that Wham! should make a series of club appearances to try and establish an underground following. Each Friday and Saturday evening a female CBS rep would pick the boys up and they'd be spirited around four or five nightclubs. To boost their numbers Andrew Ridgeley asked Shirlie Holliman to join them as a dancer, and 16-year-old Mandy Washburn made it a foursome. The quartet would arrive at a club, perform energetic dance routines while miming to a couple of Wham! tracks and then give out some free records.

Some clubs were instantly forgettable, others were more famous. At the Level One club in Neasden the group found that there was no stage and everyone in the venue crowded round to watch the dance routine. At another club Georgios' microphone came unplugged and he was jumping around with the wire dangling behind him, making it obvious even to an inebriated audience that he wasn't singing live. During an event at Stringfellow's he performed a high kick and his slip-on shoe shot out over the heads of the crowd; to make it look as if he meant it, he had to kick the other into the audience too. He spent the rest of the performance trying not to slip over in his bare feet.

Trying your hardest to garner some enthusiasm when a bunch of drunken clubgoers just wanted to fondle the women and drink lager didn't always work. Yet, despite the often lukewarm responses they received, this was a valuable learning experience for them all. Much more demanding than merely bopping around in their bedrooms to a cassette tape, it was important preparation for a possible TV appearance in the future.

The first Wham! single, 'Wham Rap! (Enjoy What You Do?)', was released in June 1982. It had been recorded with Bob Carter, whose stock was high after working on Junior's hit single 'Mama Used To Say'. Carter brought in members of the band who played on that single. Along with David Austin, Paul Ridgeley again added backing vocals. The song depicted the world as they saw it. It was hardly a rap as we know it today, more of a spoken word introduction before a heavily synthesised backing track kicked in. Stuttering Haircut 100-esque guitars washed over a funky beat while Georgios – expressing Andrew Ridgeley's attitude more than his own – sang of choosing to be on the dole rather than get a job. Hand claps, a brass section, chanted vocals – the track had it all.

The video was almost a narrative take of the song lyric.

Georgios is seen getting dressed in a white T-shirt and black leather jacket before walking round to the Ridgeley house, where Andrew's parents are telling him to get out and get a job. Then there is footage of the band and girls on a white stage, with the name 'Wham!' on a large screen behind them. The foursome perform a choreographed dance, just as they had in the clubs.

It had been the group's humorous take on rap, but the news in spring 1982 cast everything in a more serious light. Argentina had laid claim to the Falkland Islands in March and many lives were lost before the Argentines' surrender on 14 June. The song's mention of the dole and the DHSS, a major social problem, took away any humour as far as the majority of the press was concerned and most writers looking for an angle picked up on the topic of unemployment. Future Pet Shop Boy Neil Tennant, writing in *Smash Hits*, cut right to the core of the record when he said it was a 'hard, hot and witty rap . . . real excitement, hundreds of ideas, built in participation and maximum humour'. 'Wham Rap!' was even chosen as single of the week in *Sounds*.

The group, though less than a year old, was already starting to make changes. Mandy Washburn decided she was better off pursuing a career as a hairdresser but was soon replaced by 20-year-old Diane 'Dee' Sealey (aka Dee C. Lee). And Georgios Panayiotou decided to adopt the name George Michael. The first part – an anglicisation of Georgios – was easy, while the surname came from a favourite uncle called Michael. But the change came too late for the initial pressing of 'Wham Rap!'. The credit on the record read 'Panos/Ridgeley'.

Peter Powell was the first DJ to play a Wham! record on BBC Radio 1, but 'Wham Rap!' didn't sell well and stalled at number 105 in the UK chart. Mark Dean knew someone who was going to Corfu later in the summer to take photos of holiday villas for a brochure and managed to tag Ridgeley and Michael along on the trip. Once on the island they had some promotional photos taken which would mould their image for the next few years: fit and healthy, well-tanned, good-looking teenagers up for a good time. George Michael was looking especially well, having lost weight due to the energetic dance routines they'd been performing several times a night for months.

Next up was another semi-rap tune, 'Young Guns (Go For It!)'. Recorded with ABC producer Steve Brown, one of Mark Dean's connections, the song opens with a dramatic keyboard part, building to another spoken-word intro by George Michael. The lyric then bounces back and forth in a conversational style between two friends as they disagree about settling down young, a fate referred to as 'death by matrimony'. Again the song was written from experience, this time that of seeing old school friends settling down while the pair were out having fun.

The video, directed by Tim Pope, perfectly captures the conversations. It's set in a nightclub (where else?), the exchanges between George and Andrew taking place on the dance floor and at the bar. Then Shirlie Holliman arrives to disrupt the beautiful friendship before the band hit the dance floor for the usual choreographed moves. George wears his regular uniform of black leather jacket and white T-shirt, updating the James Dean / Marlon Brando image for the 1980s. 'When we began working on it and putting the whole thing down on tape,' said Michael, 'we could see from the way that it was working out that it was much more than just a straightforward song. The lyrics and the entire structure of the thing presented its way to us more in the format of a small playlet. There was a kind of conversation that was going on and so Andy, Shirlie and I put it across that way and did the video that accompanied it in the same way.'

This second single breached the Top 100 in October. Airplay snowballed and it continued to rise but CBS, not expecting such interest after the relative failure of 'Wham Rap!', literally ran out of records and it stalled while more were pressed. In the meantime

Wham! were given their first TV exposure with a slot on Noel Edmonds' Saturday morning kids' TV vehicle, *Multi-coloured Swap Shop*, getting their break because the show's producer had seen one of their earlier appearances at Stringfellows.

The importance of appearing on *Swap Shop* shouldn't be underestimated. But the biggest break came when one of the acts due to appear on *Top of the Pops* made a late withdrawal. The spot had to be filled quickly and Wham! got the call, even though 'Young Guns' was not yet a big hit and was nestled at number 42.

With no MTV in the UK and only four TV channels to watch – BBC1, BBC2, ITV and the newly launched Channel 4 – any exposure on a music programme was guaranteed to give an artist a massive new audience. This was doubly true when that programme was *Top of the Pops*. The show, presented by BBC Radio 1 DJs, was fast approaching its 1,000th episode and its traditional Thursday night slot on BBC1 had become a British institution. Having closely studied the show all his life, George Michael knew what went to make a successful appearance.

The show was filmed on a Wednesday before being aired at prime time on Thursday evening. Innervision decided that they should book the band into a hotel near the studio so that there was no chance they would be late for the recording. So Michael and Ridgeley spent the night before their debut *Top of the Pops* appearance in a crummy little hotel just off Charing Cross Road where rooms cost less than £1 per night. To make matters worse, Michael had to sleep on a child-size bed with polythene sheets, his legs sticking out of the bottom.

Though it was far and away the most important British pop music programme, as it had been since the 1960s, *Top of the Pops* had always courted controversy as to whether acts performed live in the studio or mimed. In the early days of the show, acts mimed to the recorded version of their song. Later a backing track was used, accompanied by a live in-the-studio orchestra and live vocals, before in 1980 performers again began miming to pre-recorded tracks. Wham! had no problem miming, which would simply be a recreation of their club routine.

The 4 November show was also the *Top of the Pops* debut for DJ presenter Mike Smith. He'd been fast-tracked from hospital radio to London radio station Capital, joining Radio 1 in 1982, and now he was to make his TV debut. Dressed in a knitted blue grandad-style jumper, he opened the show enthusiastically: 'It's the first chart of November, it's my first *Top of the Pops*, it's *their* first *Top of the Pops* . . .'

The acting out of parts in 'Young Guns (Go For It!)' fitted perfectly into the TV format. The conversational style, facial expressions and dance moves were all well honed. George Michael wore a sleeveless brown leather jacket with the collar turned up over his bare shaved chest, and with his tanned complexion and shin-length jeans he was the picture of young vitality. Andrew Ridgeley wore a more conservative combo, his patterned shirt tucked into his jeans. He danced with Shirlie Holliman, who had bleached blonde hair and wore an angular white dress cut to knee length at the back but barely crotch length at the front. Michael partnered Dee C. Lee. The studio crowd was in full party gear – pork pie hats, belted dresses, big hair, flicks, rah-rah skirts, vests and braces. During the performance George turned to David Austin, who was on stage miming a guitar part, and said, 'This is it. This is the rest of my life.'

Once the show was over, though, it was back down to earth with a bump as they all went home on the bus. After the show was aired on Thursday, Michael spent the next few days walking around disappointed that no one recognised him. Eventually, though, he was asked for his autograph for the first time and he felt that he was getting somewhere.

The *Top of the Pops* performance worked wonders. The single shot up the UK charts, hitting the number three spot in early December. At the time the group were not seen purely as a pop band – *New Musical Express* (*NME*) made 'Young Guns' its single of the week – but they agreed to do a photo story for teen favourite *My Guy* magazine. Michael tried to inject some humour into the piece and camped it up, wearing not one pair of sunglasses as most self-respecting pop stars did, but three pairs. But the humour didn't translate to the page very well. To end the year the band headed back to Bushey Meads School, where they played at the Christmas party as homecoming heroes.

In 1983 bands such as Duran Duran, Kajagoogoo, Spandau Ballet and Culture Club would all top the charts, a new wave of British pop which would later storm America too. On the back of the success of the 'Young Guns' single Innervision decided to re-release 'Wham Rap!' in February. This time it soared, peaking at number eight. They had appeared *Top of the Pops* on 27 January 1983. Under coloured neon lights, surrounded by balloons, the band took to the stage amid a general party atmosphere. This time Ridgeley and Michael wore the matching outfits that were to become their uniforms for the next few months, defining the band's image in the press, and which combined with the lyric to create a myth of tough street cred: blue jeans, white T-shirt, and the ubiquitous black leather jacket with upturned collar. The girls wore matching black trouser suits. Michael spent most of the performance out front alone while Ridgeley joined the backing singers at the rear of the stage, these three only coming forward occasionally. There was no pretence of instruments on stage this time; George was the star of the show. And again that show was a complete success.

In the early months of the year Ridgeley and Michael came to a decision about the future workload within the band. It was becoming increasingly obvious that George was taking on all of the songwriting responsibility; rather than soldier on under the pretence that Andrew was involved in the creative process, they took the conscious decision that Michael would be left alone to write the songs while Ridgeley went out and enjoyed himself. With this agreed, George started work in February on a new song called 'Bad Boys'. It was his first solo composition.

While George fleshed out the song a new backing band was recruited. Dreadlocked bassist Deon Estus would play with Wham! for the rest of its career. The American-born musician also added rhythm guitar to complement Andrew Ridgeley's playing. Other additions were drummer Trevor Morrell, guitarist Robert Ahwai and keyboardist Anne Dudley. The new band worked hard, but the song still took the best part of two months to complete. 'Bad Boys' was released in May, with an instrumental version of the same song as the B side, and shot to number two in the UK charts.

'Bad Boys' took the being-on-the-dole-and-not-caring attitude a step further. Written in the form of an open letter to the singers' parents, describing how they were rebelling against the plans that had been made for them since childhood, it hammered home once again the ideals of brotherhood and sticking together no matter what. Essentially it was an exclamation mark (something they were fond of) to their first three singles. (In hindsight George Michael realised that this image was not what he wanted to be remembered for and all but disowned the song; the *Twenty Five* compilation, which included several Wham! tracks, omitted these early singles.)

The video starts in black and white with a soldier returning home from National Service to a wife and son. The child starts misbehaving, shooting catapults and the like, before morphing into the 19-year-old George Michael, who proclaims himself 'handsome, tall and strong'. Now in colour, George exchanges words with Mum and Dad before going out along darkened back alleys to meet Andrew Ridgeley, after which they drive around the city streets in a large American open-topped car as steam rises from manhole covers. The final group dance scene in a backlit, smoky city street is a cross between *West Side Story* and Michael Jackson's later video, *Thriller*. George Michael's recollections of the video are less than rose tinted. 'We look such a pair of wankers in it,' he says. 'How can anybody look at those two people on screen doing what we were doing and think it's good?'

'Bad Boys' entered the charts on 14 May and remained there for three and a half months, peaking at number two while the epic Police track 'Every Breath You Take' held on to number one. Despite the odd dodgy video, things were definitely on the up. Wham! were back on *Top of the Pops* in early June to promote the single, this time being introduced by Tony Blackburn, in a vinyl blue jacket, and national treasure Jimmy Savile, resplendent in typically overstated zebra-print jacket. The band opened the show, Blackburn opining, 'This is a song about Jim and I!'

The usual white T-shirts and black leather biker jackets were given a slight twist this time. Andrew Ridgeley appeared with a guitar and wore shades while the girls wore tight white skirts and also donned shades. It was like watching 'Leader of the Pack' with Fifties rockers given an Eighties twist. George spent most of the song out front, Andrew joining him at the end almost as if to remind viewers that Wham! was actually a duo.

Even at this stage Jack Panos felt that his son's new career might be short-lived. 'When the big money came through because we were up to our third single, my father was still saying, "Save your money boy, cos it's not gonna last". And I never believed that,' said Michael. 'From the moment I got my foot in the door I believed it was gonna stay there. I found it quite amusing actually; it took him a good couple of years before he thought, "Actually I'm totally wrong".'

George Michael went back into the studio to record the next single and the rest of the songs for Wham!'s debut album. In typically confident manner, they decided to call their debut album *Fantastic*. Apart from the three singles to date, the album contained only five more tracks, though later CD versions were padded out with remixes. Despite its brevity it did manage to excite – and also crammed in four exclamation marks and a question mark – not bad for eight songs.

Michael and Steve Brown co-produced the album, neatly book-ending the start and end of each side with the four singles. It opened with the now distinctive 'Woo-woo!' of 'Bad Boys' but quickly displayed that the band had more to offer than a trio of semi-rap songs about being young and on the dole. The soulful pop of 'A Ray Of Sunshine' included the quintessential 1980s pop line 'Gotta make a lot of money', while the gang vocals and George Michael's best Bee Gees impression on the Miracles' 'Love Machine' showed the band in a completely new light. 'Wham Rap!' closed side one and the next single, 'Club Tropicana', opened side two, its motor-car sound effects leading the listener into the party – as would be evidenced in the video. 'Nothing Looks The Same In The Light' showed Michael's tender side for the first time before 'Come On!' and 'Young Guns (Go For It!)' brought the album to an end with some uptempo excitement.

The album was dedicated to the memory of ex-Executive member Andrew Leaver, who had recently died, and another old school friend, Paul Atkins, who'd been killed in a car crash. The cover shot of the boys lying back to back and staring moodily into the camera was snapped by Chris Craymer. It showed them wearing the ever-present black leather jackets with nothing underneath, the perfect image for a pair of Young Guns, and was chosen ahead of shots of the pair wearing white T-shirts and fooling around with each other. The jacket worn by Michael on the cover actually belonged to Craymer as the singer couldn't yet afford one of his own. They liked the photos so much that Craymer was booked as their photographer for the next 18 months. Eventually they went down the route of using fashion photographers for their promo shoots, inspiring Craymer to become a fashion photographer himself: 'In their own way, they were very important to me,' he says.

Don Shewey, writing in *Rolling Stone* magazine, seemed to like the music but wasn't impressed with the production values or George Michael's vocals. 'Probably the biggest problem with Wham! is that the group lacks a really distinctive vocalist,' he wrote. 'George Michael's earnest whine is as synthetic and overly familiar as the cheap keyboards so prevalent nowadays. Turn up Wham! when they come on the car radio, but remember: they won't sound the same anywhere else.'

In *Melody Maker*, Lynden Barber slammed the goody-goody nature of the supposed bad boys, their willingness to play the role of fashion models on the album cover and their attempts at rap, but did like the music, even if reluctantly. The review closed: 'Wham! are a moderate kind of pleasure boat burdened with grossly unwelcome baggage, but I guess you don't want to know about that. All you want to know is if the LP is worth buying. The only answer to that is: GO FOR IT.' The album shot to number one in the chart, helped by the latest smash hit single, 'Club Tropicana'.

With this one song Wham! changed their direction and image completely. They jettisoned the leather jackets, instead flaunting blatantly before the fans the hedonistic lifestyle to which they aspired. This perfect summer tune was just what the Conservative government ordered – young, tanned, healthy bodies splashing about and enjoying their newfound wealth, a million miles away from life on the dole. The fact that the boys had Mediterranean good looks, perma-tans and teeth from a toothpaste commercial helped. The song's bouncy bass line, jaunty piano, shakers and soaring vocals conveyed a carnival atmosphere.

For the 'Club Tropicana' video the crew flew out to Ibiza, the perfect setting for such a song. The whole production was much more professional than earlier videos with their shoestring budgets. The clip was filmed as if it were a full-length movie, with a non-musical introduction and credits at the beginning and end. In the opening shot Dee C. Lee and Shirlie Holliman are seen driving a jeep down a long dusty road into the tropical wilderness. By nightfall they arrive at a remote villa and walk into the garden. The first thing they (and the camera) see is a middle-aged, bare-chested man with a Mexican bandito moustache, wearing a straw cowboy hat and red neckerchief, looking like a throwback to a 1970s gay porn movie. As the music picks up, they walk past and turn the corner to encounter a pool surrounded by healthy young people in swimming briefs and shades. George Michael, in white Speedos, poses by the side of the pool with a pink cocktail. Andrew Ridgeley is on an airbed in the pool talking on the phone. It was the perfect picture of 1980s decadence – splashing money about while splashing in the swimming pool.

Further scenes show the boys (separately) under a shower, high jinks in the pool, lots of people swimming, trumpets in the water, people at the beach. Next we see the girls drive by the boys' broken-down jeep before, in a stereotypical Spanish touch, George and Andrew ride a couple of donkeys back to the villa. Finally all four are seen getting dressed as airline staff and heading back to work. Andrew, preening in front of the mirror, doesn't have to act too hard, while George finally fulfils his childhood dream of being an airline captain. The film closes with a shot of their plane taking off into the sunset.

One scene in the video shows George and Andrew in the pool looking up lustfully as Dee C. Lee and Shirlie walk by. In fact the image this presented was somewhat misleading. During the shoot Michael had already confided in Holliman that he thought he might be gay, though she felt he was just looking for help and might have 'had an experience'. After later discussions with Andrew it was concluded that George shouldn't tell his parents yet; if he did he'd find it very difficult to stay 'in' professionally.

'Club Tropicana' was transported to the BBC, almost literally, for a *Top of the Pops* appearance on 4 August. Mike Smith was again the presenter, this time along with the late, great John Peel. Once more Wham! opened the show. Smith explained, 'We've got sun, sea and swimming costumes for you tonight!' to which Peel pulled a face and did a little dance. The studio had been turned into a kitsch, tacky 1980s imitation of a beach with cheap silver palm trees made out of what looked like last year's fake Christmas trees. George Michael was bare chested in an open Hawaiian shirt and shorts. Fake green cocktails with umbrellas were scattered around the crowd, while couples watched from stageside seats in a low-budget attempt to capture the atmosphere of the video. Dee C. Lee and Shirlie Holliman danced around in black one-piece swimsuits and big sun hats. A large grand piano at the centre of the stage sat unused until the very end when George pretended to play it, though his hands weren't even touching the keyboard at one point.

No matter, the crowd loved it. The boys had to be smuggled out of Television Centre hiding between the crates on the back of a milk float because there was such a mob of girls waiting for them outside. Wham!-mania was just beginning.

'Club Tropicana' became the band's fourth Top 10 hit from *Fantastic*, but shortly afterwards Dee C. Lee jumped ship to marry Paul Weller and join his new band the Style Council. She was quickly replaced by another black singer, Helen DeMacque, known to everyone as 'Pepsi'. Pepsi was four years older than Shirlie and five years older than George and Andrew, but she fitted in perfectly.

Less than a year into their career, Wham! were big-time pop stars. They were also young, inexperienced kids with suffocating adulation being piled on them at every turn. Everything was starting to happen too fast and things were in danger of running out of control. Andrew Ridgeley was becoming a tabloid regular as a result of his very public drunken nights out, and although George Michael kept a lower profile in clubland he too was drinking and smoking to excess.

With an exponential rise in requests for their time as offers and endorsement opportunities flooded in, Wham! decided that now was the time to take on a manager. The prospect of setting up their first-ever tour was looming on the horizon, and they were also concerned that despite massive sales they weren't seeing much of a financial return. The band agreed to work with Nomis Management, a partnership between Simon Napier-Bell and Jazz Summers. Summers had first heard a Wham! demo tape at Island Records, while Napier-Bell had been in the music industry since the 1960s, when he had managed the Yardbirds.

The security of having managers paid immediate rewards. Soon after Wham! signed up, an American band put forward a claim for $20 million because they'd taken the name first. Other English bands have had to change their nomenclature to avoid such problems: The Beat became known as The English Beat and the Charlatans became Charlatans UK. But this case was soon dropped.

While the legal side of things was being taken care of, Andrew and George took a holiday in Cyprus. Their fame had reached the island ahead of them and as soon as George arrived he was being asked for autographs. Back home *Fantastic* became the number one album in July and stayed in the Top 100 for the next two years, though in the US it peaked at only number 83. During the break there were discussions about what should happen next. George thought that 'Careless Whisper' should be recorded properly. It was agreed that, though the band was just finding its feet, the song didn't fit the current Wham! image and should be a George Michael solo release.

In August it was arranged for Michael to make his first trip to the States to record the song with legendary producer Jerry Wexler. The walking embodiment of the history of American popular music, after serving in the navy during the Second World War Wexler had worked at MGM before joining the fledgling Atlantic Records label in the early 1950s. His list of production credits bore comparison with anyone in the business – Ray Charles, the Drifters,

Dusty Springfield, Wilson Pickett, Bob Dylan and most famously, Aretha Franklin. And he had turned the town of Muscle Shoals, in the northwestern corner of Alabama, into a musical mecca. Michael flew in to meet the producer at his Texas home and the pair travelled to Muscle Shoals together to meet the Swampers, Muscle Shoals' regular house band – Barry Beckett (keyboards), Peter Carr (guitar), Roger Hawkins (drums), David Hood (bass) and Jimmy Johnson (guitar). These were seasoned veterans who had played on a host of hits.

During the first sessions Michael was beset with nerves. It was his first time recording overseas, without the moral support of Andrew Ridgeley, with a world famous producer and an experienced band. That night Wexler showed his experience by taking Michael and the band out on a bar crawl. This broke the ice and dispersed any lingering tensions and the next morning the sessions went well, but Michael was critical of his own performance. When he'd first signed the record deal, he had it in his head that everyone in the music business ran the industry from a set of carefully planned blueprints and that artists' careers followed a set path to stardom. He was sharp enough to realise before long that this notion was wide of the mark – everything was pretty much made up as they went along. So he decided that he'd do exactly as he wanted for the rest of his career because the so-called experts knew little more than he did himself. With that in mind he decided to ignore all 'official' advice and shelve the tapes from the Wexler sessions.

Back in the UK the Nomis management team had embarked on a war of the minds with Innervision. Nomis informed the label that until things were sorted to their satisfaction, meaning a breaking of the Innervision contract, there would be no new Wham! recordings. Instead the group prepared for their first tour, for which Nomis secured a lucrative sponsorship deal with sports clothing giant Fila to the tune of £50,000.

The tour party included several relatives and old friends. George's sisters Melanie and Yioda were put in charge of hair and make-up. Cousin Andros also joined the entourage, with David Austin on guitar, Deon Estus on bass and the rest of the album's backing band along too. Pepsi and Shirlie made up an important part of the visual presentation. The sold-out Club Fantastic tour opened in Scotland with two nights at the Aberdeen Capitol. Though the band's departure from London was low key, the airport was mobbed with fans on arrival north of the border.

Rather than employ a warm-up band the group decided to get the fans in the mood by again reaching back to their clubbing roots. Gary Crowley, who had now graduated to Capital Radio, was taken along as the opening DJ act and a team of body poppers called Eklypse performed their dance routines while Crowley revved up the crowd with an hour of dance singles. The tour emphasised the growing hysteria that surrounded everything the band did, and the presence of thousands of screaming teenage – and older – girls gave rise to the phrase 'Wham!-mania'. George and Andrew were loving the attention and played up to it at every opportunity. They would walk out on stage with badminton racquets in hand and shuttlecocks stuffed down the front of their tight white shorts, then pull them out and bat them around before launching them into the seething mass of oestrogen. Sometimes Andrew would play the tease further by running the shuttlecock up and down his sweaty arm before kissing it and dispatching into the crowd. 'We wanted to put together a show that the fans would really remember,' said George. 'We didn't want to just go out on stage and leap about to the music, but put together a good piece of theatre too. It was all carefully organised, the music, the choreography, the costumes and when we felt we were ready we went out and did it!'

The first part of the show ended with a rendition of Chic's party anthem 'Good Times', before a short break was taken during which a large screen played childhood movies and old family photos of the band. The first set usually saw the band play most of the *Fantastic* album before George Michael took the stage alone for moving renditions of the unreleased tracks 'Careless Whisper' and 'Blue'.

Back at the hotel after the first show the touring party was besieged by fans. Andrew and George were spirited away but Gary Crowley and Andros were mobbed for autographs, just because they were friends of the band. Only 12 dates into the tour, after the first two of three shows at the Hammersmith Odeon, the tour was halted when Ridgeley managed to write off his green Ford Capri in an accident and Michael was struck down with laryngitis. A total of 11 shows were cancelled but they were immediately rescheduled for the restart of the tour on 13 November.

Innervision struck the next blows in the escalating battle with Nomis, antagonising the band in the process. They took out injunctions that stopped Wham! from talking to other labels and barred them from recording for anyone else. They also issued the 'Club Fantastic Megamix' without the band's approval, a final step which sealed the label's fate as far as any workable relationship with the band was concerned. Rehashing three of *Fantastic*'s non-singles ('A Ray Of Sunshine', 'Come On!' and 'Love Machine'), it was a blatant attempt by Mark Dean to cash in on the pre-Christmas market. But with little or no support from the band, the single struggled to number 15 in the charts during December 1983.

Nomis were quick to distance the band from the release, putting out a statement which said: 'It's absolutely disgusting. I just hope the radio doesn't play it. It would be so irritating to hear something you think is so bad.' It was a sad end to an otherwise triumphant year. The anger George Michael felt at not being in full control would simmer on into the new year – and then things would take a turn for the worse.

FOUR

BIG

1984–1985

big

1 large, as in size, height, width, or amount: a big house; a big quantity.

2 of major concern, importance, gravity, or the like: a big problem.

3 outstanding for a specified quality: a big liar; a big success.

4 important, as in influence, standing, or wealth: a big man in his field.

5 grown-up; mature: big enough to know better.

6 doing business or conducted on a large scale; major in size or importance: big government.

7 magnanimous; generous; kindly: big enough to forgive.

8 boastful; pompous; pretentious; haughty: a big talker.

'We were out and out pop. We thought it was the most honest thing to do. We didn't want to be subversive in any sense. We wanted to be huge stars. I knew that I could do it. I knew that I had the capability, craftwise, to put us ahead of groups like Duran Duran and Culture Club, so I just went for it.'

George Michael

'He has one of the best voices I've ever heard. Technically it's way ahead of mine. When I first saw George and Andrew Ridgeley together they reminded me of when Bernie Taupin and I first started writing songs together. He's also a great songwriter. I'd put him up there with Paul McCartney.'

Sir Elton John

In the seemingly ever-spinning revolving door at the top of the UK charts, Frankie Goes To Hollywood made the biggest impression during early 1984. Their controversial song 'Relax' went to number one on 28 January and stayed there until March. Once again the gauntlet had been laid down. Duran Duran also held top spot before Wham! knocked them off in June. Frankie then returned to knock Wham! from the perch. This seemed to go on for the whole year. But at the end of the 12 months one group was king – 1984 was the year of Wham!.

Coming down from the touring high, there were serious business matters to iron out before the band could capitalise on their status. The pop world moved notoriously fast. Wham! might have been a successful brand in 1983, but they would have to work extra hard to keep their fan base growing in 1984. So it was even more frustrating that instead of cashing in, the band were made to wait in limbo while a five-month legal stalemate ensued.

For the various members of Wham!'s cast, the break had quite different effects. Because Shirlie Holliman was paid per performance, the long spell without work meant she had no money coming in. Andrew Ridgeley was less than sympathetic to her situation and suggested that she go and get a job. It was around this time that the pair split up, though Holliman continued to work with the band until the end.

Ridgeley himself used the time as he had previously, in partying as hard and as often as he could. George Michael on the other hand carried on writing, in order to ensure that everyone else could keep earning when the legal dispute was over. During this period he wrote what would become one of Wham!'s most famous songs, 'Wake Me Up Before You Go-Go', and one that would ensure Christmastime royalties for the next two decades and beyond, 'Last Christmas'.

By now the early ideas for songs had all but dried up. 'We've now completely exhausted all of that early material,' said George at the time. 'We only worked carefully on a few songs which we felt would help us get the recording deal. A few we held back and did later, but "Careless Whisper" was really the last of that early output. It's now down to the tough work of producing a steady stream of new material, and it isn't easy. But we both love the whole process of writing songs. It's exciting to come up with an idea and then go into the studio and watch the whole thing come together. When people then go out and buy that song in their hundreds of thousands it's a rewarding experience.'

One Saturday night in early 1984 inspiration struck. '[Sometimes] you think of someone sitting down at a piano or with a guitar and tape machine and really working hard at it,' recalled George. 'In this instance, Andy and I were sitting together at my house and we were watching *Match of the Day* in the evening. We'd just been chatting and cheering on the teams, when suddenly I yelled out and ran upstairs.'

'I wondered what on earth he was up to,' said Andrew Ridgeley. 'He seemed to be up there ages and I went to see what was going on. When I found him, he was singing into his tape recorder and when he'd finished he just turned and told me that he'd had a marvellous song come into his head whilst he'd been watching television and that if he hadn't rushed upstairs to put the ideas down then he'd probably have forgotten it.' The song was 'Last Christmas'.

During March the miners went on strike in the UK. It would become a bitter war of attrition which would last for just under a year and effectively spell the end of the country's coal-mining industry. In the same month that the strike began, Innervision reached the end of the road. With Mark Dean's mounting legal bills seriously threatening to bankrupt his company, CBS, rightfully mindful of their initial investment, stepped in and took Wham! off the label's hands. CBS moved the band to their Epic subsidiary, loaning more money to Innervision at a low interest rate to compensate Mark Dean for the loss of his prize asset. It was a sad end to the association between Dean and the band. Dean had got in too deep with CBS, but if he hadn't had faith in Wham! when he did George Michael would quite likely have missed his father's deadline of getting a deal or getting a job. He might have been lost to the industry altogether.

As soon as the new deal was in place Nomis wasted no time in getting Wham! back in the public eye. 'Wake Me Up Before You Go-Go' was released in May, with a re-recording of 'Careless Whisper' ready for release later in the summer of 1984. Before these latest potential hit singles could be pressed the band had to film videos for each. The importance of a good video had been growing ever since the 1982 launch of MTV. From a marketing standpoint, the video was becoming almost as important as the song – and especially in America, where Nomis really wanted to break the band.

For 'Careless Whisper', Epic gave Wham! a relatively massive budget, £30,000 for two days' shooting in Miami. Michael, Ridgeley and David Austin flew out with Melanie Panayiotou to work with Carina Camamile, a seemingly inexperienced music video producer. It was during the shoot that Michael had his first real 'diva moment'. His hair kept going frizzy in the humidity of mid-spring Florida, and his sister Melanie had to give him an on-the-spot haircut after he said they'd have to discard the early takes because of his unruly hair. The extra day of shooting required to replace the ditched footage cost a further £17,000. It must go down as one of the world's most expensive haircuts.

With £47,000 – which could have bought a very nice house in 1984 – spent on the 'Careless Whisper' video, the video for 'Wake Me Up Before You Go-Go' would have to be made on a shoestring budget. Carina Camamile was again the producer for the clip, which was filmed at the Brixton Academy in south London. The costs were kept down by shooting a performance piece, for which invited Wham! fans filled the audience free of charge. The video's opening shots were to provide the band, and indeed the decade, with one of its most enduring images. They wore all-white outfits, including the famous baggy T-shirts with the slogan 'Choose Life' printed on the front in enormous black letters. These T-shirts would become the ultimate teenage fashion accessory of 1984. The band, at the back of the bright white stage, wore similar T-shirts but with 'Go-Go' printed on the front. In the second half of the video, the band appeared on stage wearing an assortment of day-glo outfits, while George, in pink sweatshirt, tight shorts and bright yellow fingerless gloves, rolled his eyes at the camera. It was a routine, he later admitted, that should have given viewers a good idea about his sexuality.

The song itself had been titled after George spied a note that Andrew Ridgeley had left for his parents. Having by mistake written 'Wake me up up', he had added the jokey ending 'before you go go'. Michael turned this into an insanely catchy and uplifting chorus and the band had another major hit. Michael's vocals were his most assured to date, while the progression of the musical craft and lyrics from the songs on *Fantastic* was striking. The big band horn section, coupled with references to pre-war dance the Jitterbug and 1950s sweetheart Doris Day, gave this squeaky-clean pop a timeless feel. 'I think "Go-Go" is undoubtedly the most remembered Wham! song because it is that much more stupid than anything else,' laughed George Michael. 'I still look at that video and think it worked really perfectly for that song. Really poppy, really colourful, it totally captures that whole period. But although I see it working as a video, it makes me cringe for myself. But I was completely into the idea of being screamed at, I was very young and I can't pretend my ego didn't need that.'

There had always been a party air about Wham!'s appearances on *Top of the Pops* but when 'Wake Me Up Before You Go-Go' reached number one it was an all-out celebration. Balloons floated down from the rafters as the band partied their way through the song in all-white outfits, the boys' T-shirts this time reading 'Number One' instead of 'Choose Life'. George's shirt had been further modified by his mum and sisters, who had spent the previous night sewing hundreds of little silver buttons over the lettering. 'How annoying must we have been,' asked Michael years later, 'to be so tacky and cheesy. But we just thought it was being funny.' Michael played out his hip-swinging, big-clapping dance while Pepsi and Shirlie backed him up in white T-shirts, pleated white mini-skirts and white boots. The song became the feelgood hit of the summer, spending 16 weeks in the charts.

Wham! were still not completely shunned by the 'serious' music press. In late July the cover of *Melody Maker* blared 'Wham! In The Flesh' while the boys smouldered, topless, from the front page. Inside the band were given a two-page spread and space for George Michael to talk candidly to Helen FitzGerald about his suspicion of the music press. He defended the band's live shows, pointing out that the audience had its fair share of the male population and that they weren't all 16 to 18 years old. He spoke of the backlash that had begun against the band because they dared to say what other bands kept to themselves – that they unashamedly wanted to be big, wanted to sell lots of records. But he also showed the first signs of frustration at not being taken seriously. 'Here I am, 21 years old, I've written six Top 10 singles, written, sung, produced and arranged a number one, I've just released a solo single and what do people want to ask me? Where I buy my shirts from and what my favourite food is!' He finished, emphatically, 'We both vote Labour, we're not sexist, racist, bigoted in any way and oh, we're not gay either.'

For the revamped version of 'Careless Whisper' Michael brought in the much sought-after session keyboardist Andy Richards to synthesise parts of the backing track. 'Careless Whisper' proved to everyone, the singer included, that George Michael would be a viable solo artist in the years to come. Though it was written when he was still a teenager, Michael demonstrated a grasp of music and lyrics in the song that belied his years. This was adult music, though that didn't stop it also becoming a massive hit at school discos up and down the land. After an opening of soaring synth melodies and acoustic guitars, the first verses give way to the most famous saxophone solo of the decade, played by Steve Gregory. This tender ballad, piled high with melancholy, was a complete departure from the fun of 'Go-Go'. In later years Michael was almost unhappy that the song had done so well, saying that to write something so flippantly and see it become so loved was disheartening, but on the other hand it proved that he had the talent without having to think too hard about it. He'd unwittingly provided the closing song to be played at every disco and club for years to come; it's perfect for that late night/early morning smooch, even if the lyric is talking about betrayal.

In the video the sax solo plays over a night-time cityscape straight out of *Moonlighting*. Michael, dressed in lounge suit, sings directly into the camera while clips are interspersed showing him romping around with his first girl; in some of these shots he wears a baseball cap to hide his frizzy hair. Then a second woman arrives in a classy Eighties sports car before luring George on to a yacht in her bathing costume. The two women meet, the first girl flies away and George is left standing on a balcony, looking wistfully at the Miami sunset as he rues his mistakes.

When it was released in August, 'Careless Whisper' bounded up the charts, knocking Frankie Goes To Hollywood's 'Two

Tribes' from number one where it had been lodged for the past five weeks. 'Careless Whisper' spent 17 weeks on the chart, providing Epic with its first million-selling single while pocketing George Michael something in the region of £300,000. The 12-inch single version also included the Jerry Wexler version of the song. George had now achieved number one singles in the same calendar year as both a solo artist and a member of a band. Meanwhile, in the USA the single went to the top of the *Billboard* chart on the back of some heavy CBS promotion. At the age of 21 George had topped the charts on both sides of the Atlantic. He appeared alone on *Top of the Pops* in late August wearing a collarless white shirt, rolled up to the elbows and tucked into his jeans. With his hair growing to full 'Princess Di' effect and looking very tanned, he was the vision of Greek masculinity, 1984 style.

Michael was clearly enjoying the competition with the likes of Duran Duran, Culture Club and Frankie Goes To Hollywood. He liked the challenge of writing and producing something that would be commercially successful as they sought in turn to knock each other off the top of the charts. By the end of the summer he had written enough new material for the band to record their second album. Following on from the tongue-in-cheek title *Fantastic*, they called their sophomore effort *Make It Big* – which was their aim for America. The album was recorded in just six weeks at Chateau Minerval, the southern French studio where Duran Duran had recorded *Seven And The Ragged Tiger* and which had also played host to Pink Floyd. With a band comprised of old stalwarts Deon Estus (bass), and Trevor Morrell (drums), along with Hugh Burns (guitar) and Tommy Eyre (keyboards), Michael took over all the main duties for the album, while much of the time Andrew Ridgeley was absent. Michael not only wrote, sang and played on the album, this time he produced it as well. Despite having no training, he was able by sheer instinct to come up with highly radio-friendly arrangements that people loved to hear.

During the sessions Michael was invited to meet Elton John and his wife Renate in St Tropez. He also flew back to London for a benefit show with Wham! in support of the families of coal miners caught up in the long-running strike. Wham! were to appear in the last of a series of shows hosted at the Royal Festival Hall, but when the rest of the group weren't available Michael and Ridgeley agreed to appear alone, deciding to mime their parts. It was a misguided decision – when Michael introduced one song, a different backing tape started playing. The press hounded them for it, and to make matters worse Michael was quoted as having made unsavoury comments about the National Union of Mineworkers' boss, Arthur Scargill. Michael had met Scargill at the show and thought the union man was enjoying the attention and the strike a little too much, while thousands of his members needed financial help – hence this show – just to be able to buy food.

Michael also found himself appearing with increasing regularity in the gossip pages of the national press. *Private Eye* pointed out that his haircut was very similar to that of Princess Diana. 'The hairdryer was working overtime in autumn 1984,' Michael admitted to the *Daily Mail* in 1990. 'I was sporting the baroque hairdo with the sculpted, blond locks. Some people thought I had the same hairdresser as Princess Diana. Some days I made the covers of the tabloids. Some days Princess Di made the covers of the tabloids. Some days I think they just got us mixed up.'

The satirical ITV puppet show *Spitting Image* also poked fun at the duo, depicting them as a pair of walking white pants with a mouth full of shining white teeth on the front. They were portrayed performing a spoof song that seemed to sum up many people's view of the band: 'Hair, teeth, lips and a perfect bot'.

Wham! returned to the charts in the autumn with a new single and album. 'Freedom', chosen as the single to promote the new album, duly produced another number one hit. This clap-along anthem had been written during the sessions in France and was recorded there in a single day. The title is somewhat misleading: Michael sings of not wanting freedom but instead preferring a monogamous relationship. The opening horns dissolve into an infectious beat that drives the song along at a fast pace and the fist-pounding chorus is pure George Michael magic, with not a little Motown influence showing through.

To promote the new material the group appeared on many TV shows including *Razzmatazz* and Terry Wogan's early-evening chat show, plus the now customary spot on *Top of the Pops*. This time DJ Mike Read introduced the band. He looked like he'd been watching the 'Careless Whisper' video too much, dressed as he was in shades and a white jacket with the sleeves scuffed up to the elbows. Michael had changed his image again for the performance, letting his highlighted hair grow and wearing a baggy black suit and black T-shirt, while Andrew Ridgeley also wore a suit. While the boys shimmied back to back, the girls looked classy in sparkling red dresses and long black gloves. The backing band, in front of the banks of shaped neon lighting, were clad in tuxedos.

Make It Big was mixed in Paris and released in November. Again, it exemplified quality over quantity, as once more just eight songs were included. 'Wake Me Up Before You Go-Go' set the scene, closely followed by the band's most mature song to date, 'Everything She Wants'. This was a perfect slice of funk-pop in which Michael sings about a partner who takes everything he earns, money being the mid-Eighties subject of choice. 'Heartbeat' sounded like mid-1970s Bruce Springsteen until Michael began to sing and 'Like A Baby' was sub-par 10CC with some Spanish guitar. The aforementioned 'Freedom' picked up the pace, the Isley Brothers cover 'If You Were There' trotting nicely along in its wake before the theme of money returned on 'Credit Card Baby'. This horn-driven Sixties pastiche again dealt with the topic of George's girl spending all his money for him. The obvious album closer, 'Careless Whisper', proved perfectly suited to that role. Though a couple of the songs now sound dated, overall the album has aged pretty well. And it really did manage to make the band big, especially in America where George's range of vocal styles – from falsetto to white-boy soul – was lapped up.

Rolling Stone magazine again reviewed the album. This time Christopher Connelly grasped the band's appeal perfectly, calling *Make It Big* 'an almost flawless pop record, a record that does exactly what it wants to and has a great deal of fun doing it. Sure, it's slight stuff and too thinly orchestrated at times, but George Michael can write and sing rings around fellow teen dream Simon Le Bon. Everyone has a guilty pleasure. Why not let Wham! be yours?' American record buyers agreed – the album hit number one in the US charts.

The album cover was again kept simple, showing the boys lounging in suits, black for Michael, white for Ridgeley. *Miami Vice* would never look the same again. *Make It Big* tied in with everything that upwardly mobile Conservative Britain was about in 1984. The album became as much a staple of Eighties culture as Rubik's Cube, legwarmers and *The Breakfast Club*.

This depiction of the lavish lifestyle of the young and successful was hammered home with a £10,000 champagne reception at London's Xenon Club, attended by representatives of the music industry such as Bob Geldof, Nick Heyward and members of Duran Duran and Spandau Ballet. *Make It Big* went straight in at number one in the UK, staying in the charts for a year and five months.

Wham! were now at a stage where each successive album was expected to be accompanied by a worldwide tour. The Big Tour opened at Whitley Bay Ice Rink on 4 December. For what was portrayed as such a prestigious tour, the opening venue was modest to say the least, but with no other large venues available in the north-east they were booked in for three shows sandwiched around trips to Glasgow, Dublin and Leeds. The UK leg of the tour was only just hitting its stride when George Michael hurt his back during an excessively energetic dance sequence at Leeds Queens Hall. For the second UK tour running the band had to cancel some shows, this time five gigs which were put back until February and March the following year. But they did manage to perform dates at Wembley Arena on 23, 24, 26 and 27 December, providing quite a Christmas present for around 50,000 fans. The tour would prove to be hard work and Michael lost an average of five pounds per show due to dehydration. Andrew Ridgeley also gave his all on stage and was a key part of the live show, managing to keep going despite the numerous stories of his excesses that were now regularly popping up in the tabloid press.

George Michael was also out and about a lot, but he managed to keep any liaisons away from the press. This was quite a feat in itself, for the hysteria had reached even higher levels than that surrounding the 1983 tour. 'It's hard for people to appreciate that the screaming,' Michael explained, 'although initially very flattering – you feel like you've been blessed with something – does eventually make you feel like an object, a sex object. You have to have gone through the initial excitement to relate to it. Then you get terrible guilt feelings when you lose the excitement.' This feeling of being adored as an object rather than a talented musician and performer was beginning to wear away at Michael.

The December tour dates coincided with a burst of chart activity for George Michael. The first manifestation came via a charity single. Bob Geldof had been one of millions of Britons moved by BBC newsman Michael Buerk's reports of the famine sweeping through Ethiopia, and especially by the accompanying images. Geldof and Midge Ure immediately set the wheels in motion to produce the most famous charity record of all time, 'Do They Know It's Christmas'. On 24 November he had collected together a cast of around 40 performers spanning the whole spectrum of 1984's pop superstars, including George Michael (Andrew Ridgeley allegedly overslept, which is why he wasn't on the record). Phil

Collins, Tony Hadley of Spandau Ballet, Status Quo, Sting, Bono, Paul Young and Bananarama were just some of the participants in the project, which was given the name Band Aid.

At the Band Aid sessions Michael felt snubbed by some of the other performers. Within the music industry, he felt, Wham! was becoming something of a teenybopper joke to the more 'serious' artists. Paul Weller approached him and had a go about his Arthur Scargill comments. Michael was quite firm in his belief that, in his words, Scargill was a 'wanker', and he told him so. And if Michael's charitable credentials were under the microscope, he passed with flying colours, donating the royalties from his next single, a cool £250,000, to the famine relief fund.

Band Aid's 'Do They Know It's Christmas' was a surefire bet for the Christmas number one spot. Released on 3 December, it went straight to the top, selling over three million copies. Meanwhile Wham! had issued 'Last Christmas', which slotted in nicely behind at number two. In a clever marketing ploy, Epic added 'Everything She Wants' to make the release a double A side. Once Christmas had passed they could continue to promote the single, flipping it over to give it a second wind.

'Last Christmas' was a Phil Spector-ish blast of seasonal pop replete with eminently singable, heartfelt lyrics, sleigh bells and a touch of longing and regret – the perfect Yuletide mix. The accompanying video also followed the perfect Christmas recipe. In it a group of big-haired friends get together for a trip to a remote ski lodge where they dress the tree and all sit down for Christmas dinner together. It has become not just one of the best-remembered videos of the Eighties but possibly the most famous Christmas video of all time. Royalties for repeat plays seem to be secure for ever more.

After the Christmas buzz had passed – probably by the end of Boxing Day – record buyers started purchasing and playing 'Everything She Wants', pushing sales past the one million mark. The video for this track was a mix of black and white concert footage from the December 1984 shows and close-ups of George Michael singing directly into the camera lens. 'Everything She Wants' was the song used on the first *Top of the Pops* of the new year, on 3 January 1985. George Michael bounced around with flowing hair, wearing an untucked shirt, grey jacket and jeans, a look that would be trendy in 20 years' time. Andrew Ridgeley had a massive mullet, and wore mega-loud grey, black and white tartan trousers with matching knee-length coat. In front of a giant neon '1985' sign Pepsi and Shirlie danced in black polo necks and strings of pearls. In the USA, 'Everything She Wants' topped the singles chart, while it also made number seven in Australia and number two in Canada.

After *Top of the Pops* Wham! set off for shows in Japan, Australia and the United States. This time Jack and Lesley Panos came along for the ride. Like much of the tabloid-reading fan base, they were still unaware of their son's excesses, especially while on tour. In Japan Michael's spiralling after-show partying continued. After one show he didn't manage to make it back to his hotel, even though his parents were staying there. Members of the crew had to go and collect him at noon from another hotel where he'd spent the night with three women he'd just met. He stumbled out into the daylight with a dazed look on his face, clearly still drunk. During the February US tour, according to Andros Georgiou as quoted in Michael's own book, *Bare*, Michael was sleeping with anyone and everyone he could, from fans at shows to air hostesses. While Michael claimed that he didn't like being used as a sex object, it didn't appear to stop him from sleeping around. In contrast Andrew Ridgeley, having split up with Shirlie Holliman, didn't complain about it – he enjoyed it to the extreme. But the real Georgios Panos was still insecure about his looks and his sexuality.

While in Japan George and Andrew were asked to shoot a little TV promo video to a backing track of 'Freedom'. They used the shoot as a chance to take the mickey, changing the words to, 'It doesn't matter that you're slightly porky/Ever since that day we met in Torquay' and adding, 'You're the fish face I adore'. When quizzed by the Japanese press, they said this was a British term of endearment.

In between these overseas dates, the band flew back to the UK to collect a Brit Award for Best Group and a prestigious Ivor Novello Award (named after the gay Welsh singer and composer who'd gained massive fame during the first half of the twentieth century) for Most Performed Song of the Year, presented for 'Careless Whisper'. At the same ceremony Elton John presented George Michael with the award for Songwriter of the Year 1984, making him the youngest-ever recipient of the award. Finally Michael was seeing some recognition for his songwriting craft and hard work. But he wanted much more – and the rest of the year would seal Wham!'s fate in that regard.

FIVE

FREEDOM

1985–1986

free·dom

1 the state of being free or at liberty rather than in confinement or under physical restraint: he won his freedom after a retrial.

2 exemption from external control, interference, regulation, etc.

3 the power to determine action without restraint.

4 political or national independence.

5 personal liberty, as opposed to bondage or slavery: a slave who bought his freedom.

6 the absence of or release from ties, obligations, etc.

7 ease or facility of movement or action: to enjoy the freedom of living in the country.

8 frankness of manner or speech.

'The one person I really wanted, the one I thought my life would revolve around, didn't want me. It hit me hard. The relationship screwed me up because I am usually the one who does the leaving. It was messy and I am used to being loved. It was unfair. It had nothing to do with me as a person, as an individual with two legs, eyes and dark hair. It had everything to do with me being a pop star. I was spoilt in so many ways, going straight from school into the band, having no money problems, being able to sleep with whoever I wanted whenever I wanted, and my career going exactly as I liked it, then someone pulled the carpet away. I drank myself stupid for months. I was in a very bad way and started losing my temper for the first time in my life. I got into fist fights with friends, threw photographers against walls and acted very macho.'

George Michael, *Today,* 1990

In March 1985 blood donors in the UK were screened for the AIDS virus for the first time. Health minister Kenneth Clarke announced the move in an effort to calm growing public paranoia about the virus. During 1984 there had been a reported 132 AIDS cases in the UK, up from just four cases in 1981.

In the spring of 1985 George Michael moved to a flat in Knightsbridge before Wham! set off on tour. He was still keeping a relatively low profile while Andrew Ridgeley filled the tabloid pages with his drinking, love life and love of fast cars. In the USA 'Everything She Wants' went to number one, becoming the band's third consecutive American chart topper with the help of the George Michael-produced black and white concert video, which received a lot of airplay.

Meanwhile Simon Napier-Bell was working hard on a publicity coup for the band. He had been holding meetings with the Chinese Minister for Culture, Wang Ping Shan, to discuss the possibility of Wham! playing a pair of shows in Peking and Canton. If this came to fruition the band would be the first major western pop group ever to be allowed into the planet's most populous nation – which of course was also potentially the biggest record-buying market on the planet.

'The basic reason for going to China was not to introduce our wonderful culture. It was to do something,' said George Michael. 'How many things does a band do that are of any significance whatsoever? Just for once, it was nice that you were the first and, quite possibly, the last.' After lengthy negotiations, two dates were agreed, Peking on 7 April and Canton four days later. On the way over the band would also play two shows in Hong Kong on 2 and 3 April. The Wham! organisation paid the bill for everything related to the trip, an estimated £500,000. They hoped to recoup some money by making a film of the tour and securing a deal to sell records and tapes to the Chinese public.

A large cast and crew were taken along for the shows. Keyboardist Tommy Eyre was given the job of musical director and the regular band signed up: Deon Estus, Trevor Morrell and Hugh Burns, plus percussionist Danny Cummings, a brass section of Dave Baptiste, Raul D'Oliveira and Paul Spong, backing vocalists Leroy Osbourne, Janet Mooney and Janey Hallett and a trio of dancers, Shirlie Holliman, Pepsi DeMacque and Trevor Duncan. George's sisters were employed as well. Melanie, who now worked as a hairdresser in London, took care of make-up. Yioda, who had been teaching languages at a school in Nottingham, quit her job to take charge of the wardrobe department.

To finance the making of the tour film, Nomis set up a company called Big Boys Overseas and brought in 23-year-old producer Martin Lewis. Lewis was to go on to greater things, including *The Secret Policeman's Ball* for Amnesty International, but his choice of director for the Wham! movie was a misguided one. He gave the job to Lindsay Anderson, a 61-year-old Scotsman known for his work in the Free Cinema movement of the 1960s. Oxford-educated Anderson had cut his teeth as a film critic after the war before making his own films in the 1950s. His documentary *Thursday's Child* won an Oscar in 1954 but his most memorable films, *This Sporting Life*, *If* and *The White Bus*, had come in the 1960s. He was a strange choice to document a pop band such as Wham!.

The tour party arrived in China for a banquet of honour, to be held on 5 April in Peking. Back home the visit made headlines on the main BBC news programme that night. Throughout the trip Michael and Ridgeley were filmed constantly and followed religiously by a pack of the UK press who had been allowed into the country especially to follow the tour. Tickets for the show included a free Wham! cassette with every purchase and many fans queued all night to ensure a place. However, the Chinese Cultural Ministry was keeping a firm hold on proceedings. The estimated 10,000 fans in attendance for the first show at the Workers' Gymnasium in Peking were told quite clearly that dancing was not permitted and that they had to stay in their seats. On stage Wham! too were under the scrutiny of the authorities, and had been told that they weren't allowed to play 'Love Machine'.

Backstage George Michael admitted that he was nervous before going on, which was unusual. At 7.45 pm prompt the show began. After a local introduction the band put on an energetic show which bemused and entertained the crowd in equal measure. The main problem was the language barrier – with most in the crowd not knowing what the songs were about.

With four days between shows the band had time to take in the sights and attend more PR events, all their activities being captured on film. The second show, in Canton on 11 April, was played to a more lively crowd, despite warnings from the government – the Minister of Culture had said, 'Go to the show but don't learn from it!' Nevertheless many in the audience did get up and dance in their own way, which was quite unique as they'd never seen a band play live or been able to watch how westerners danced on TV. At the end of the show George Michael returned to sing 'Careless Whisper' in a white suit, looking more like Don Johnson by the day.

Michael said afterwards that the trip had given him a new perspective on communism. He was shocked at the way anything outside the normal, everyday lives of the public seemed to baffle them. On the whole he felt depressed and used by the whole experience.

The footage of the tour that Lindsay Anderson cut into his edit of the film did not go down well with Wham! or their management. Anderson had skilfully produced an insight into China at a moment when western influence was just starting to become apparent, but Wham! presumably wanted an MTV-friendly edit with more concert footage. Anderson was removed from the film and a second version was prepared by Strathford Hamilton and promo video collaborator Andy Morahan. This new edit, titled *Foreign Skies*, was issued in 1986, making its debut on the big screen during Wham!'s last show at Wembley Stadium.

The hour-long *Foreign Skies* opens with footage of a UK show. The band are then shown arriving at the airport, in scenes overlaid with footage of a Chinese woman picking out notes on a kind of zither and shots of Buddhist temples. So far, so un-MTV. Then it's a chronological run through the trip. The plane arrives in Peking, using footage later used in a new video for 'Freedom', the band passes through passport control amid a ruck of photographers, they rather uncomfortably meet the Chinese welcoming committee, pose like politicians on a walkabout for photos with local women and children and then are bundled into big black cold-war limos and whisked away. Staying at Peking's best hotel, the band meet more middle-aged Chinese dignitaries; George Michael grins like an embarrassed schoolboy while the Chinese, not for the first time, look quite bemused.

The band visit the Great Wall, there's footage of George looking out over the battlements. Overall it's quite predictable and dry, though one moment of humour arises at a reception garden party at the British embassy where a group of lords and ladies seem to be discussing the embassy's cricket team. Andrew Ridgeley, on the periphery of the conversation, adds 'I'm a footballer!' In fact Ridgeley features quite prominently in the film, buying a jacket from a local store and giving a Wham! tape to a bunch of elders hanging out at the market. There's also footage of an informal game of football in a local park. The band and crew chase around for a bit, Michael is seen wearing a green peaked cap with a red star on the front, while Ridgeley is in his full Queen's Park Rangers kit. The film ends with footage of the concerts.

The fallout from the trip and disagreements over the film continue to this day. The BBC reported that it made a loss of around £1 million. Anderson died in 1994, leaving his archive to Stirling University, and in 2006 his anger at the way the film was handled came to the public's attention for the first time. In his private paperwork he described George Michael as a 'shivering aspirant plucked out of the street, who turns almost overnight into a tyrant of fabulous wealth, whose every command his minions must dash to execute'. Whether Michael's commands were very different to those of any other millionaire pop star is unknown, but Anderson added that he was tied to 'arbitrary orders from George Michael, who doesn't know what he's talking about . . . a young millionaire with an inflated ego. I was struck by his total disinterest in China. His vision only extends to the Top 10.' This may well have been true; maybe Anderson's brief hadn't been made clear enough and his emphasis was weighted differently.

The director had also given the university a copy of his 90-minute cut of the film, *If You Were There*. Having gained permission from Sony, who in the intervening years had bought CBS, Stirling University archivist Karl Magee planned to show the film in 2006. He was ready to go until Michael's camp got wind of it and pulled the plug. 'It wasn't a fast-cut MTV-style video but a slow fly-on-the-wall type of film which had probably more about China in it than it did about Wham!' says Magee. 'In Anderson's version there are only four songs performed by Wham! in China and they happen at the end of the film. After they remade the film there were 12 songs and very little about China.' Michael's current manager Andy Stephens was quoted in the *Independent* as saying 'It's a dreadful film. It's a rogue copy that was supposed to have gone away and we don't want it to be seen in public. It's 20 years old and it's rubbish. Why on earth should we allow it to be shown?' Obviously Stephens felt that the showing of the film to a group of students would have been harmful to his client. 'Anderson catches China on that turning point,' adds Magee. 'When all the consumerism and Western influences started to make an impact.'

Ultimately the trip failed on almost all fronts apart from that of giving a minuscule portion of the Chinese population a good night out. The film was a disaster, as were relations with Lindsay Anderson, the band lost money hand over fist, the hoped-for record sales never materialised (the Chinese said they would pay in bikes as money was not allowed to leave the country), the band had a dimmer view of the country than before they went and the Chinese government had won a propaganda victory by getting the band to bankroll its own performance without being able to cash in afterwards via record and tape sales.

Those close to the band were aware that cracks were starting to appear in the Wham! armour. George Michael was increasingly happy to make solo appearances, especially if it freed him from teen adulation and placed him in a light more becoming of a serious writer. In May he accepted an invitation to appear at a Motown anniversary show at the legendary Apollo in Harlem, New York City. Introduced by veteran comedian Bill Cosby, George first sang a solo rendition of 'Careless Whisper' dressed in a blue suit and long blond hair. Part way through Smokey Robinson joined him to sing a verse or two, the pair rattling off some impressive harmonies to end the song. George also sang with Stevie Wonder.

Back in the UK, Wham! then joined Elton John at Live Aid on 13 July 1983. The concerts in London and Philadelphia were the centre of world attention; over a billion people watched the events unfold on TV, putting their hands in their pockets to the tune of £150 million. After The Who finished 'Won't Get Fooled Again', John took the Wembley stage shortly before 9 pm and ran through a quartet of hits. Kiki Dee joined him for 'Don't Go Breaking My Heart', after which Wham! came out for 'Don't Let The Sun Go Down On Me'. Andrew Ridgeley, very much in the background, performed backup vocals with Dee. The grand finale of 'Do They Know It's Christmas' followed soon afterwards. Like many acts that day, George Michael's status, even his street credibility, was raised by his performance, though he thought that performance had been decidedly average and he'd been out of tune for the first couple of verses. A seed had been sown in the public mind that Michael was an adult solo performer rather than a member of a teenybopper band.

In late August Wham! returned to North America for another nine shows in cities that had been passed over in the spring. This time they were supported by large stars in their own right. Chaka Khan, who had been releasing singles for seven years, had recently hit the charts with 'I Feel For You' and 'Eye To Eye'. The Pointer Sisters were even longer established but had hits in 1984 with 'I'm So Excited', 'Jump (For My Love)' and 'Neutron Dance'. During these nine massive stadium shows spread over 17 days Wham! played to over 250,000 fans. The band also previewed a new song, 'The Edge Of Heaven'. Edging slowly towards his later solo look, George had had a sharp new haircut and took the stage heavily stubbled. He was also wearing his most outrageous outfits to date. One of these combined a mustard yellow tasselled jacket and matching hipster trousers; as he was bare chested underneath, these slunk right down four or five inches below his belly button, only just leaving his modesty intact.

The tour was followed across the country by rumours of a romance between Michael and actress Brooke Shields. Shields had begun life as a model, courting controversy when she appeared in a jeans advert with the slogan, 'Do you want to know what comes between me and my Calvins? Nothing.' Eventually the pair met, but it turned out to be little more than a mutual photo opportunity. The predicted romance failed to blossom.

Another story following the band around was discontent within the camp over the backing band's treatment on the road. It had become the custom for George Michael and Andrew Ridgeley to be billeted in a different hotel to the rest of the band and tour crew, both for security reasons and because it was felt they were entitled to higher-quality accommodation. But this time the crew felt that the difference was too wide. Before the end of the tour, Tommy Eyre had quit.

The crew were also well aware that George Michael's mood was different to that on previous jaunts. Having been uncharacteristically short-tempered on tour, after the band arrived back in the UK he was involved in an all-out fist fight with David Austin outside a nightclub. Shortly afterwards he was snapped grabbing a member of the paparazzi outside another club. Things were obviously weighing on his mind. He'd been in a short-lived and tortuous relationship (he has never revealed who it was with), and he was losing the buzz that had previously come from the hysteria surrounding his every move.

Michael decided that he'd had enough and needed to break away. He called Andrew Ridgeley, Jazz Summers, Simon Napier-Bell and lawyers Dick Leahy and Bryan Morrison to Langan's restaurant in London for a lunchtime meeting. There he told them straight out that he wanted out of Wham!, that the party was over. He explained that he was fed up with the character he was playing, that it wasn't the real George Michael, and he couldn't bring himself to write another album of Wham!-type material. It was time to move on.

It was decided that no announcements would be made yet. The band wanted to go out on top and their last few months were planned carefully. At the age of 22 George and Andrew had achieved everything that they had set out to do as a pair of Bushey Mead teenagers. In three years Michael had gone from feeling unattractive, unhappy with his own reflection, to being a sex symbol admired by millions of girls, and some boys. But already that wasn't enough. He'd tried to solve his problems via drink and then drugs – in 1990 he admitted to the *Daily Mirror* that he'd taken 'loads' of ecstasy, starting when he first visited Los Angeles with Wham!. 'I took it when I was really depressed about five years ago. It's not a great thing to do when you're depressed, that's why I stopped taking it. I don't benefit. I don't escape with drugs. Pretty well the same as I don't escape with booze. If I have a problem, it's there with me and I can't get rid of it by drinking or taking drugs.'

But for now things would carry on as normal as far as the outside world was concerned. Wham! headed into a London studio to record 'I'm Your Man'. This non-album single was released in November 1985 and returned the band to number one. Written in the catchy, anthemic mould of 'Freedom', 'I'm Your Man' was another stomping singalong classic. Some sources claimed the song had been inspired by Brooke Shields; their brief encounter probably wouldn't have facilitated such a powerful song, but then who knows? George Michael certainly wasn't telling. The band were in fine fettle on this track, with horns, bass and soaring backing vocals providing an almost wall-of-sound production quality. The promotional video was also impressive, Ridgeley and Michael acting out little cameos as ticket sellers outside the famous Marquee club in London. When Ridgeley gets fed up and walks off Michael berates him in his campest voice, 'Sell 'em yerself, sell 'em yerself.' Michael calls his manager to complain about the gig and in a humorous exchange drives Napier-Bell to tears, leaving Michael trying to console him down the line. The band then take to the stage for a performance. Michael, in black leather fingerless gloves, bangs away on a tambourine and is clearly having fun. With his belt of bullets, open-shirted hairy chest and stubble, he looks more Greek than ever before.

George Michael's friendship with Elton John bore further fruit when he sang on 'Wrap Her Up' for John's *Fire And Ice* album, also appearing in the video and adding backing vocals on the hit single 'Nikita'. Thanks to the collaborations with Elton John, George spent December with four singles in the UK Top 20. 'I'm Your Man' and 'Wrap Her Up' were joined by seasonal reissues of 'Last Christmas' and Band Aid's 'Do They Know It's Christmas'. At Christmas he finally agreed to do a US Diet Coke commercial for a whopping $3.3 million. However, he did insist on certain rules: he wouldn't be filmed drinking or even holding a can of the product, he wouldn't let any of his music be used and his face was only seen right at the end of the clip. The ad was pulled from rotation soon after its debut in the USA and was never used in the UK.

At the end of the year George, Andrew and a couple of male friends took a well-earned holiday in Australia, which was just about as far from the prying British press as they could get. Andrew Ridgeley had been dubbed the 'vomit fountain' and 'Randy Andy' in the papers. In contrast, for some reason George Michael's sexual conquests weren't selling their stories to the press, but Michael was reported in the tabloid press as having been seen taking poppers (amyl nitrate), the gay scene's drug of choice at the time, in a London club. (Around this time he'd also started using marijuana.) People were beginning to ask questions about his sexual preferences, even if those questions didn't appear in print. George wanted to guard whatever might be going on and was happy to be snapped out on the town with various women – over the years stories had run about possible relationships with Helen Tennant, Gail Lawson and Kay Beckenham. But he was fed up with having paparazzi living on his doorstep, fed up with being portrayed as little more than a teen idol. He wanted to move into the mature adult world where his music would be taken more seriously.

As 1986 began some industry sources were gossiping that the end was nigh for Wham!. It was already clear that George Michael had what it took to be a star in his own right, while Andrew Ridgeley seemed to be more interested in motor racing and felt his future lay there rather than in the music industry. Wham! fans didn't realise it, but the group's final show was only a matter of months away.

Again the band collected a number of awards early in the year. At the 13th Annual American Music Awards in Los Angeles they won Favorite Video and weeks later at the Brit Awards they were given an award for Outstanding Contribution to British Music. For a band that had only released two albums this smacked of an end-of-career tribute, and the rumours intensified.

Amid the speculation George Michael flew out to Paris to record a new song, one which he saw as the beginning of his solo career proper. Like his previous solo effort, 'Careless Whisper', 'A Different Corner' was a mournful ballad about lost love. Michael said that the story behind this song was drawn from his own personal experience but he never revealed the identity of the person on whom his affection was focused. (In 2006 American photographer Brad Branson claimed that 'A Different Corner' had been written about him, and that Michael had played him an early demo version of the song.) Michael himself explained, 'I had to write something. I had to get it out and I did it in a couple of days. It was the first time I used my own experience and emotions for a song. The pain comes back when I perform or hear it. At first I couldn't even listen to it, especially when I was trying to get over the emotions I was singing about.' The lines in the song about 'fear of being used' certainly chimed with his interviews, where he had bemoaned being seen purely as a sex object and not a feeling person.

Heavy synth rhythms open the song and recur throughout, while Michael's vocals range from almost whispered desperation to soaring anguish. The promo video was also quite dramatic, but very simple. Dressed all in white, Michael lounges around in a white room filled with white furniture, white bean bags and a white telephone. Michael ditched the all-white look for his performance of the song on *Top of the Pops*, going instead for a rough look in battered leather jacket and jeans tucked into brown cowboy boots. He sang the song at the microphone in front of some of the BBC's best backlit white plastic tubes, the kind that might still be in place in some small-town nightclubs. And with the end of Wham! in sight, fans lapped up this single, giving him his second solo number one in as many attempts.

In late February Michael was a guest on Michael Aspel's TV talk show *Aspel & Company*. He announced on the show that Wham! were splitting up, that they would play one last show and then that was it. He went on to explain that while he loved making the music, he was growing to hate everything else around it. A perfect example of what he wanted to escape from came via the *Sunday People* on 6 April. The newspaper claimed that ex-Executive members Tony Bywaters and Jamie Gould, no doubt in order to promote their unknown band Ego, had revealed that George Michael had been married as a teenager to a Greek Cypriot, a marriage which was not legal in the UK. It was poppycock, of course.

Like the tongue-in-cheek titles *Fantastic* and *Make It Big*, the final Wham! trio of EP, album and show came under the simple moniker of *The Final*. The show was scheduled for 28 June at Wembley Stadium. It was back to what really mattered, the music, and Michael was working hard on a new song. 'The Edge Of Heaven' was chosen as Wham!'s goodbye present to their fans. The lyric contained plenty of sexual references but because the word 'sex' wasn't actually used the censors didn't seem to care, even if those references seemed to be sado-masochistic, and heavy breathing greeted each chorus. Talk about leaving millions of fans wanting more. A finger-clicking intro was the prelude to a rough George Michael vocal with a hard-hitting bass line. Saxophones cried out as Elton John on piano and David Austin on guitar joined the going-away party. The video was similar to that for 'I'm Your Man', but this time large screens behind the stage showed old videos and clips of the band, giving a mini summary of their short career. As the song faded out, the words 'Goodbye' and 'Thank You' flashed up on the screens.

Wham!'s final week was unsurprisingly very busy. Two warm-up shows, last-minute preparations for Wembley and a *Top of the Pops* recording all had to be fitted in. They visited the BBC with 'The Edge Of Heaven' predictably sitting at number one, and their last appearance, like their first three and a half years earlier, was presented by Mike Smith. He introduced them not as Wham! but as George Michael and Andrew Ridgeley. George wore a BSA leather jacket with 'Rockers Revenge' written across the back. The full band appeared, but without Pepsi and Shirlie. In all there were four guitars on stage, none of them actually being played.

The Final show took place at a sunny Wembley Stadium on Saturday 28 June 1986. During one of the many interviews he gave before the show George Michael explained that they'd done everything they wanted to in just four years and he needed the challenge of a solo career: 'How can you end Wham! any more perfectly than in front of 72,000 people, still good friends, with a record at number one?'

In the United States, the compilation album *Music From The Edge Of Heaven* and the single 'The Edge Of Heaven' both reached the Top 10 in the weeks after *The Final*. An extra song recorded for *The Final* was a cover of 'Where Did Your Heart Go?' by Was Not

Was. Filmed for *Top of the Pops* at the same time as 'The Edge Of Heaven', the performance was screened in early July. But after the euphoria of The Final show it was rather weak, an uninspired last representation of Wham!'s creative output.

In the aftermath of The Final show Andrew Ridgeley wanted to throw himself into motor racing. Having eased into the sport by taking part in celebrity events where the participants simply had to make sure they got around the circuit in one piece, after Wham! – and once lingering insurance issues had been resolved – he could step up to try Formula Three racing. He would later move to Monte Carlo to avoid a hefty tax bill and pursue his new interest. But he had been unable to race from the start of the season in March until after Wham!'s last show in July, and the French Formula Renault series was a serious business, used by young drivers as a stepping stone to a possible Formula One career. The likes of Alain Prost and Kimi Raikkonen had graduated from its ranks in the past. These drivers were focused 100 per cent on their goal while for Ridgeley it was merely a way of enjoying himself. He himself later admitted that he didn't have the concentration necessary to make the grade.

With Andrew Ridgeley away in France, George Michael was hit with the reality that he was alone in the music world. Though he'd been the musical brains behind Wham!, he was well aware that Ridgeley was a crutch for his worries and insecurities. Michael took time in the press to pay tribute to his friend, saying he couldn't think of anyone else he'd ever met who could have filled the role so well. The luckiest moment of his life had been when he met Ridgeley and in hindsight he felt that it had all been part of some master plan.

Michael was at a turning point, suffering emotionally and losing his confidence. When he later talked about this period of his life, he explained that in the weeks before The Final show he'd been coping with the end of a short relationship that had hurt him severely. In true George Michael fashion he'd chosen not to kiss and tell; instead he'd kept it all in and suffered in silence. The relationship hadn't worked, he said, because of the situation he lived in as a pop star. It was like being shown that he couldn't have everything – the relationship and the position of fame.

The experience would stay in the back of his mind for some time, shaping his career choices in the early 1990s. 'Wham! were dead,' he told the *Daily Mail*, 'but my problems hadn't disappeared with the band's demise. Andrew and I were still good friends, but broken relationships, a bout of heavy boozing and a fair bit of drugs hadn't made my life any easier. Somewhere along the line I had to make a radical change.'

PART TWO

•

1986–2007

SIX

TOUR

1986–1989

tour

1 a travelling around from place to place.
2 a long journey including the visiting of a number of places in sequence, esp. with an organised group led by a guide.
3 a brief trip through a place, as a building or a site, in order to view or inspect it: the visiting prime minister was given a tour of the chemical plant.
4 a journey from town to town to fulfil engagements, as by a theatrical company or an entertainer: to go on tour; a European concert tour.
5 a period of duty at one place or in one job.

'I think at that age – I was only 25 when I did the Faith tour – there was such a feeling of emptiness about the level of fame that I'd achieved that I couldn't see the good things about it. I couldn't really experience the highs because I was too busy wondering what was going to make me happy, if this incredible luck was not going to make me happy. And I guess loneliness is really intensified if you are being admired by thousands of people every night very loudly, and then going back to your hotel room alone. I guess really it was the loneliness of the experience that, when I look back, I mistook for genuine unhappiness with the touring.'

George Michael

'At the end of Wham! I needed a new challenge. So I set myself the challenge of getting up there on the American level with Madonna and Jackson, that circle of people. That was my goal. And then having got into that position I realised that it wasn't really going to do anything for me. I can honestly say most of 1988 was a complete nightmare for me.'

George Michael

George Michael was not Madonna, he was not Michael Jackson, nor was he Prince. He couldn't live in the public eye by putting on an act as they did, both on and off the stage. He'd quickly tired of being 'George Michael' for the sake of the media. 'I didn't know how much longer I could stand losing my privacy. But it is all gone now. It is like having your life documented for approval or disapproval, down to the minutest detail. We would understand if we were royalty, but we are not. It makes you feel trivial. It can be a little embarrassing.' The Wham! persona, all teenage fun and juvenile humour, was not the 'real' George Michael, or at least it was only a small part. Having yearned for fame all of his life, once he had it he didn't want it any more. He wanted his real life back.

'I woke up one morning, and I realised that there had been a period in Wham! when I had actually completely forgotten who I was,' he told *Q* magazine. 'I had this depression for about eight months. For a time I thought I really didn't want to get back into the music business when we finished Wham!. The problem was just that I had developed a character for the outside world that wasn't me, and I was having to deal with people all the time who thought it was.' Hence the decision to unravel the 'monster' he'd created and start from scratch.

The yearning for a normal life included disentangling himself from the dependence on other people that had built up over the last three years. One of these tasks, trivial to some but important to Michael, was learning to drive. Having only passed his driving test just before The Final, in another show of independence he went out and bought his first car – a Mercedes. Now he could do away with the chauffeurs who'd been ferrying him around.

Michael continued his purging of the past by parting company with the Nomis management team. This, though, he hadn't planned in advance. While in Los Angeles, where he spent much of the second half of 1986, he was informed that the *Hollywood Reporter* was running a story headlined 'Wham! Sold to Sun City'. Michael exploded. Without telling his major client, Simon Napier-Bell had been looking to float or sell the business while it was still on a high from Wham!'s success. Napier-Bell had lined up a £5 million deal with a South African company called Kunick Leisure, who would own the company while Napier-Bell and Jazz Summers were retained as consultants. The key feature of the deal was that the new company would continue to manage George Michael's and Andrew Ridgeley's (if he had one) solo careers.

The problem as far as Michael was concerned was twofold. One, he hadn't been told at any stage about what was going on. And two, Kunick Leisure was partly owned by Sol Kerzner, the man behind Sun City. This South African holiday resort had been the centre of controversy concerning western artists and the country's apartheid government as it offered large sums to attract world-famous acts to break sanctions against apartheid. In 1985 the star-studded Artists Against Apartheid group (Bono, Bruce Springsteen and Bob Dylan were among the many artists involved) had recorded the song 'Sun City', saying they would never play there while apartheid was in place.

When Michael saw the report he immediately called Nomis and flew back for a meeting in London with Napier-Bell and Summers. The singer was almost beside himself. How could they do this? he asked. He felt he had a good ten years left as a solo artist. The managers soon realised that they'd made a big mistake – if they lost their prime asset, the deal would undoubtedly be called off. Napier-Bell tried to pull out of the South African arrangement but it was too late. Michael left the meeting and never spoke to the pair again, ignoring their calls and communicating only via his lawyer. With no George Michael to manage, the South Africans pulled out. Nomis collapsed, Napier-Bell and Summers going their separate ways.

Simon Napier-Bell had always known that George Michael didn't entirely trust him – Michael openly said that Napier-Bell was an 'asshole' – but he was an asshole he'd rather have on his side. Make no mistake, Nomis had done a lot for Wham!, especially in America. But ultimately Michael needed to hold power over his own decisions and Nomis had stepped over the line. Like Inner-vision before, the arrangements had been useful for George Michael for a while, but as soon as things went astray he cut all ties with no chance of a reconciliation. But now he was adrift on a sea of uncertainty. Ridgeley, Wham! and Nomis were all out of his life and he was living in the USA. It was a difficult time.

Michael spent most of the rest of 1986 in Los Angeles, drinking, spending time with model and friend Kathy Jeung when she was in town, but generally he was unsure about his future and depressed. He'd always worked hard to keep his weight under control, but he didn't seem to care so much now he was taking ecstasy. Then, when it wore off, he'd have massive down periods. When he saw his parents and family he put on a brave face as usual and said everything was OK, but families usually have a way of knowing that something is wrong even if it's not brought up in conversation.

Pre-dating the sexual controversy that would involve him in the summer of 1987, Michael appeared on Channel 4's unusual chat show, *Sex with Paula*, in which Paula Yates interviewed her guests about intimate matters while lying on a bed. George appeared in a turquoise jumper with a garish white pattern on the front, while Paula was dressed in a black shoulderless ball dress. Michael was quizzed about his preferences and writing songs about girls. When asked about his fantasies he skirted around the subject, claiming his mother would be watching. But he did say, 'I couldn't possibly tell you, but ask me for a demonstration later!'

Later in the year Andrew Ridgeley flew to Los Angeles to visit his old pal. Even when talking to Ridgeley, Michael had been keeping things bottled up and when Ridgeley arrived at Michael's house he was shocked at both the singer's appearance and mood. During Ridgeley's visit the pair had a heart-to-heart in which Michael poured out all his insecurities and worries. The next day he felt like a weight had been lifted from his shoulders. The old Ridgeley optimism had worked wonders yet again. Life suddenly seemed much better, and Michael decided to start work on his first solo album.

In November CBS-Epic took up their option for George Michael's solo career, which was to last for the next five albums. At Christmas George flew home to be with his parents and seemed fitter and happier than he had in months. Early in 1987 he decided to sort out his lack of management and employed Rob Kahane, his booking agent and promoter in the United States, to take on the role. They had first worked together when Michael had sung at the Motown show in New York. Now that Nomis was out of the picture, he approached Michael offering to manage him. Hired initially to take care of Michael's North American interests, his responsibilities were soon extended to the entire globe.

Kahane's first job as Michael's manager was to accompany the singer to Detroit, where a collaboration with soul legend Aretha Franklin was planned. Franklin's management had approached Michael to suggest an arrangement that the two camps knew would be mutually beneficial: Michael would provide her with an entry to UK fans while she would add credibility to his adult marketing in America. The song they would be recording had been supplied by Climie Fisher, the songwriting duo of Simon Climie and Rob Fisher. Best remembered for their own 1987 hit 'Love Changes Everything', they had already supplied songs to Franklin, Smokey Robinson and Pat Benatar.

The song, 'I Knew You Were Waiting (For Me)', and the accompanying video were completed during two days in December, ready for a January 1987 release. Michael knew he was a white boy who'd walked into a hotbed of black soul music when he and Kahane arrived at the studio and realised they were the only white people around. The producer was Narada Michael Walden, another legend in his own field. The winner of Grammys for Best Album, Best Song and Best Producer, Walden had worked in genres as diverse as soul, country, rap and jazz and produced for Stevie Wonder, Tom Jones and the Temptations. And *Billboard* magazine had named him one of the ten best producers of all time. If George Michael had felt nervous at Muscle Shoals, here the pressure was intensified tenfold. 'Standing in a studio looking across at Aretha trading lines was something that I would never, even a couple of years ago, have dreamed of,' said Michael.

But he carried it off superbly. When 'I Knew You Were Waiting (For Me)' was released in January 1987 it was an instant sensation. The mix of pop, soul and R&B and the two very distinctive yet compatible voices was a powerful one. Franklin's vocal gymnastics at the song's climax outshone Michael's performance, but then they would have outshone almost anyone.

Before Michael flew home the couple filmed a video at a nearby soundstage. One of the massive video screens used during The Final at Wembley was again utilised, adding a new and interesting dimension but pushing the cost for what was basically a film of the two singing in a studio up to a staggering £150,000. George enters what looks like a warehouse where the giant screen shows Aretha singing her lines. Then the roles are reversed, with Michael on the big screen and Aretha singing in the 'warehouse', before they are brought together, bouncing their lines back and forth while footage of famous old duets from the past is shown behind them in black and white.

The single was a blinding success, providing Franklin with her first American number one single for exactly 20 years and her first ever in the UK. In the UK charts at the same time was Pepsi & Shirlie's 'Heartache'. 'Our manager called to say that "Heartache" was number two in the UK,' recalled Holliman. 'Guess who kept us off the number one spot? George and Aretha! Oh well. But we made number one in a lot of other countries.'

Buoyed by yet another success, Michael bought his first property in north London, among the old money in Hampstead. He reportedly paid cash for the house, a cool £2 million. It was a further sign that he was gaining some stability in his life. Happier than he had been for many months, Michael was writing new material with renewed vigour and with the aim of releasing his debut solo album before the year was out. He was determined to show the world his 'real' music. 'Some people just thought we were prats,' he said, reminiscing about Wham! 'They thought that bloke poncing around in the pretty blond hair with the shorts and the teeth was me. They couldn't understand that it was me trying to be the ultimate performer. In fact, we were the first group since the days of The Beatles who didn't relate their personalities to their music.'

The first post-Wham! George Michael solo single was released in June 1987, and if this was music which represented his personality it surprised a lot of people. 'I Want Your Sex' would give many casual listeners the wrong impression. Just as Bruce Springsteen's anthem 'Born In The USA' had sounded to some like a patriotic call-to-arms when it was actually a damning indictment of the Vietnam war, many people decided that George Michael was promoting promiscuity with his new single when it was in fact a simple message about keeping one sexual partner. In the UK it caused the biggest pop music outcry since Frankie had said 'Relax' three years earlier. And all this with a song which Michael had almost donated to David Austin to help him launch a solo career of his own.

The reaction was due in part to mounting hysteria in the UK about the AIDS virus, which was becoming a hot topic in the press due to poor education on the subject. It was reported that morticians were refusing to embalm the bodies of AIDS victims, that the police were wearing protective equipment due to the fear of being contaminated on the street, while the term 'gay plague' was regularly bandied about. Paranoia was rife and being gay was more stigmatised than ever. Promoting sleeping around, as Michael was apparently doing with this song, must be both irresponsible and dangerous.

But if he wanted to move into more adult territory, he certainly succeeded with 'I Want Your Sex'. Musically it was funky and carried a typically 1980s upfront drum sound, with staccato keyboards coming in and out of the mix. Vocally he switched between low-down, dirty provocation and a semi-breathless Prince imitation. The track was completed before the rest of the album, Michael playing all the instruments himself and providing all the vocals. The album version, 'I Want Your Sex (Parts I & II)', lasted over nine minutes, Part II opening with a strident horn section which, though uncredited, was highly unlikely to have been played by Michael. Despite, or perhaps because of, the controversy, the single hit number two in America and number three in the UK.

Part of the controversy caused by the song came from people's misguided reaction to the video. 'When I released "I Want Your Sex" and the music video, I didn't think the image would have such a lasting effect,' said Michael. 'The image still seems to overshadow the music.' At face value the video is just a couple of steps away from soft porn. Kathy Jeung struts around in stockings and suspenders, or lies blindfolded on a bed with Michael. There are close-up shots of body parts writhing around the sheets (Michael used a body double), clips of water being poured on to naked flesh and the like. What critics seemed to miss, or ignore, was that Michael is filmed writing on Jeung's naked body with a stick of red lipstick. The words he writes are 'Explore' and 'Monogamy', which couldn't make the point of the song or video any clearer.

The video was nevertheless banned from UK television and the song itself from the radio after 6 am and before 9 pm, thus taking away most of his potential listeners. Michael desperately needed his fans to be able to hear and see his new image and new product and they were being denied the opportunity. Irritated by the media response, (Radio 1's Trevor Dann dismissed the song as 'silly'), Michael decided to take control of the situation. He ensured that copies of the video were sent to cafés and bars up and down the country to play on their own in-house TV systems in order to give the clip an airing. He also put a veto on the BBC being sent any more copies of the video, record or CD, justifiably upset that he was being censored for promoting sex in a stable relationship while rap and rock videos showed much worse.

As would become common throughout his career, when faced with a problem, Michael offered himself directly to his audience so as to put his point across without being misquoted or misrepresented. In the wake of 'I Want Your Sex' he offered a lengthy interview to Channel 4's *Jonathan Ross Show*. Ross had only just broken into television and the slim, impressively quiffed interviewer sat with a clipboard of questions, looking as if he was working on a school project. After a round of mundane questions they cut to the chase and discussed Michael's new single. The singer explained that he wanted to make a moral statement by being direct. While he had anticipated that the BBC would ban the song because of the use of the word 'sex', the fact that the IBA (which governed the UK's independent radio stations) had also banned it – effectively halting all daytime play – shocked him. He wanted to put the record straight, he explained, because most people had heard things about the song without actually hearing it for themselves. He also said that he was tired of answering questions about the song which, he explained, 'was my take on just one aspect of relationships'. For a month he felt as if he'd been voted in as the young person's official spokesman on sex. At the end of the interview Michael told Ross that he'd been offered various film roles, including one part playing a Greek-Jewish revolutionary, but he'd turned them all down and would wait for a few years.

The Ross interview was soon lampooned in the *NME*, zooming in on the host's relentless questions about Michael's sex life and Michael's holier-than-thou answers. Claiming to be 'That George Michael Interview By Jonathan Ross In Full', it opened (Ross has a lisp, making it difficult for him to pronounce his 'r's correctly, 'Jonathan: Well, George, I weckon it's weasonable to say that you're a wakish, woguish, waspscallion and a bit of a sexpants to boot. Are you getting enough?' And it went downhill from there.

Elsewhere the controversy saw Michael grace the cover of the *NME* on 20 June. Under the prophetic title 'Decadence! George Michael exposes himself' he was given a centre spread to talk about his new solo career in an issue otherwise filled with Robert Cray, Genesis and Curiosity Killed The Cat. Inside, beneath the caption 'Tart with a Heart', he again discussed the 'I Want Your Sex' ban. His main bone of contention was that the record would only be played late at night; if he couldn't be bothered to listen at that time, he asked, then why would anyone else? He went on to discuss his image in America, which was still very much linked to Wham!. In the UK, however, 'I Want Your Sex' had gained him a new audience. It was kept from the top spot only by Whitney Houston's 'I Wanna Dance with Somebody', with Johnny Logan's 'Hold Me Now' at number three.

The final touches were put to the forthcoming album, to be titled *Faith*. 'I had faith in what life was going to deliver,' said Michael, 'that I was going to get the things I wanted.' The bulk of the work had been done at Michael's favourite London studios, Sarm, and at PUK in Denmark. Close to Portobello Market, the Sarm complex houses four studios and provides a vastly experienced staff who have since worked with Coldplay, Oasis, Radiohead, Doves, Muse and Alicia Keys. George Michael used its comfortable environment when working on *Faith*, gladly paying the extra fees in order to write in the studio as well as recording there. He played many of the instruments himself, including the drums, but the final mixes were augmented by some familiar helping hands. Hugh Burns, Deon Estus, Andy Duncan and Robert Ahwai from the Wham! days were all present, as was Paul Gomersall who had worked with George on *Make It Big*, while Chris Cameron added the famous church organ to the title track. 'On *Faith*, the musicians were around all day, every day,' recalled Gomersall. 'Deon Estus on bass, Chris Cameron on keyboards and Hugh Burns on guitar. But he has always appreciated that his listening audience wants to hear George Michael, so he now tends to do most of the work himself.'

The single 'Faith' was released in October to further promote the album. The combination of a musical style very new to the singer and an iconic visual image, promoted via the heavily played video, sealed the track's place in pop history. With acoustic guitars and a clap-along beat Michael sounded like Elvis at Sun but looked like Elvis on the '68 Comeback Special. 'Faith' opens with a church organ reprising Wham!'s 'Freedom'; this gives way to light percussion and that guitar part as Michael begins to sing. The organ was a poppier version of the rumbling church organ that had opened U2's 'Where The Streets Have No Name' on *The Joshua Tree* in the spring of 1987. '[It] was inspired by a couple of relationships that didn't happen,' recalls Michael. 'Very soon after the break-up of the group and before I started seeing Kathy, there were people with whom I thought about starting relationships and eventually decided against it. Because I knew I was on the rebound and I wanted to be with someone for a different reason than that.'

The video came prepacked with the new improved George Michael image. The opening shot shows a Wurlitzer jukebox playing a seven-inch record of 'I Want Your Sex'. Part way through, another record flips down and the organ opening to 'Faith' starts to play. Michael appears, shot in black and white except for his blue jeans, which are in colour. The camera starts low down and rises, revolving around him, lingering as it passes his backside, while he stands like a statue in ripped blue jeans, with designer stubble, crucifix earring, BSA leather jacket, metal-tipped boots, shades and a low-slung guitar. This was the George Michael image of 1987–89; he later told Michael Parkinson that at the time he walked around dressed like that almost every day. And at the age of 24, this image would bring him a whole host of new female fans, almost eclipsing Wham!-mania.

The *Faith* album was George Michael's career peak. The variety of song styles, his vocal range and the arrangements were all impressive; containing half a dozen singles, it was almost a greatest hits selection on its own. Even the non-singles are memorable. Opening with the cathedral majesty of 'Faith', the sophisticated eastern influenced pop of 'Father Figure' and the funk of 'I Want Your Sex (Parts I & II)', he'd laid out his new career before the end of side one. 'One More Try' is a heartfelt ballad just behind 'Careless Whisper', 'Hard Day' an archetypal 1980s pop-funk fusion and a US dance hit, while 'Hand To Mouth' features one of Michael's most involved, almost political, lyrics to date. It also contains the line 'she ran to the arms of America', eerily similar to the words 'the women and children who run into the arms of America' from U2's song 'Bullet The Blue Sky', also released in 1987. 'Look At Your Hands' laments the state of an ex-girlfriend, while 'Monkey' and 'Kissing A Fool' were further hit singles, the jazz stylings of the latter being a complete departure from the rest of the album and a pleasant surprise to end with.

Among the album artwork were five symbols denoting 'faith', 'music', 'money', 'religion' and 'love'. The album's portraits, taken by photographer Russell Young, gave the singer an image which still resonates decades later. Michael himself set up the studio lighting for the photo shoot and they made several attempts to get a shot for the cover with the singer wearing a suit while a tape of the album played in the background, but it didn't feel quite right. Young claims he then went and borrowed a leather jacket for Michael to try (though he'd worn a similar BSA jacket around the time of *The Final*) and the *Faith* image was created, unshaven and with a large gold cross dangling from his ear. Designer stubble was born in an instant. Apparently it was worth millions to the beard-clipper industry.

Reviewers were almost ecstatic over the album. 'At times he's almost too good,' wrote Mark Coleman in *Rolling Stone*. 'The concluding number, a pseudo torch song called "Kissing a Fool," recalls one of Barry Manilow's forays down Memory Lane with painful accuracy. It's a sentimental dead end. But the rest of Faith displays Michael's intuitive understanding of pop music and his increasingly intelligent use of his power to communicate to an ever-growing audience.' Released in November 1987, *Faith* would stay in and around the US Top 10 until May 1989, selling nearly 10 million copies, and it was in the UK charts for well over a year.

The launch party for *Faith* indicated how George Michael's career had rocketed. In earlier days Wham! had hosted a £10,000 champagne launch; three years later *Faith* was launched with a

£100,000 drinks bill. But the guest list was equally suspect. Apart from Elton John and Bob Geldof, the party was populated by celebrities such as breakfast TV presenter Anne Diamond, Curiosity Killed The Cat and soap actress Anita Dobson. At the end of 1987 the *Sun* newspaper said that Michael spent £6 million on presents, including cars for his parents, sisters and Kathy Jeung.

No other pop star could touch George Michael in 1988 and he became, briefly, the biggest star on the planet. It all started with the release of 'Father Figure' as a single in January, designed to keep the *Faith* bandwagon rolling in the post-Christmas depression. The new single, an intimate pop ballad with hints of a massed gospel choir, continued to promote his new adult image. The video, co-directed with Andy Morahan, portrays Michael as a hunky yellow-cab driver in New York, unshaven, smoking a lot, in a white vest while driving around a vision of Eighties beauty, a woman with unfeasibly large shoulder pads in a large white coat. Later she appears as a catwalk model and is seen in the bedroom with Michael; as in other videos of the time, the women wear black stockings and suspenders like models out of a mid-1980s lingerie catalogue. Better received in the US than in the UK, 'Father Figure' was at number one for two weeks.

While the single was selling well, Michael collected more awards. At the Royal Albert Hall in London he won the award for Best British Male. Nominated for Favorite Male Artist at the American Music Awards, he captured a Grammy for Best R&B Performance by a Duo or Group for his collaboration with Aretha Franklin.

Though he hadn't much enjoyed being on tour during Wham!'s later years, Michael realised that to establish his new image with fans around the world he would have to commit to a lengthy jaunt across the globe. With what he hoped was a more mature album to promote, he expected – perhaps naively – that he would have a more mature audience and be able to throw off the shackles of having girls screaming non-stop for the entirety of a show. MTV were invited to film his tour rehearsals. He explained that he wanted to keep the level of excitement high throughout the show as he had with Wham!. He was planning to play all the songs from *Faith* and add in a few Wham! oldies for good measure, plus 'Lady Marmalade' and Stevie Wonder's 'Love's In Need Of Love Today'. Choreographing the show was 25-year-old Paula Abdul. Well known as a dancer, she was about to embark upon a pop career of her own, breaking through in 1988 with the album *Forever Your Girl*.

'I hate the process of travelling and being protected,' Michael said. 'It's a 24-hours thing, you can't just go home and forget what you do for a living. But I am excited about the actual performing.' If he wanted to put himself up there alongside giants like Michael Jackson, Prince and Madonna, he knew that he had to go through it, if only once. Opening in February in Japan, the tour would work its way down to Australia, then west to North America via Europe. He would perform 160 concerts to millions of fans during the year. With such a large-scale undertaking Michael knew that he wouldn't be able to retain as much control as normal. Instead he focused on managing things that he could directly influence, for instance taking along a personal trainer and his own chef.

To warm up the crowd before each show Janet Jackson's *Control* album was played. When the time was ready George Michael took the stage in darkness. He stood still, legs apart, fists clenched, eyes closed and head back as a powerful spotlight beamed down on him from above, looking as if an alien abduction was about to take place. Meanwhile the introductory organ chords of 'Faith' rang out across the arena before – surprise, surprise – the band broke into 'I Want Your Sex'. Michael viewed the tour very much as a work in progress. He would frequently video shows, watching them later with the band to see where improvements and adjustments could be made. In Europe he sang a long, semi-a cappella introduction to 'Everything She Wants'; it was a great fit with the material from *Faith*, even if the live version was in danger of being spoiled by some over-the-top, disco-tinged bongo drums.

For the first time George Michael, by his own admission, was acting like a diva. He had an entourage wherever he went, his old friends had a hard time even getting to talk to him after shows and he was liable to more tantrums than normal. Andros Georgiou and David Austin flew out at various times to lend moral support, but even they had conflicts with the minders about access to Michael. Kathy Jeung travelled with him on tour, though some reports said that they had separate rooms.

'The more people you employ, the more people you have in your life who can't be honest with you and that's what I find most distressing about touring,' said Michael. 'You're responsible for so many people's livelihoods. I prefer to be with unbiased company, put it that way. People are terrified of me. I don't know why. I very rarely fire people. They'd have to do something really out of order. Maybe it's the size of my position. I'm quite distant even from the band, but I find it very distressing to get close to people who can't really be honest with me. I like to know if I make a joke and the room laughs that it was funny. I'm not saying that anybody really licks my arse but it's evident, when you really analyse it, that at the end of the day I pay their wages. It frightens me. Being around people who can't tell you to fuck off. Whereas the people I spend time with in my personal life tell me to fuck off on a very regular basis!'

'One More Try' was the next single, released in April to promote the European leg of the tour. Again it went to number one in the USA where it was lapped up alongside the big ballads of the million-selling MOR artists. The video was very MTV-friendly: George sulked around a dusty old house, a backlit stained glass window casting him in silhouette as he walked among dust-covered chairs and writhed against the wall while wailing away in anguish.

For the European dates Michael rented a villa in St Tropez. From here he played the ultimate superstar, flying by helicopter to the local airport and taking a private jet to cities around Europe for the shows, returning 'home' each night rather than staying in the city where he had performed. This gave him a semi-stable base from which to work and provided an escape from the endless parties and clubbing.

Andrew Ridgeley tagged along for some of the European shows, staying in St Tropez and even joining his ex-partner on stage at the NEC in Birmingham for a rendition of Wham!'s 'I'm Your Man'. Having Ridgeley along with him emphasised how lonely Michael was as a solo artist.

On 11 June Michael returned to Wembley Stadium, this time performing at the Nelson Mandela tribute concert. Like Live Aid, this effort to pressurise the South African government to release the ANC leader brought out a long list of stars – Michael appeared alongside singers such as the Bee Gees, Eurythmics, Wet Wet Wet, Bryan Adams, Peter Gabriel, Whitney Houston, Youssou N'Dour and Stevie Wonder, and comedians such as Graham Chapman, Stephen Fry, Billy Connolly and Harry Enfield – and reached a massive global audience, with 600 million watching on TV. Keen to avoid being overtly political, but also uneasy about promoting his latest material, Michael decided to sing a trio of cover versions, Marvin Gaye's 'Sexual Healing', Stevie Wonder's 'Village Ghetto Land' and Gladys Knight's 'If I Were Your Woman'.

As in the Wham! days, Michael had been struggling with throat problems on tour and gigs were cancelled, no doubt because he was battling to be heard above the constant screaming. He had visited numerous doctors around the world about his throat, but none of them had been able to come up with an answer; he was usually fobbed off with the explanation that it was 'tour fatigue'. Now, during his prolonged stay in England, he visited a London specialist who found a cyst growing in his throat which would require surgery to remove. The decision was made to get through the Earls Court residency first, then have the surgery in London. Having managed that he decamped back to St Tropez for much-needed rest before heading to North America.

Each leg of the tour was usually heralded by a new single and a press conference. In the summer 'Monkey' became the fifth single to be taken from *Faith* and a remix of the song reached number one on the US dance chart, the first time that either George Michael or Wham! had achieved this. The video was a mix of live footage from the current tour and studio footage of Michael wearing tight black trousers with a white shirt and braces, a hat pushed back on his head like other late Eighties acts.

As for the press conference, Michael did well to contain his disdain. Normally at such events news journalists would ask the same old questions or make wild speculations, and this time was no exception. There were rumours about Michael's health; AIDS was mentioned, just as would be the case with Michael Stipe a couple of years later. It seemed as though when any singer of 'questionable' sexuality had health issues or wanted to step back from public life a little, the mainly homophobic press of the late Eighties and early Nineties instantly jumped to the conclusion that AIDS was the cause.

By the time Michael kicked off the North American leg of the tour in the autumn, around six million copies of *Faith* had been sold in the USA alone. This leg was a real test of his throat condition – he was scheduled to play an exhausting series of over 40 consecutive nights. But his vocal cords passed with flying colours. He was big news in the States and the likes of Madonna, Janet Jackson, Rob Lowe, Demi Moore and Whitney Houston attended his shows. He was also pleasantly surprised that although he had a massive, and loud, female following, the album and tour tickets were also being bought by a whole range of new fans: soul fans, rock fans and pop fans.

In September the video for 'Father Figure' won the award for Best Direction – jointly shared between Michael and Andy Morahan – at the MTV Video Music Awards, and was nominated for both Best Art Direction and Best Cinematography. After more shows the longest tour of Michael's career came to an end in Florida on Halloween. 'I expected to be dealing with a completely different audience on this tour,' said Michael once the dust had settled. 'I expected a lot less screaming and I didn't really get what I wanted, so maybe I'm overcompensating in the raunch department to make up for it. I don't find it shocking though. If I was a guy watching the show I'd think it was funny. If I was watching someone being that cocky up on stage, I'd think it was fun. It's what made Mick Jagger watchable, it's what makes Prince watchable. I don't expect the critics to disassociate that performer from me as a person because they don't, they just think, fucking big-headed wanker. But it's difficult for me to think of those repercussions when the audience are obviously getting off on it so much. I think it's really funny at the end of the show, it's such a pathetically harmless thing to do, when I put my back to the audience and I take my jacket off really slowly and the place goes absolutely mental. It's just so funny! It's really funny.'

The last release of a busy year was the laid-back jazz of 'Kissing A Fool'. The black and white video, set in a 1930s-style speakeasy, complete with period microphones, the band on stools and spread between piles of broken crates, captured the song's mood perfectly. Critics more accustomed to George's pop and soul leanings weren't sure he had carried off the shift in direction. In fact it's a perfectly good, if low-key, end to the *Faith* cycle.

The plaudits kept coming at the start of the last year of the Eighties. George Michael had begun that decade singing about being on the dole and had gone on to become the biggest star on the planet. The latest batch of awards were some of his most important and most controversial to date. *Faith* won Album of the Year at the Grammys and International Hit of the Year at the Ivor Novello Awards, where Michael also won Songwriter of the Year again. In September Madonna presented him with the Video Vanguard Award at the MTV Video Music Awards. But at the 16th Annual American Music Awards in Los Angeles he, or rather the selection committee, stirred up quite a controversy. Michael won the award for Favorite Pop/Rock Male Artist, which was usually the preserve of white artists, but he also walked away with the awards for Favorite Soul/R&B Artist and Favorite Soul/R&B Album, awards usually presented to black artists. The black community were outraged. Film-maker Spike Lee and rappers Public Enemy started the outcry, claiming that black artists, always bypassed for the mainstream awards, were now even being shoe-horned out of their 'own' genre. For George Michael's part, he was just happy to win. He hadn't asked for the awards, hadn't had any say in receiving them, they were just dropped onto his lap.

While the arguments raged around him he kept a low public profile, taking the time to look back on a fantastic decade. As a solo artist he'd thrown everything into challenging the big two, Madonna and Michael Jackson, the biggest solo stars in the world. During the 1980s Jackson had gained a record nine US number one singles and Madonna seven; Michael was sandwiched between them with an impressive eight. Admitting later that he hadn't been able to control his ego and had really wanted to try and topple those at the top, he realised in hindsight that he probably would have gained no more happiness from such an achievement. As maturity set in he decided that happiness would come from his private life, not his professional one. It was a real turning point.

During 1989 he put down more roots, buying a second home in Santa Barbara for $3 million. The house was an architect-designed property, with 16 glass walls affording panoramic views well beyond the five acres that also came in the deal. Built in 1985, the house was constructed as a series of hexagonal shapes inspired by the designs of Frank Lloyd Wright. Michael had various changes made, including a new viewing deck from which he could watch the sunset.

'I must admit I go out less and less,' he told *Q* magazine. 'Now and then I have to go to pretty well the same places where I know I'll get a bit of breathing space. But I think if you can come through Wham! and the exceptional exposure we had around 1984 and 1985 and you still have a social life, still go out and get pissed out of your head, then you're doing OK. My big problem is I haven't got the ability to tell people to fuck off. I have the right to tell people to leave me alone. But it's not worth it to me now to be in a roomful of people and by the end of the evening five or six people have a real aggression toward you. I'd rather just be pleasant and tell people nicely. When I'm on tour I don't have any protection so I'm either rude to people and end up with everyone hating me, or I'm polite and waste my evening answering the same questions over and over. So I tend to get pissed out of my head and just try to enjoy myself. It is getting harder and harder but I think compared to a lot of people I still get out quite a lot on my own.'

Having begun to step back and slow down, at the age of just 26 George Michael decided to write an autobiography. In *Bare*, put together with the help of author and journalist Tony Parsons, he talked openly about his childhood, Wham! and his fledgling solo career. But he didn't reveal his biggest secret. On page 222 of *Bare*, Andros Georgiou talks of the offers he has turned down to tell his cousin's 'inside story'. But years later Andros changed his mind and decided that he would be interviewed for the Channel 5 documentary. After the end of the *Faith* tour, he recalled, Michael had invited him to a meal. With perhaps a little exaggeration, he claimed that George had drunk three bottles of wine before he found enough courage to tell him that he was gay. Andros was stunned, even more so when George told him that he'd been sleeping with one of Andros' male friends. The world's biggest heterosexual sex symbol was gay.

The understanding of his own sexuality and the adulation he'd been subjected to on the *Faith* tour had made Michael realise that the problems he'd encountered towards the end of Wham! hadn't been solved by going solo. He needed to stop being a star for a while and take a different approach to promoting his music, and most of all work out what he wanted in his private life.

'If I was not someone who knew about women, I wouldn't have the audience I have,' he said. 'People don't want to hear that, but it's the truth. I spent the first part of my adulthood not being in love, fucking around, fucking men, fucking women, thinking I was bisexual. I had no proof of anything deeper. I'd spent most of my professional life being told what my sexuality was, which was rather nice as I didn't know. It could have gone on indefinitely if I'd kept working and taking public admiration as a replacement for the real thing.'

But the culture of America would probably struggle to understand why someone wouldn't just want more and more adulation. Michael was bound to suffer something of a backlash. As he said during his evaluation of the end of the *Faith* period: '[I thought], Oh my god, I'm a massive star and I think I may be a poof. What am I going to do? This is not going to end well.'

SEVEN

WITHDRAWAL

1990–1994

with·draw·al

1 The act or process of withdrawing, as:

a. a retreat or retirement.

b. retreat of a military force in the face of enemy attack or after a defeat.

c. detachment, as from social or emotional involvement.

d. a removal from a place or position of something that has been deposited.

e. discontinuation of the use of an addictive substance.

f. the physiological and mental readjustment that accompanies such discontinuation.

'I love England. Tax-wise it's very expensive here but I couldn't give a toss really. I've got more money than I know what to do with anyway. I can't pretend that I need any more money or that I need to hang on to my tax money. I've always paid my full tax. In the Wham! days people were always saying, take a year out of the country, but I just don't see the point in having money if you're not where you want to be. It makes the world an open prison if you can't wake up somewhere you want to be. What's money for, you know?'

George Michael

'There will come a day when what I am doing is no longer what the public want. I hope I'll see it coming. I think there will be a point where I can't match what I have done before. It happens to just about every artist and the way I am dealing with it is that I hope, because I started so young, that when the time comes there will be other avenues. I want it to happen gracefully because I see so many people fall and it's terrifying for somebody in my position.'

George Michael

The new decade would bring massive changes to the music industry. Grunge and Britpop would rule the airwaves, everyone and their dog would get a home computer and start downloading music, and glorified talent shows like *Pop Idol* would soon transform the pop scene.

Having moved to Los Angeles, Andrew Ridgeley made a surprise comeback in 1990. It shouldn't have been a surprise – George Michael had mentioned it in interviews almost two years earlier – but the money coming in from Wham! had set Ridgeley up for life, so it wasn't something he had to do. And the fact that he hadn't been involved in any songwriting for almost ten years made the 'comeback' even more of an eyebrow raiser. Not that the album, *Son of Albert*, was ever going to be given much of a chance by the music press. They'd decided a long time ago that Ridgeley was a 'talentless hanger-on' and they weren't about to change that opinion, no matter how good his album might be.

Ridgeley had co-written eight of the ten songs, his collaborators including David Austin and Hugh Burns, and he'd co-produced the record with Gary Bromham. The opening 'Red Dress' included samples of motor racing cars and heavy guitars; if you didn't know who the artist was, it sounded like Bon Jovi or Aerosmith. Ridgeley sang in a distinctly American style, if not exactly with an American accent, and as the album progressed it became clear that this was a hair-metal album, without the hair – Ridgeley was going a little thin on top. 'Shake' was released as a single but couldn't crack the Top 50, while *Son of Albert* peaked at number 130 before sinking without a trace. It was a shame, because there was definitely an audience for this type of music, competent if not wholly original. But fans of Whitesnake were hardly likely to be caught buying an album by an ex-member of Wham!.

Meanwhile, at the other end of the balance sheet, *Forbes* magazine named George Michael the biggest earner in the 'entertainment' industry, ahead of Michael Jackson and Mike Tyson. 'Money does give you a lot of confidence,' admitted Michael. 'I know that no one can ever pull the rug out from under me. I am worth a lot of money and I know I can spend it on what I like today and it won't affect my pocket tomorrow. It's an incredible freedom to have. Money is such a big problem in most people's lives, but it is a problem I am lucky enough to have avoided. My only extravagance is cars. I spend a lot of money on them because they're like toys to me. And I buy clothes for prices I wouldn't have dreamt of paying years ago.'

Michael spent more time in Santa Barbara and various vacation spots around the USA before heading back to England and the familiar confines of Sarm West Studios in London. The new songs he worked on here signalled that his next album would mark a change in direction. During the quiet period between June 1989 and June 1990 he completed *Listen Without Prejudice Vol. 1*, a ten-song collection which took him a further step away from Wham!, and even a step away from the poppier moments of *Faith*. Holed up with engineer Chris Porter, he had recorded most of the tracks himself, playing bass, keyboards, guitar and percussion, though stalwarts like Deon Estus did make fleeting appearances. This was truly adult music. For George it was an intensely personal album, closer to the music he'd always wanted to make.

But his label didn't like where he was going. For George Michael there were problems on the horizon at Sony / CBS. The old guard at the company were being weeded out and the people that Michael had worked with for years, those he knew and trusted, were being ousted. This purge, combined with his desire to change the way he was portrayed in the media, set him on a collision course with the company.

After *Faith* and the accompanying furore of 1987–88, he wanted to step back from the chores of promotion. He expected that the album would sell well – as would anything he released – without him whoring himself to every newspaper and teen magazine. 'I think if I step outside the promotion and marketing of George Michael, doing all the videos and the big tours and interviews, then I have every chance of surviving as a successful musician and a balanced human being,' he said. 'I've achieved every other goal, I've done just about everything that I could and that's my goal now. I hope the public understands. I don't want people to feel pissed off or to feel Madonna is trapped in the way that Jackson's become trapped. And that was my next option. There's a point of no return, and I think I've stopped just short of it. I'm lucky, I know, because I still live the life I want to live. I do what I like. I still travel about. I'm quite sure Madonna can't remember the last time she travelled from country to country on her own. Obviously this isn't an ordinary life. But I do normal ordinary things, and I know, with time, I'll be able to do more and more ordinary things. If I don't do that much promotion, if you don't push, it gets easier.'

When the 'suits' at Sony heard the tapes of *Listen Without Prejudice Vol. 1* they were stunned and disappointed. Obviously they were expecting *Faith Vol. 2*. One of them went so far as to quip that this was George Michael's *Nebraska*. (*Nebraska*, released in 1982, had been Bruce Springsteen's acoustic album. Springsteen had decided that the stark demo versions of the songs he'd written for the album were more powerful than the band versions he'd tried to record and so he'd used them on the album. Critics loved it but it sold poorly, fans finding it too much of a departure from his normal output.)

What was more, he didn't want to tour and wasn't keen on filming videos for any singles that might be issued. 'I had to walk away from [touring in] America, and say goodbye to the biggest part of my career,' he said. 'I knew [that] otherwise my demons would get the better of me.' Michael wanted people to listen to the music on this album without an image with which to prejudge it.

'I've realised that I have a lot more respect for my own music than I used to have,' he explained. 'I actually believe in what I do as a musician now, divorced completely from the imagery. And I've come to the point where I know that creating imagery makes me unhappy now.' He emphasised that his purpose in withdrawing from the public gaze was not to create some kind of mystique around himself, but warned: 'I want people to know that for the foreseeable future, unless there's something really important to say, which I don't think there will be, I'm going to kind of disappear. I've made a platform for myself now from which I can make music and that's all. It's not me going, oh, I'm such a serious musician who takes himself so seriously that people should only hear the music. It's just now I think the music is strong enough to stand up on its own, and my priority now is to keep myself happy.'

His decision to hold himself back drew comment from the strangest of places. Frank Sinatra was moved to write a letter to the *Los Angeles Times* on the matter:

> When I saw your Calendar cover today about George Michael 'the reluctant pop star' my first reaction was he should thank the good Lord every morning when he wakes up to have all that he has. And

that'll make two of us thanking God every morning for all we have. I don't understand a guy who lives 'in hopes of reducing the strain of his celebrity status'. Here's a kid who 'wanted to be a pop star since I was about seven years old'. And now that he's a smash performer and songwriter at twenty-seven he wants to quit doing what tons of gifted youngsters all over the world would shoot Grandma for – just one crack at what he's complaining about. Come on, George. Loosen up. Swing, man. Dust off those gossamer wings and fly yourself to the moon of your choice and be grateful to carry the baggage we've all had to carry since those lean nights of sleeping on buses and helping the driver unload the instruments. And no more of that talk about 'the tragedy of fame'. The tragedy of fame is when no one shows up and you're singing to the cleaning lady in some empty joint that hasn't seen a paying customer since Saint Swithin's day. And you're nowhere near that; you're top dog on the top rung of a tall ladder called Stardom, which in Latin means thanks-to-the-fans who were there when it was lonely. Talent must not be wasted. Those who have it – and you obviously do or today's Calendar cover would have been about Rudy Vallee – those who have talent must hug it, embrace it, nurture it and share it lest it be taken away from you as fast as it was loaned to you. Trust me. I've been there. Frank Sinatra.

Michael did grant an interview to the *South Bank Show*, ITV's long-running cultural documentary programme, which typically aired late on Sunday night. The show's presenter, novelist and intellectual heavyweight Melvyn Bragg, talked to the singer on a whole range of topics during the one-hour special. Along with Michael Parkinson, Bragg was to become Michael's most trusted TV interviewer.

With no more interviews scheduled, it was time to let the

music do the talking. 'Praying For Time', selected as the lead-off single from the album, scored yet another Top 10 hit in the UK and another number one in the US. The single, which would also open the album, showed that Michael had been listening to John Lennon's early solo recordings. The vocal effects, the understated acoustic strumming and the big ideas all harked back to the early 1970s, which was no bad thing. The lyrics dealt with the subject of people going hungry while the rich cover their eyes to the problems of the world. Given his favourable record of contributing to charities, he was one millionaire who could just about get away with singing such lines.

The album was released soon afterwards and again spawned numerous hit singles, despite limited promotion by either Michael or his label. With its simple piano arrangement, a cover of Stevie Wonder's 1974 song, 'They Won't Go When I Go', sounded like Michael could have been singing at a Memphis church on a Sunday morning, especially when the impressive backing choir harmonised. It was a live recording too. 'Something To Save' was more acoustic guitar pop with a powerful vocal performance, while 'Mother's Pride' hinted at Michael's later much publicised anti-war stance. The timing was uncanny – just as the album was released, Saddam Hussein's Iraqi army rolled over the border into Kuwait, sparking what would become the first Gulf War. The chugging 'Soul Free' sounded a little too indulgent, but the closing 'Waiting (Reprise)' ended the album perfectly. Gentle but intensely autobiographical, this final song told of his career to date, the problems he'd faced and why he wanted to change direction. Essentially it was a road map from Wham! to the end of this album: 'Is it too late to try again? Here I am.'

'With other albums I have been exhausted and by the end, glad they were over. With this one, I felt like carrying on and on,' he explained. 'It was a slightly more adult album, but I didn't feel that *Faith* was a very young album, I felt that *Faith* captured a middle ground. And also remembering that most of the people who bought *Faith* would be three years older, I don't think that the market I was appealing to was particularly different. I think that the market that I had attracted in *Faith*, in the United States maybe more than in other territories, a lot of that market was attracted on a visual basis. But musically I didn't think there was a huge disparity between the two albums.'

Despite Sony's initial reservations about the album, critics on both sides of the Atlantic loved it. Awarding it a five-star review, Mat Snow reported in *Q* magazine that 'George Michael is completely at ease in the studio, detailing the songs with brushwork that is fine without ever distracting from the big picture. Pop LP of the year? Probably. Now roll on Vol 2.' *Rolling Stone*'s James Hunter focused in his review on Michael's shift to a more adult stance:

> For the most part the album succeeds in its effort to establish Michael's seriousness and deliver him from caricature . . . This time around, George Michael has begun to think that he should provide something to his fans beyond fun and games. Fun and games at Michael's level needn't be underrated, as he sings on 'Freedom! '90', such stratagems happened to yield a captivating sound for millions of people who like to listen to the radio. On this anxiously titled album, though, he's operating from the proposition that a damn good sound is only the starting point for how much pop music can achieve.

Reviews like these helped propel the album to the top of the UK chart, even though it was up against Prince's new effort, *Music From Graffiti Bridge*. The album came in a sleeve showing a photo of an insanely crowded beach, and nothing else. No picture of George Michael. No album title. No indication of whose album it was. Nothing.

For listeners who hadn't been paying close attention to his growing rift with Sony, the next single, 'Freedom! '90', with its accompanying video, showed exactly what he was trying to achieve. Whereas Wham!'s 'Freedom' had been about not wanting to be set free, 'Freedom! '90' was just the opposite, trashing industry ideas that a pretty face and an MTV-friendly video were all that was needed to be successful. Michael wanted freedom from his label, freedom to record what he wanted and freedom to promote it or not, however he saw fit.

The message couldn't have been clearer. The video cost £300,000 and Michael didn't even appear in it, instead hiring a bevy of supermodels to lip-synch to his words. In a parody of the opening of the 'Faith' video, a CD player is shown in close up as a laser starts to read the spinning disc. On top of the stereo is a CD case for the album. The song begins, and the models, both male and female, walk around a derelict high-ceilinged apartment singing along to a jaunty piano that predates Primal Scream's 'Loaded' by a year. Elsewhere in the film the messages are even more obvious: a Wurlitzer jukebox explodes and the famous BSA leather jacket, suspended on a coat hanger, spontaneously bursts into flame.

The models used to illustrate his point – including Cindy Crawford, Linda Evangelista, Naomi Campbell, Christy Turlington and Tatiana Patit – became the stars of the clip, which received oodles of MTV play. 'I really enjoyed making the film with George,' said Cindy Crawford. 'I don't pose naked often, but I was quite happy to do it for this video because George made it almost a work of art.' In September 1991 Michael's decision to use models in the video was vindicated when it was nominated in five categories at the MTV Video Music Awards.

The release schedules for the UK and the US crossed over, so that when 'Freedom! '90' was released in one territory, 'Waiting for the Day' was released in the other and vice versa. The latter, a tender, mellow track, faded out with Michael quoting from the Rolling Stones' 'You Can't Always Get What You Want', which earned Jagger/Richards a co-writing credit. Michael had discussed the writing of this track with Melvyn Bragg on the *South Bank Show*, telling the interviewer that he'd sampled James Brown's 'Funky Drummer', slowed down the beat then layered acoustic guitars on top.

Michael ended the year as the 128th richest man in the UK, according to the *Sunday Times* Rich List, with an estimated fortune of £65 million. Among musicians only Paul McCartney, Elton John and Mick Jagger were ranked higher. But these weren't his direct competitors, and Michael was struggling to find who he should be benchmarking himself against. 'I've got a real feeling of growth now,' he explained. 'Although I'm really proud of this album and I feel it really represents me, I have this completely secure feeling inside me that the next one will be much better. I've really learned to relax when I'm making music now. The pressure's off me. I don't have to worry about getting to number one, I can just concentrate and enjoy the music. At the moment I'm not in competition with anybody because I have different objectives. In a way I wish that there was someone in the same area that I'm in now so I'd have a sparring partner. But I don't really feel threatened by anyone. In the first part of my career I was threatened by all the other big pop bands like the Frankies and Duran and in the last period it was Madonna and Jackson and Prince. Now that I've made a transition in my head and have moved away from that territory I don't know who there is to compete with.'

At the start of 1991 war was looming in the Middle East and on 17 January Operation Desert Storm began. One hundred hours later the Iraqis surrendered and Kuwait was cleared of their presence, although Saddam Hussein was allowed to stay in power, sowing the seeds for further conflict a decade later. George Michael flatly refused to tour the songs of his new album; instead, almost rubbing Sony's nose in it, he decided to set out on the Cover to Cover tour, during which he would sing only cover versions. He explained that he was attracted to the idea of paying homage to songwriters, adding, 'As a singer it should be a real joy for me, and playing live has never been a joy for me. I don't particularly enjoy singing my own songs.' His choice of covers was quite diverse, oldies from the Doobie Brothers and Gladys Knight rubbing shoulders with Seal and David Bowie. And he sometimes departed from the brief, slipping in 'Careless Whisper', 'Freedom' and 'Everything She Wants' while allowing even 'Mother's Pride' and 'Freedom! '90' from the new album an airing in the encores.

Midway through these dates he jetted to South America for the massive Rock in Rio festival. This was the second such event, the first in 1985 having featured Queen and AC/DC. Other acts on the 1991 bill at the Maracana Stadium were Guns N' Roses, Happy Mondays, INXS and Santana. Various bands took turns headlining over the nine nights, A-Ha making the *Guinness Book of Records* when 195,000 people crammed in on the night they headlined. On the second night, in front of a crowd of 170,000, the largest Michael had played in his career, Andrew Ridgeley made a guest appearance.

The most earth-shattering event on the trip, though, was yet to come. Michael was sporting his new short-cropped hairstyle with goatee beard, wearing a leather waistcoat. Brazilian Anselmo Feleppa, a designer at his father's clothing factory, had front row tickets for each of the shows and managed to catch Michael's eye, putting the singer off with his attention to the extent that, he later said, he spent more of the show at the other side of the stage. After the show Feleppa managed to get an introduction to Michael at a party on a private island. Meeting Feleppa, Michael said, changed his life.

For the next six months, explained Michael, he'd never felt better in his life. Feleppa was soon introduced to all of Michael's friends, though not to his immediate family. Michael said that Feleppa 'broke down my Victorian restraint, and really showed me how to live, how to relax, how to enjoy life'. The singer had been sleeping with men for several years but this was to be his first lasting relationship. The pair fell in love, and Michael knew that he was on a path that he could never retrace. 'It's very hard to be proud of your own sexuality when it hasn't brought you any joy. Once it's associated with joy and love it's easy to be proud of who you are.'

With no tour to promote, Sony continued to hype the album by issuing as many singles as they could. 'Heal The Pain', 'Cowboys And Angels' and 'Soul Free' were all lifted from the album ('Soul Free' was only issued in Australia), none of them making the Top 20. 'Cowboys and Angels' was probably too long, at over seven minutes, to make much chart impact.

On his return from Brazil, Michael continued with his Cover to Cover dates. Once the shows were over CBS still wanted him to tour the US to promote *Listen Without Prejudice Vol. 1*, and still he refused. This time he flew off to spend time with Feleppa on a private yacht off the Brazilian coast. The couple then travelled to George's Santa Barbara house, as the singer was to be best man at cousin Andros' wedding in Los Angeles.

'In pursuing stardom, I've wasted a lot of time,' Michael had told *The Times* in 1990. 'I don't think I'd realised how meaningless chasing the celebrity circuit was until I'd taken it as far as I could. In the Eighties you didn't have to do much more than keep repeating what you had done and, as long as your youth was holding up and you're not letting anybody down agewise, you don't have to worry about much more than that. I just wanted the attention of thousands of women, I suppose. I was a very insecure child. Most huge stars are driven by these insecurities. I wasn't that attractive and I just had this feeling that if I could become a pop star I could make up for my shortcomings. What happened was that at some point I realised I could do a lot more than that – you could take yourself to a level where you are almost untouchable, which, I suppose, is where I am.' Over the summer he stayed in the States and demoed some material for a possible *Listen Without Prejudice Vol. 2*, which was eventually scrapped. Instead he turned his attention to the charity project *Red Hot & Dance*.

Just five months into their relationship, Anselmo Feleppa confronted Michael with potentially devastating news. It was a terrifying wait and the outcome was not good. The Brazilian was infected with HIV, and Michael might be infected too. Feleppa insisted on being treated in Brazil and Michael spent some time back in the UK.

Then, on 24 November, the world was shocked when Queen's Freddie Mercury died at his home in Holland Park, London, officially due to pneumonia-related complications from AIDS. The whole country mourned, not just the millions of Queen fans. The band put out an official statement:

> We have lost the greatest and most beloved member of our family. We feel overwhelming grief that he has gone, sadness that he should be cut down at the height of his creativity, but above all great pride in the courageous way he lived and died. It is a privilege for us to have shared such magical times. As soon as we are able we would like to celebrate his life in the style to which he was accustomed.

After a lull following the original publicity explosion in the 1980s, AIDS was now front page news once again. Once Mercury's ashes had been scattered on the shores of Lake Geneva, the music industry went into AIDS charity overdrive. A Concert for Life was organised in which a host of stars paid tribute to Mercury. George Michael joined forces with Elton John to record 'Don't Let The Sun Go Down On Me', with proceeds going to AIDS charities.

After Christmas it went to number one on both sides of the Atlantic and raised a bucketload of money, Michael's donated royalties alone topping $500,000. Queen's own classic 'Bohemian Rhapsody' was reissued, again to raise money for AIDS charities, and it too went to number one. Michael broke down in tears while being interviewed about Mercury's death. The interviewer assumed that the tears were for Mercury, and to an extent they were – but they were more for Feleppa and what he was going through.

Michael travelled to London to spend Christmas 1991 with his family, while Feleppa returned to Brazil. Keeping his innermost feelings and fears to himself yet again, Michael spent the time worrying that the man he loved, the man whose existence was unknown to his family, might be dying. He didn't even know if he was dying himself. Although he was surrounded by his family it was a lonely time. Even close friends who knew about his relationship with Feleppa didn't know about the HIV result; the Brazilian had forbidden Michael from telling anyone. His family weren't even aware that he was gay, though his mother had always privately suspected as much.

George Michael's frontline involvement with AIDS charities and fundraising events caused more questions to be raised about his sexuality. No one in the press officially knew about Anselmo but newspapers and magazines prodded and poked for a scoop. Rumours were coming out of America, where a publication was supposedly about to spill the beans. The pressure was growing to such an extent that Michael felt he had to put out a statement of his own: 'George wishes it to be known that a report emanating in America suggesting he is considering giving an interview about his private life is wholly without foundation and, as in the past, he will not be giving interviews on the subject.' At least, not for the moment.

The next, and most memorable, tribute to Freddie Mercury took place at Wembley Stadium on 20 April 1992. Queen played, with a series of vocalists taking the lead. Focused as it was on a single person rather than a cause, the whole event was intensely emotional. George Michael gave a powerful and impassioned performance, not just because of Mercury but because of his hidden feelings for Anselmo Feleppa. 'It was probably the proudest moment of my career,' he said. 'It was me living out a childhood fantasy to sing one of Freddie's songs in front of 80,000 people.' It was a bitter irony that while Michael was paying tribute to his childhood hero, the love of his life was secretly going through the same pain.

George Michael's next AIDS-related project was the *Red Hot & Dance* album. This was a follow-up to *Red Hot & Blue*, released in 1990, on which the likes of U2, Iggy Pop and Erasure had performed covers of Cole Porter songs. The album was filled with remixes of tracks by Madonna, Seal and Lisa Stansfield among others, while Michael donated three new tracks – 'Too Funky', 'Happy' and 'Do You Really Want To Know' – from the shelved *Listen Without Prejudice Vol. 2* album.

Released as a single, 'Too Funky' almost was too funky, but not quite. Opening with a sample, 'I'm not trying to seduce you. Would you like me to seduce you?' this was Michael's most danceable track for quite a while. The track drifts close to house music, with samples popping up throughout and Michael taking on various vocal styles. The video, for which he again utilised a gang of supermodels – this time they included Tyra Banks, Nadja Auermann, Estelle Halliday and Linda Evangelista – was set at a fashion show, Michael himself playing the part of a cameraman seated behind a television camera and watching the action from afar. The supermodels were depicted mixing with drag queens backstage and taking it in turns to strut down the catwalk in ever more weird and wonderful creations, including feathery lion manes, a 'motorbike' outfit complete with handlebars and rear-view mirrors, and a *Metropolis*-inspired metal robot costume. The video was co-directed by Michael and shot in Paris during early 1992. The single did well, going to number ten in the States and number four in the UK.

But the album as a whole bombed. 'It went completely wrong for reasons that I thought were beyond my control,' Michael explained. His growing impatience with Sony and their apparent unwillingness to support his projects was discussed during the court case in 1993. 'I was going to give them a track from *Listen Without Prejudice* to remix. Then later on, when I decided that I was not going to make a dance album or even half a dance album, I decided almost immediately after that to give those three tracks that I was considering, or three of the four tracks I was considering for *Listen Without Prejudice Volume 2*, to *Red Hot & Dance*.

'I think its importance was, firstly, as a charity album, and secondly as an album which had three brand new compositions and recordings of mine on it. And therefore,' he added, 'it should have been of some importance, I would have thought, to Sony worldwide, simply because it included new material from one of their artists.'

He also hit out in the *Mirror* newspaper. 'The many people around the world who will benefit from the *Red Hot & Dance* project need all the support we can give them,' he said. 'It is a shame this fact was overlooked. This lack of support was apparent in the *Chart Show*'s refusal to play the "Too Funky" video. It seems this negative approach has more to do with people's perception of George Michael than anything else.'

This perceived negative approach was mind boggling. Was it because he wasn't touring? Was it because some in the press thought he was gay? Michael himself believed that by walking away from success he had committed 'a very American form of blasphemy'. 'They were like, "You're making a hundred million dollars, people love you, how can you quit?" But I knew that to develop as a gay adult, which I had never really been, I had to do it.'

By October 1992 things had escalated to the point where George Michael simply wanted to get away from his label. He flew to New York for a meeting with the head of the Sony Corporation, Norio Ohga. Michael's legal position was simple. He wanted to be released from his contract with immediate effect, even though he was still signed for a total of six more solo albums to be spread over the next 11 years. He left the meeting confident that he might be able to reach a settlement, but Sony weren't going to let him get away without a fight. When they refused to act, Michael decided to challenge them in the courts.

The rest of the year, and the start of 1993, was dedicated to two major projects: preparing evidence for the upcoming court case and making the most of the time he had left with Feleppa. But like any couple facing terminal illness, the time they had together was never going to seem enough. Michael was convinced that Feleppa would receive better treatment in the US or Europe than he was getting in Brazil. Feleppa though was adamant that he wanted to be treated in Brazil, away from the prying press. For the sake of his family in particular, he didn't want his illness turning into a circus, which was bound to happen if George Michael was linked to him publicly.

The pair remained a couple until the end. Feleppa finally died of a brain haemorrhage on 26 March 1993. Michael was still of the opinion that he might have lived if he'd had treatment elsewhere, and was convinced that the only reason he hadn't was the threat of media intrusion. It added more fuel to Michael's hatred of the press.

Michael didn't attend the funeral, for fear once again of turning the service into a media circus, but the next day he admitted to his parents that he was gay. They took the news well. His father took a little time to get used to the idea, but his mother was more concerned that he'd gone through the whole Feleppa trauma by himself. Not long afterwards Michael visited Feleppa's grave with Anselmo's mother, an event about which he later wrote the song 'You Have Been Loved'.

Soon after the funeral Parlophone released the *Five Live* EP. This featured Michael's performances of 'Somebody To Love' and 'These Are The Days Of Our Lives' with Queen and Lisa Stansfield at the Freddie Mercury tribute concert, as well as recordings of 'Killer', 'Papa Was A Rolling Stone' and 'Calling You' made on the Cover to Cover tour. Again the proceeds went towards AIDS charities. Michael's sleeve note read:

> I think a lot of people, not necessarily people who have anything against gay people, are probably taking some small comfort in the fact that although Freddie died of AIDS he was publicly bisexual. It's a very, very dangerous comfort. The conservative estimate for the year 2000 is that forty million people on this planet will be infected by HIV, and if you think that those are all going to be gay people or drug addicts, then you are pretty well lining up to be one of those numbers. So please, for God's sake and Freddie's sake and for your own sakes, please be careful.

As was his wont, Michael seemed almost intent on putting himself through pain for reasons that he was still keeping private. Throughout the spring he agreed to a series of interviews to promote the *Five Live* EP, on which all his grief for Freddie Mercury and Anselmo was expressed. While giving nothing away about himself, he told MTV: 'It's really sad to me that people think in order to work towards a cure, you have to be afflicted yourself. If people look at me and they think I'm a gay man, fine. If they look at me and think I'm straight, that's fine, too. It makes no difference. The important thing for the kids, whether they be straight, bisexual, gay, whatever, is to be aware, there's a definite threat. They are all going to come into contact with people who are afflicted by this disease. There are plenty of people who will die because they felt it was something that was never going to happen to them.'

In June Michael reached the milestone of his 30th birthday.

Despite the trauma he'd been through that year he hosted a wild party in a large marquee at Newmarket racecourse. The venue was chosen because Jack Panos had a horse running at the racecourse, Michael having gifted his father an expensive stud farm a couple of years earlier. The party had a 1970s fancy dress theme and guests were bussed in from pickup points in Watford so the location wouldn't be leaked to the press. It was extravagant, but Michael could afford it. In 1993 the *Sunday Times* Rich List claimed he was worth £80 million.

After the party, Michael had just three months before his case against Sony was due to open. He later admitted that if it wasn't for the pain of losing Feleppa he might not have gone as far as the courtroom, but it was to become the perfect vessel for his pain and resentment.

The preliminaries to the case had now begun, and Michael's legal brief won the right to access the contracts of other artists on the Sony roster. Bruce Springsteen, Michael Jackson and Billy Joel were just three of the acts whose deals were scrutinised. The whole music industry watched with more than a passing interest: if George Michael won it would send shock-waves through the business. The high cost of buying CDs, especially in the UK, was the subject of debate in the press and people were keen to see what information would come out during the proceedings regarding how much artists earned per disc sold.

On the eve of the case Sony put forward an offer to Michael's legal team in an effort to avoid going to court. The offer included an inclination to end the contract, though with certain financial provisos. Michael's camp saw this as an unofficial admission that Sony expected to lose the case; Michael, feeling particularly belligerent, decided to go for the kill.

The opening salvos had been fired via the press as far back as 1992. Sony made a statement in the *Independent* newspaper which claimed they had clear and unwavering commitment to their artist:

'Together our relationship with him has been mutually fruitful. Our contract with George is valid and legally binding. We are saddened and surprised by the action George has taken. There is a serious moral as well as legal commitment attached to any contract, and we will not only honour it, but vigorously defend it.' Michael's music publisher, Dick Leahy, was quoted in the same article. 'It's about the style of management,' he said. 'Under the old management there was an understanding that their top worldwide artists would develop over time, and change direction when they needed to. Now it's all short-term thinking. All a record company has to do is market what he gives them, and he feels he wasn't marketed adequately. He feels Sony got their priorities wrong and made a lot of mistakes.'

George Michael was also quoted: 'Since the Sony Corporation bought my contract, I have seen the great American music company that I proudly signed to as a teenager become a small part of the production line for a giant electronics corporation. Musicians do not come in regimented shapes and sizes, but are individuals who change and evolve together with their audiences. Sony obviously views this as a great inconvenience.'

Proceedings finally opened at London's High Court on 11 October 1993. Justice Jonathan Parker would be judging the outcome; Graham Pollock was defending Sony while Mark Cran acted as QC for George Michael. Each day the singer turned up to listen to the sometimes technical legal matters that were argued over by counsel before the case proper could start, his parents looking on all the while from the public gallery. As the trial wound on, Michael would start and end his day by playing squash and pounding away on a treadmill in an effort to burn off his anger and anxiety. He sat in court for 17 days before being asked to take the stand himself for a draining three-day stint.

Beginning his evidence, Michael told the judge that he wanted to back away from the limelight. He explained why he had titled his last album the way he had, why he hadn't toured and why his picture wasn't on the cover, and cited Sony's alleged lack of support over his image change. But he refused to say out loud how much he was worth, instead writing the number on a slip of paper which was passed to the judge. It was revealed that Michael had grossed just short of £100 million for Sony. Out of this mind-boggling figure, Michael had been paid 7.4 per cent and the label had taken 52.5 per cent. Sony hit back by saying that he'd known it was an exclusive contract and that he'd been more than happy to take the £11 million advance when he'd signed back in the 1980s.

Michael spoke at length about his disappointment at the perceived lack of support given to him on the completion of *Listen Without Prejudice Vol. 1*. 'The main thrust of my disappointment in Sony UK at the time [was] how they spent their money, was that they sustained regional advertising on the album. I was shocked that there was no advertising going on in London, and I was shocked that they had not promoted the B side that I had prepared to help them in the charts with "Waiting For That Day",' he told the judge. 'I obviously didn't feel at the time that they were totally committed. I found it surprising that for their biggest selling artist they waited before they advertised in London, which presumably has got to be one of the strongest areas. I must admit, even though they did a very good job over the course of the album around the country, I was surprised that they felt they had to test areas before they could spend money in London.

'My reason for wanting to part with Sony is because I don't believe that one particular area of the world which is very important to me has any belief in me or any motivation to exploit my work. If there's a relationship between artist and record company it should be a mutual thing. If an artist wants certain songs on the radio I would have thought the record company's position with that artist, especially after almost ten years, would be to try and support that.

'I'm not really complaining. I am saying that I was satisfied with

George and David Austin become 'Tony' and 'Des' for *My Guy*.

George and Andrew Ridgeley on stage in July 1986.

The boys celebrate 'Wake Me Up Before You Go-Go' reaching number one in their iconic sloganeering t-shirts.

George joins Elton John for Live Aid at Wembley Stadium in July 1985.

George attends court for the first day of his case against Sony in 1993.

Parents Jack (*left*) and Lesley Panos leave the Howard Hotel in London in 1994. They refused to comment after their son lost his court battle.

George accompanies Princess Diana in the royal box during the World Aids Day Concert in 1994.

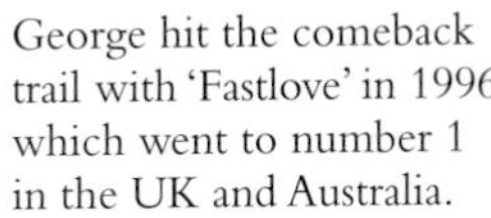

George hit the comeback trail with 'Fastlove' in 1996 which went to number 1 in the UK and Australia.

above left The press core hung around while George had his meal at Spago's after the infamous press chase in April 1998. Here he is snapped leaving the restaurant.

above right George and Spice Girl Geri Halliwell pictured at the Equality Rocks show in April 2000.

left George and partner Kenny Goss at the Ritz in Paris attending a party thrown by Donatella Versace.

George at the Japanese press conference to launch *A Different Story*.

Helen 'Pepsi' DeMacque and George's sister, Melanie, attend a screening of *A Different Story* in London in 2005.

George returned to the touring circuit in 2006 with his triumphant *25Live* show.

George became a regular on the Michael Parkinson chat show, here he talks during a May 2007 appearance.

George leaves the Brent Magistrates court on 8 June 2007 after being sentenced to 100 hours of community service.

above George debuted his new song, 'White Light,' at the London 2012 Olympic Games Closing Ceremony.

right George and partner Fadi Fawaz enjoying some free time in Australia.

left and above As news of George's passing on 25 December 2016 spread, memorials were left at his London and Oxfordshire homes.

the job they did and that even though I do believe that with more extensive advertising *Listen Without Prejudice* would have sold more in this country, I still am happy with my position here because the music was heard on the radio. I'm afraid I have to refer you again to the fact that the radio promotion has absolutely nothing to do with CBS UK.'

Sony claimed that the whole case was a cover for Michael's inability to fulfil the contract because he was suffering from writer's block. Further arguments raged over the relationship between Sony's management and Michael himself. The label had to admit that relations had deteriorated when Michael's brief pointed out that they were in possession of a recorded telephone conversation in which CBS president Don Ienner had referred to Michael as 'that faggot client of yours'.

The case would drag on until April 1994, incurring massive legal fees on both sides. But on 1 December 1993, Michael took time out to appear at the World AIDS Day concert at Wembley Arena at the special request of the Princess of Wales. The 'Concert for Hope', held to raise funds for the Princess' National AIDS Trust, was presented by a very dapper looking David Bowie in a grey suit. k d lang and Mick Hucknall played as support acts for Michael, who appeared in an understated, slim-fitting single-breasted tartan suit of green and blue. The circular stage was spotlit from four corners as screams welcomed the opening words of 'Father Figure'. Michael turned the excitement up a notch further for the next song, jump-ing around the periphery of the stage clapping his hands above his head as the opening bars of Seal's 'Killer' rang out. Every little dance move drew more screams. He slowed it right down with a couple of ballads, thanking 'the lady who made this all possible' before demonstrating that he still had it as the ultimate showman, getting the entire crowd on its feet for 'Freedom 90'.

✧

Back in court, after the closing arguments had been heard, the verdict took a further two months while the judge deliberated and set out his reasoning in a 280-page ruling. On 21 June the parties were recalled to court. Queues started to form outside the High Court at 7.30 am, fans and photographers jostling for position. When the judge read out his ruling, it was soon apparent that Sony had prevailed. His decision hinged on two major factors: first, George Michael had renegotiated the contract during its course, when he'd signed for the £11 million advance, and second he'd always had full and proper legal advice and had entered into the contracts knowingly. Michael left the court in silence but later made an official statement to the press:

'I am shocked and extremely disappointed. It means that even though I both created and paid for my work, I will never own it or have any rights over it. And perhaps most importantly, I have no right to resign. In fact, there is no such thing as resignation of an artist in the music industry. However, I am convinced that the English legal system will not support Mr Justice Parker's decision or uphold what is effectively professional slavery.'

He vowed that he would never record for Sony again and pointed out that while he'd had money deducted from his earnings to pay for recording costs, Sony still owned the very same recordings. Meanwhile, Sony somehow found it appropriate to say that they looked forward to working with George Michael again.

After taking time to review his options, Michael spoke to David Frost on Carlton TV about his frustrations over the case. He continued to argue that his contract was essentially an extension of the very first one signed with Innervision. 'It wasn't a perfect deal because all the way through, I never signed a new deal . . . Every single deal that I have done, every single renegotiation that I've ever done, whether it be with CBS or Sony, has been an extension of the deal that I signed when I was 18 years old, which effectively bound me for, I think it was ten albums altogether. It was five and an optional five which is effectively the whole of my career. I've never been able to sign a piece of paper as a new deal. I've always been trying to update that deal that I did when I was 18, so I've always been held to that part of the deal that I signed when I was 18 years old.' He also pointed out that when the news broke in court that he'd been paid an £11 million 'advance', it was actually taken from royalties that he'd already earned. Sony, as he put it, were always operating in the black.

'You are almost always signing people in a very vulnerable position, and I definitely was in a very vulnerable position. I was at the age of 18, and many bands are signed that young. Some are signed a little older, but whenever they're signed, they're desperate. There isn't one other industry that operates on this basis. If I were an author, and I fell out with my company in the way that I have, the worst I would have to endure was the fact that they would have the first option on my next book, so you're talking about two books. It's a ridiculous situation to sign a contract when you're 18 years old, and be held to it for your entire professional career. Why, why, would any court uphold that situation? The judge seems to have found, in my case, that I reaffirmed this contract at the given point of my renegotiations, but did I really have any choice? The choice that I had was to go along with that length of term, or to do what I've done now, which has been incredibly difficult.'

He understood that not everyone on the street would be sympathetic to his argument as he was so rich, but he also wanted to point out that his wealth shouldn't prevent him from taking a stand for what he truly believed was right: 'I thought it was a very strange judgment. The judge was kind enough to point out that he believed I was very honest and candid in the witness box, so I did my best to be truthful. And at the same time, he completely accepted everybody on Sony's side. Everybody that appeared in defence of Sony, he completely accepted that they were all telling the truth. The ultimate truth is Sony didn't need me to begin with.

Sony as a corporation, and even as a record company, is so massive that they can do without George Michael perfectly easily. The UK company would miss me, the company as a whole would not miss me because it has so many major artists. What they did mean to do with this court case was hold on to their standard contract, and with this judgment they've managed to do that.' That was, of course, the main point as far as the company was concerned. If they let George Michael 'get away with it', who would be next?

Michael was determined not to be beaten. He said 'I am now convinced that, without a total artistic and personal compromise on my part, the sad deterioration in my relations with Sony worldwide is irreversible. I shall obviously take full legal advice, but the initial view is that we have very strong grounds for an appeal.'

In August 1994 Michael entered his official appeal, but despite arguments that it should be heard sooner rather than later because of the effect upon his career, he was told it would have to go on the lengthy waiting list just like everybody else. In the aftermath of the ruling Michael decided to dispense with the services of Rob Kahane, implying that he'd been unhappy with his input during the legal battles. (The judge had called Kahane a 'thoroughly unreliable and untrustworthy witness . . .) By the autumn his head was finally clear enough for him to be able to write music again, and his feelings about Anselmo Feleppa came flooding out. With the traumatic year almost behind him, George Michael was back on form.

EIGHT

GRIEF

1994–1997

grief

1 keen mental suffering or distress over affliction or loss; sharp sorrow; painful regret.

2 a cause or occasion of keen distress or sorrow.

'I thought it was punishment because I turned round at the end of *Faith* and said, "You know what? I'm going insane, and I know there's another way to do this". I thought, is it because I wasn't grateful enough for my talents? In terms of coming close to saying I don't want to live, that would have been after my mum died. I had this overwhelming feeling that the best was behind me. I so loved my mum, and respected her. I'd have to be seriously mentally disturbed to even consider suicide because of what it would do to the people who were already devastated from losing my mother.'

George Michael

'I can't be bothered with being aloof anymore. I think being aloof served me very well, especially in that period when my life was a f**king nightmare, when Anselmo was ill and my mum died and everything. Not anymore.'

George Michael

George Michael wrote 'Jesus To A Child' in the autumn of 1994. Within days he'd recorded it and was on stage performing it live. And not just any stage – this one was in front of Berlin's Brandenburg Gate, he was being backed with an orchestra and the show was being beamed live to millions of European TV viewers. The venue, chosen to host the 1994 MTV Europe Video Music Awards, saw Michael courageously return to form with this stunningly beautiful song about Anselmo Feleppa. His first new song since 'Too Funky' in 1992, it showed him at his emotional best.

This was the first time he'd put his feelings towards Feleppa into a song. As he later explained, even if people didn't know he was gay, the song's lyric of the male 'Jesus' figure could or should have made it clear that he was singing about a relationship with a man. Listeners might have chosen to think that he was singing in character, but how many straight men have sung in character as being gay?

It wasn't as though the press had not given enough away. In interviews published around this time Michael spoke for the first time of his 'friendship' with Feleppa. 'I don't understand this idea that my sexuality was shrouded in any sort of mystery,' he said later. 'I mean, there were three-page articles about Anselmo in the papers. There was one by Tony Parsons, who I thought was a good friend. If Tony Parsons writes an article that I had taken part in about my dead lover, where is the mystery? He outed me. Basically, I told him all this stuff as a mate, because my life had changed so much and I wanted to tell him what I'd gone through. And he put it all into print. But I didn't deny it, so all those statements stood. So where the fuck was I not out? Until you sit down in front of the press and say "I am gay" you're not considered to be out. And I wasn't going to do that.'

At the Berlin show, Michael's manager Andy Stephens wondered what Sony's reaction to the new song would be. There was still no movement on his contract and relations with the label were at stalemate, though tentative background negotiations were to continue into 1995. To confirm his own stance, Michael had also chosen to perform 'Freedom! '90' that night; before he broke into the song, a selection of supermodels on platforms rose on to the stage wrapped in blankets, then paraded before the TV cameras.

In February Michael's compassionate side again came to the fore when he, along with Eric Clapton, helped the family of Nigel Browne win a hefty compensation payout. The two musicians had both previously employed Browne as a bodyguard, Michael during the Faith tour in 1988. Browne had been killed in a helicopter crash and after the court case the family's lawyers publicly thanked both musicians for their help.

Despite such acts of kindness, with his career still hanging in limbo Michael was struggling against depression, increasingly turning to cannabis to alleviate the dark mood hanging over him. An offer of a helping hand came from a most unusual source. Michael had first come across Princess Diana when she'd invited him to perform at the World AIDS Day concert in 1993. Michael later revealed that he'd been invited to Buckingham Palace by the Princess on several occasions. He finally agreed to meet, and for a while he and Princess Diana became close friends.

'I think we clicked in way that was a little bit intangible,' he said. 'It probably had more to do with our upbringing than anything else. She was very like a lot of women that have been attracted to me in my life because they see something non-threatening. Maybe because I take care of my sisters and I'm so protective of my sisters, women seem to smell that. There were certain things that happened that made it clear she was very attracted to me.' When asked if they'd slept together he responded, 'I knew it would have been a disastrous thing to do.'

After their lives had gone their separate ways Michael, along with 20 million others, watched Martin Bashir's infamous interview with the Princess on the BBC's *Panorama* TV show in which she admitted adultery, sowing the seeds of her eventual divorce. Michael recalled that he was upset while watching the show because he thought she seemed unwell and vulnerable. He also felt more than a twinge of guilt, as he'd been keeping his distance from her to the point of avoiding returning her phone calls. Knowing he couldn't provide what she wanted, he'd assumed that she had lots of help and support around her, that it would be intrusive for him to contact her. After 1995 he never saw her in person again.

Michael himself was in danger of falling off the map. Finding it almost impossible to write music, he seemed to be living on marijuana and Prozac. Eventually, through a haze of cannabis smoke, he threw himself back into writing songs. He managed to quit the Prozac but found that the weed helped his creative process, and in the state he found himself in he was willing to use whatever he needed to get his writing confidence back. 'It was quite inspiring,' he admitted. 'The album that resulted from it was the most creative I'd made at the time. Unfortunately, it is a writing tool now, which is one of the things that makes it hard to give up.'

A year after losing his court case with Sony, Michael finally negotiated his release from his contract. He flew to New York, agreed that the contract would be put up for sale and flew home a happy man. There were conditions: one clause bound him to record three new songs for a 'best of' collection that would be issued before the end of the decade. In July 1995 he signed a new deal which would see his music distributed by Dreamworks SKG in the USA and by Virgin in the rest of the world. The buyout fee was $40 million and he was offered a very generous 20 per cent royalty rate.

Plans were put in place for a return to the limelight in 1996, and a new album was pencilled in for May. The only problem was that the new songs were taking a long time to form fully. Engineer Paul Gomersall, who had recorded with George since the Wham! days, worked closely with the singer at Sarm's Studio Two, Michael's studio of choice. 'Compared with what I experienced on the *Faith* sessions at PUK in Denmark, it was very different this time around,' recalls Gomersall. 'George was a lot more in control, and playing most of the keyboards and bass guitar. We've used a lot more computers and synths on the album than George was previously accustomed to, and now that the technology has improved so much, along with his grasp of it, he was doing a lot more himself, as opposed to bringing in a lot of musicians.

'He arrived with the songs in his head, and whenever he was ready to lay something down, he would call the guys into the studio and spend a few hours getting a basic backing track on tape, and then they'd leave. After working alongside a producer and an artist on many occasions, I find it very refreshing to work on a purely one-to-one basis, as I have done with George. The artist is effectively producing and I have a direct line to him. It's always healthy for an artist in George's position to listen and react to a second artistic opinion, and I do offer such words of wisdom, but because he has always known exactly what he wants, especially in terms of vocal and musical phrasing, he generally ignores me! I think most people would agree that his track record more than suggests George is his own best producer.'

The songs on the resultant album, *Older*, were more introspective than ever before. As the title suggests, Michael was considering the passing of his life and that of others to the ultimate end, death. The previously debuted 'Jesus To A Child' became the first single in January 1996 and went to number one in the UK. The video, which Michael now talked about as being the key way of getting a song remembered, showed various highly symbolic images, including two male models in wooden crates reaching through holes to hold hands. In another scene a male figure was shot down by an arrow. Michael himself was shown in close-up, half his face obscured by shadow, singing with real emotion.

With the album's release date fast approaching, a second, upbeat single was given an airing. As suggested by the title, 'Fastlove' concerns one-night stands and getting down to it as quickly as possible without any preamble. This highly danceable song was a little out of place on the album, being the only really upbeat track among the 11 included. Three and a half minutes in, the song introduced the same melody sample that Will Smith would later use on the smash hit 'Men In Black'.

The video for 'Fastlove' gave Michael his strongest visual image for some years, the sharp production and slick performances proving that he now took the medium very seriously. Michael is seen in what has become an iconic 'speaker chair', choosing various holographic fantasy figures which cover all kinds of freaks and fetishes. At one point, as he revolves in his chair, he's seen wearing a pair of headphones with the word 'Fony' written on them, a little dig at his old label. The final shots of the video were also the last to be filmed. The various models featured in the shoot were filmed under a shower dancing to the tune, and Michael himself was convinced to give it a go.

By the time *Older* was released in May, a full six years after *Listen Without Prejudice Vol. 1*, the American press had clearly grown tired of waiting. Writing for *Rolling Stone*, Al Weisel quickly dismissed the motives of its writer but had to admit he liked the album. 'Michael hasn't lost his talent for writing pop songs as contagious as the Ebola virus, if only slightly more cheery,' he deadpanned. 'Michael desperately craves respect, not content with simply being an accomplished writer of silly loathe songs about relationships gone bad. Although he occasionally sounds like the Prozac queen Elizabeth Wurtzel singing "It's My Party" in an empty karaoke bar, for those who can get past Michael's pretentious melancholy, *Older* is a surprisingly enjoyable record.'

Michael freely admitted to smoking a lot of cannabis during the writing and sessions for the album. 'Oh yeah,' he said. 'It's the only way to work. I light a joint at the end of "Spinning The Wheel". You hear a lighter, then you hear it burning and me going [inhales] then, Pahhh, and the next track starts. I don't want to sing about drugs though, how boring. The media and music industry have been incredibly irresponsible in making drugs essential to youth culture. Look at how the Happy Mondays were written about and Oasis are written about. It's fine if you've got a habit and the money to do it, but it does nobody favours to make out it's an integral part of making music. I made lots of music before I took drugs that was just as good. I'm a grass and occasional ecstasy man. I wish I'd never taken ecstasy because I wouldn't know what I was missing. I've never thrown up on it. Never had a headache. I'm very good with drugs. But I find cocaine offensive – it's the new alcohol. It's fashionable to take heroin again, so you've got perfectly intelligent people doing the most stupid thing. It's looked at as heroic. It doesn't matter how horrific *Trainspotting* is if you give it the coolest soundtrack of the last five years. I didn't take drugs until my fucking bones had stopped growing. At least I was the shape of an adult.'

The UK music scene was awash with Britpop, guitars were the in thing. Nevertheless *Q* magazine was impressed. Under the byline 'George Michael: more thoroughbred than clothes horse', Paul Du Noyer awarded four stars, writing, 'He resolutely remains in Anglo-soul mode, and some people just don't hear anything good in that stuff. But if you recognise a rare talent for fusing truth and beauty in mainstream pop music, then George Michael is still your man.'

Opening with a strong one-two punch of 'Jesus To A Child' and 'Fastlove', the album is seemingly filled with singles. 'Older' and

'Spinning The Wheel' follow, both of which were to climb high in the UK. In fact the album would yield six UK singles, all of which reached at least number three in the charts. Much of the album was mid-tempo and dark, reflecting the singer's own personal life in the past three years, which was bound to permeate every pore of the songs as Michael was writing, performing and producing almost everything himself. 'It Doesn't Really Matter' was a late-night message to a lover about the benefits of moving on with life, 'The Strangest Thing' picked up the pace with an eastern-influenced flavour, and 'You Have Been Loved' proved that he could still bring listeners to the brink of tears with a trip to his lover's grave.

Older not only put Michael back in the public eye, it gave the award committees something to think about. The 'Fastlove' video was nominated for Best Dance Video and Best Choreography by MTV and later in the year Michael won the MTV Europe award for Best Male. After being presented with the award by Björk and Richard E. Grant, Michael said, 'The first half of the Nineties was pretty crap for me and 1996 has made it all worthwhile.' He was truly appreciative of the fans' reaction to *Older*.

Around this time Michael was keeping himself busy setting up his own record label, Aegean, with Andros Georgiou. Their main hope of breaking into the pop market came via a 32-year-old Irishman by the name of Toby Bourke. Michael was supportive enough to introduce him on *Top of the Pops*, but Bourke didn't take part in radio or TV interviews, perhaps because he might let the cat out of the bag about Michael's sexuality. However, keen readers would have already known Michael was gay from the articles about the death of Anselmo Feleppa, though until Michael spelled it out, the press wouldn't actually 'out' him for good. The day-to-day running of the label seems to have been in Georgiou's hands, but after copies of Bourke's debut single dried up and the shops ran out, the writing was on the wall. The label ceased trading soon after the millennium with losses amounting to over £100,000.

In June 1996, 33-year-old George Michael met 38-year-old Texan Kenny Goss at the Beverly Hot Springs Spa, just off North Western Avenue in Los Angeles. 'Actually, we have two stories,' says Goss. 'There's the one that we tell people and the one in which we actually met. There's a really posh spa called the Beverly Hot Springs. It's a very straight, above-board spa but, you know, if we tell people we met in a spa they always get the wrong idea. So we often tell people that we met at Fred Segal [a favourite store for celebrities in Los Angeles], but that sounds really camp.' Goss was a self-made millionaire in the sports equipment business. The singer asked him to dinner, though he wasn't sure if Goss was gay. In fact he wasn't completely sure until they had a second date at the Maple Drive in Beverly Hills. On that night Michael managed to trip down some stairs and tore a ligament – but it didn't keep him from the romantic enagagement.

Goss' family lived in Coleman, Texas, just over 100 miles south-west of Dallas. His mother, Ozzell, was a housewife (she passed away in 2000), his father, Earl (who died in 2003), sold fire protection equipment. Kenny shared a love of expensive cars with Michael, but said his greatest fear was 'living in the shadow'. Whether that applied to the shadow of being the partner of a rich and successful international pop star is uncertain. But either way, the pair hit it off.

Chart momentum was kept up with the August release of 'Spinning The Wheel', which reached number two. This was a chugging piece of mid-tempo pop with an urban intro, pan pipes, funky beats and horns all over the place. The song talks of a lover putting the singer in danger through his sexual activities with others. Having lost a partner to AIDS, this was a subject that Michael felt was close to home. The black and white video was set in a kind of down-market 1920s 'cotton club'. Michael and the band sit around on stools, intercut with images of trapeze artists and dancers.

To end the cycle of promotion for the album, George Michael

was able to fulfil a musical ambition by playing a set for MTV's *Unplugged* series. For 'pop' performers the setting, without electric instruments or gadgets, often sorted the wheat from the chaff; only the truly great could strip down their songs to the basics and prove that they could stand alone. Filming took place on 11 October at Three Mills Island Studios in East London, and Michael proved that he could still produce a mean live show, even if it now meant wearing a suit and tie and sitting on a stool rather than racing around a stage in leather jacket and jeans. 'Freedom! '90' opened the show to the packed audience of a few hundred. 'Fastlove', stripped of the dance accoutrements of the album version, was performed with a saxophone treatment that gave it new life.

Such an intimate setting allowed Michael's charisma to come through. He joked with the crowd at one break that he would rather have stayed at home to watch the Liverpool-set soap opera *Brookside*. When a couple of technical hitches occurred and his earpiece wire came loose he declared, 'I'm not plugged in.'

'Father Figure', 'Hand To Mouth', 'Star People', 'One More Try' and 'Waiting For That Day' all made the acoustic transition. He even proved that Wham! could work in an acoustic setting with 'Everything She Wants'. The whole evening seemed to have a magical aura. It was the only show in which he ever paused to say hello to his mother, who was in the audience with the rest of his family. 'I just lost myself in singing that night,' Michael said. 'I have great affection for that evening because I know she was so proud of me.' It would be the last time she ever saw him play.

A week after meeting Kenny Goss, George had phoned his mother back in England to tell her about his new friend. Since coming out to his family he had no longer had any problem discussing personal matters with her. During the conversation Lesley told her son that she'd found a little growth on her shoulder, but that she was being treated and that everything was fine. The little spot, however, turned out to be skin cancer. Treatment continued and she went into remission for three or four months, and for Christmas 1996 she was allowed home to be with the family. But the melanoma was extremely virulent; it came back with a vengeance and she died soon after its return. Apparently she'd known all along that she had only a very small chance of survival, but – just as her son tended to do when he had a serious problem – she had kept it to herself.

George, with his father and sisters, was at her bedside at Charing Cross Hospital until the end. The suddenness with which it came took everyone by surprise, but George was devastated. He had been completely unprepared for this, and found himself spiralling into darkness as life went by in a blur. In February, when he won the Brit Award as Best British Male for the third time, he was in no state to appear at the show. Instead Elton John read out a note apologising for his absence: 'I would have loved to have been there and say thank you to everybody who has made music part of my life for 15 years.'

Soon after Lesley's death George Michael appeared on Chris Tarrant's Capital Radio show to make a donation of £166,000 to the station's Help a London Child weekend, which had been running since 1980. Michael had already written and recorded 'Waltz Away Dreaming' for the charity, listeners pledging money in order to hear it over the airwaves. This raised £35,000, Michael then added £70,000, topping it up with a further £96,000 to push it over the £200,000 mark. 'I hope everyone who listens to the song appreciates what it means to me,' said Michael. 'I didn't think I'd have a good day like this for a long time. I had a fantastic time just listening to the radio.'

'After my mother died, luckily I had just met Kenny,' he explained elsewhere. 'So he was my lifeline. I think if Kenny hadn't been there, I don't know if I would've got through that, I really don't. Because from the day that I found out about my partner [Anselmo] to the day that I could say I was actually on the mend from my mother it was just constant fear, either fear of death or fear of the next bereavement. I took it very, very badly, very badly indeed. I feel like I lost a big chunk of my life to that kind of bereavement. I'm so appreciative of what I have now, so appreciative of the simplest things, it really makes a difference.'

Years later Michael would discuss his belief that the departed Anselmo Feleppa had looked down from heaven and sent Kenny Goss to him just as he needed him most, when his mother's cancer was diagnosed. Kenny was vital in helping Michael to pull through the most difficult period of his life. The singer felt that the greater powers of life were saying he couldn't have everything. Money and success on one side was being balanced by the loss of those closest to him on the other.

'I was so convinced I was going to lose her, that in my own way I was grieving well before she died,' he said. Michael granted an interview to his *Bare* biographer Tony Parsons for what he thought would be a record company biography, but it ended up being serialised over three days in the *Mirror*. 'I'd talked to him as a friend,' said Michael. 'Even though I was telling the truth, it was degrading in "Mirrorspeak". I didn't want to talk about important things in the *Mirror*. I lost dignity.

'When my mum died, it was the one time that going through my internet sites made me feel good, people genuinely wishing you well is a blessing. From the minute I sorted myself out, everything seemed to fall apart. It's lucky it was that way round. If these things had happened when I was a young man, it would have been too much. When you've gone through the shit I have, you understand the value of pop music, of how fantastic it is to whack on a great record and go where it takes you. I fucking needed that plenty in the last couple of years. I really understand what it is to be able to do that for people. I don't want to write more songs about misery, writing about it doesn't seem to stop me from getting more of it.'

While Michael was trying to come to terms with his mother's loss the promotional bandwagon rolled on. 'Older' was released as a single in January 1997 and 'Star People '97' followed in April. In a setting of understated percussion and a lilting trumpet, Michael used 'Older' to reflect on his life and the passing years. The moody vibe was transferred to the video, which showed Michael walking around a hillside village in what looked like New Mexico. The sepia-tinged shots were filled with religious imagery, including glimpses of a statue of the Virgin Mary.

'Star People '97' took a swing at the cult of celebrity. 'I don't think I would ever have been part of that,' he claimed. 'I always wanted to be famous for being good at something. I wanted to be so good at something that I would be untouchable. Most stars started out as children that felt out of control or oppressed and wanted to show the world and their parents that they were worth something. There are so many people out there now that are prepared to sell their lives to make themselves famous, and that makes them completely vulnerable. I'm not saying it's right or wrong. I just don't understand it.'

On 31 August the world was stunned by the news that the Princess of Wales, along with her companion Dodi Al-Fayed and driver Henri Paul, had been killed in a car accident. Like everyone else, Michael was stunned. 'I hadn't seen her for a couple of years by the time she died,' he recalled. 'We nearly got together on that St Tropez trip [where she'd been photographed with Al-Fayed]. I was supposed to go onto the boat, and I'm quite glad I didn't because it would have been so fresh when she died. I mean, I was so upset by it anyway, but had I seen her just before I think it would have been even more upsetting.' Within weeks of her death the final single from *Older* was issued, the emotional 'You Have Been Loved'. It was almost ironic that this song, with its graphic description of Michael's visit to Anselmo Feleppa's grave, should have been released when it was. Still grieving for his own mother, looking back at the death of his lover and dealing with the loss of the Princess, it's no wonder that Michael later said he felt that he was surrounded by death. 'You Have Been Loved' was donated to a charity album released as a tribute to Princess Diana.

George Michael spent the rest of 1997 in private, reeling from the deaths that seemed to knock him back one after the other. He continued to keep a low profile during early 1998. The cycle of singles from *Older* had run its course, there was still no sign of a tour and he was staying away from the press as much as possible. He was spending most of his time in Los Angeles. Who could have predicted what would happen next?

NINE

PHOENIX

1998–2002

phoe·nix

1 (sometimes initial capital letter) a mythical bird of great beauty fabled to live 500 or 600 years in the Arabian wilderness, to burn itself on a funeral pyre, and to rise from its ashes in the freshness of youth and live through another cycle of years: often an emblem of immortality or of reborn idealism or hope.

2 a person or thing of peerless beauty or excellence; paragon.

3 a person or thing that has become renewed or restored after suffering calamity or apparent annihilation.

'In the UK, since my left hand outed me to an audience of millions on that fateful day in 1998, my personal life, or rather my imagined personal life, has rarely been out of the tabloid press.'

George Michael

'I quite like the fact that I'm the last person that anyone expected to do it. Being humiliated so badly in the press was a good starting point for me being honest. It gave me the guts to do it. But now I see it as a mission. To say, "Look, I know you like me, and

I know you like my music. But at the end of the day I'm gay. And I'm a slut." Some of us are and we should be fine with that.'

George Michael

It's not that strange to see a celebrity in the Will Rogers Memorial Park. Rogers, cowboy, philosopher, film star and mayor of Beverly Hills, had this park named after him in 1952. Previously it had been part of the front lawn of the Beverly Hills Hotel, which is now located across the street. That's why celebrities visit it – the gentle landscaping, immaculate gardens and fish ponds make it a perfect place to meet a friend or have a picnic. John Wayne is said once to have landed in the park in a helicopter, while Rod Stewart proposed to Rachel Hunter there in 1990. But on 7 April 1998 it became forever linked to George Michael.

Just over a year after his mother's death, Michael was spending a lot of time with Kenny Goss at his Los Angeles home. He'd also been playing host to Spice Girl Geri Halliwell. Some papers had started rumours of a romance, especially after the two were photographed walking hand in hand. 'It's not a "celebrity friendship",' Halliwell told *Q* magazine. 'I can't stand that Hello! darling, lovey lovey. We're both famous and part of the music industry but we've both lost a parent, both from Watford, both have a Mediterranean parent, both been ugly kids and blossomed. Nobody wants to talk about death. Then I heard George talking about losing his mother, I was a fan, I thought I was going to marry him, and I was so drawn to him. I gave him my telephone number, gave him big eyes and tried to flirt with him, thinking I had a chance. How wrong was I? I got second best and we became friends.'

During 1998 Halliwell was staying out of the UK for tax reasons. Michael extended her an invitation to stay with him and Kenny for a while, and she accepted. 'We were telephone buddies and when I left the group, he invited me to stay for three days. I stayed for three months. I don't know what I'd have done without that guy, he was an absolute angel. To begin with, he didn't know me that well, but I had nobody, I was so lonely. I needed someone to give me a cuddle and say it's all right. George and Kenny were everything to me, the moral support I needed to get through that time. I share my doubts and fears with him. He said, "There's no rush, nobody's going to forget you, if what you're doing is good it will stand the test of time." I play him things, but it's like taking it home to your parents, desperately wanting their approval. I crap myself every time. He's brutally honest: sometimes I walk out with my head in my hands and sometimes I'm going "Yes!" I've never been friends with anybody famous before.'

But gossip-column items about George Michael and Geri Halliwell were soon forgotten after what happened next. On the day in question George had been working at his home on the bonus tracks for the forthcoming 'best of' compilation. That afternoon he drove down to the park. He had been there before. A member of the British paparazzi had photographed him hanging around there the previous year but the photos had never been published.

There were a few people in the park going about their business. One of them, undercover police officer Rodriguez, was on 'potty patrol' – looking out for homosexual men picking each other up in public conveniences. His department was supposedly 'acting on information' that the park was a hotbed of gay activity, even though only two arrests had been made during the previous year.

After a while Michael thought that there were only two people around, himself and a cute-looking guy he'd spotted. Reports vary about what happened next, but it seems that Michael then went into the men's room and was followed by the undercover cop. Michael was at the sink washing his hands when the officer walked in. 'They don't send Columbo, they send someone really nice looking,' Michael said later. The policeman stood watching the singer from a cubicle, pleasuring himself. Michael started to do the same, at which point the policeman walked out. When Michael followed a few moments later he was arrested. If the cop hadn't followed him no crime would have been committed and there would have been no arrest. From that perspective it could be called entrapment.

'I was stupid,' Michael told MTV. 'It was a stupid thing to do, but I've never been able to turn down a free meal. The fact is there was absolutely no one else in the vicinity, whatever the police arrest report says. It was just me, well actually it was two undercover cops, only I couldn't see one of them. Two undercover cops and a randy pop star. So there was no one there. If someone's waving their genitalia at you, you don't automatically assume they're an officer of the law.'

George Michael spent the next three hours at the spotlessly clean Beverly Hills police station. When he was put in a holding cell he couldn't believe the irony of his situation; lying on the concrete bed was a copy of the gossip magazine *National Enquirer*. 'I'll be on the cover of that next week,' he thought to himself. Arrested under his real name, Michael was charged with lewd behaviour. He was released on $500 bail and ordered to appear the following month.

The use of Michael's real name meant that the news wires didn't pounce all over the arrest, while the charge of lewd behaviour was vague about what he was supposed to have done. Due to the eight-hour time difference between the UK and Los Angeles, the official police statement about the incident didn't make the UK news until the following evening, when a spokesman for the Beverly Hills Police Department said, 'Members of our crime suppression unit were monitoring the park yesterday, they did go into the rest room and did observe Mr Michaels [sic] engaged in a lewd act. He was by himself. The officers observed the act and arrested Mr Michaels [sic].'

On his release George called Kenny to tell him what had happened. Andros Georgiou was in town and he went to Michael's house that night for dinner. Michael explained to them that this was something he'd been doing for a while, something that at the time they hadn't needed to know about. He wasn't looking forward to speaking to his father about it, though – but when he phoned, Jack Panos was behind him all the way, saying George should tell them all to 'sod off'. The singer gathered a great deal of strength from his friends and family that day.

When the news broke back home the tabloid response was predictable. The *Mirror* claimed that Michael had lured the officer into the toilets, while the *Sun* screamed 'Zip Me Up Before You Go Go'. The next day the park was full of the press, trying to find out exactly what had happened. The men's room quickly became the world's most photographed loo. Michael's house was surrounded, while helicopters buzzed overhead. Even his neighbours were interviewed.

In hindsight the incident was Michael's subconscious way of outing himself. He would have gone through life without ever sitting down in a face-to-face interview with anyone and saying 'I'm gay'. Still very depressed about his mother, he knew he shouldn't have gone into that toilet – he said he'd had a bad feeling about it – but he had done so anyway. And he'd chosen to do it in Beverly Hills, which gave the incident an inherently 'showbiz' aspect. 'If it hadn't happened that day, it was going to happen very soon,' said Michael. 'But going through two bereavements gives unrivalled perspective. The first day I was freaked out because I'd literally just got out of depression. I thought, somebody is trying to finish me off here, I cannot be this unlucky, when do I get a fucking break? I couldn't believe it had happened.'

With the press pack sniffing around outside, Michael decided to defy the unwritten law that says celebrities in this situation should hide behind their curtains. Instead he went out for a meal at nearby Spargo's. At 10 pm a black stretch limo pulled up and Michael was bundled into the back. The cameramen set off on a hectic chase behind him down the winding roads, jumping red lights, determined to be there for that all-important photograph when Michael stepped out of the car.

The singer ate his meal, said hello to Lionel Richie and Tony Curtis, who were eating there that night and was home by midnight. It was the first indication that Michael wouldn't be running from this incident.

The next day he took this approach a step further. In an attempt to make a pre-emptive strike against the British Sunday papers, he put himself forward for an interview with CNN. He knew that his Friday recording in Los Angeles would air in the UK on Saturday night, while CNN also offered a worldwide platform for him to give his side of the story.

The singer was clearly stressed as filming began. After a few minutes he asked to take a break, after which he came back in and recording started over again. What he had to say was intensely personal and brutally honest. 'This is as good a time as any,' he said to interviewer Jim Moret. 'I want to say that I have no problem with people knowing that I'm in a relationship with a man right now. I have not been in a relationship with a woman for almost ten years.

'I don't feel any shame. I feel stupid and I feel reckless and weak for having allowed my sexuality to be exposed this way. But I don't feel any shame whatsoever.' He'd never been reticent, he explained, in expressing his sexuality through his songs. 'I write about my life. I do want people to know that the songs that I wrote when I was with women were really about women. And the songs that I've written since have been fairly obviously about men.'

The interview itself made the TV news in the UK. The worst-kept secret in show business was now well and truly out in the open, but by approaching the situation head on he'd handled it perfectly. By early the next week the front pages were given over to Anthea Turner's love life.

George Michael didn't actually appear in court. His legal team entered a plea of no contest and took the punishment of an $810 fine and 80 hours' community service as well as a ban from Will Rogers Park. At Michael's birthday party that summer the invitations said 'Go to the bathroom before you come as all conveniences will be locked to protect the host.'

When George Michael returned to the UK he was given an entire episode of the *Parkinson* show to himself. It was the first time he'd appeared on Michael Parkinson's long-running talk show and as he was announced he received one of the loudest and longest ovations in the show's history. George, who was in good spirits throughout, started by telling the host how his mother used to let him stay up and watch when he was a child. He humorously added that she might not have been so thrilled that he'd managed to get a show to himself because 'I had to take my willy out in order to get on!' He explained that he'd talked about the incident so much to ensure that he wouldn't have to talk about it in the future. If he ever felt pressured into a position by individuals or history, then he would react against it so he didn't have to hide inside a walled compound.

The interview was wide ranging and delved deep into Michael's emotional past. He wasn't a depressive, he said, but the 1990s had been a decade of loss: Feleppa, the court case, his mother and now his dignity. He said he'd never felt confused about his sexuality, but that a combination of there being so much sex available to a pop star and the fact that he felt underdeveloped emotionally and had never had a real crush or fallen in love at school meant it had taken longer for him to figure things out. 'The day I knew I was gay was when I knew I was in love with a man,' he revealed. 'The confusion ended when I was about 26. I thought that, especially in England, most people had a good idea. The press knew I was gay, but until they could get something nasty they were playing the game.'

Finally he explained that even though in his early twenties he'd wanted to have children, as he got older he'd gone off the idea, thinking he'd feel the responsibility to the point of not being able to do what he wanted to. Basically he'd lost the desire to be a father and having the vocation of music had taken over his sense of purpose.

With that he was gone. Talk of a tour to coincide with the 'best of' was shelved and he resumed a more private life, at least for the time being.

The final reply from George Michael in the Will Rogers Park saga was a song he wrote for his 'best of', *Ladies & Gentlemen*. 'Outside' is essentially a disco-themed thumbs up to outdoor sex, but it was the video that made all the news. The film opens with a spoof porn movie. A middle-aged businessman washes his hands in a public toilet, watched by a buxom, blonde-haired young lady. As the scene plays, spoof credits in a made-up language appear over the top. The young girl is identified as Heidi Kockenblauer, while the imaginary director is Marchelo Uffenvanken. As the girl pouts her lips, about to kiss the man, she suddenly turns into a wrinkled old female cop and the man is arrested. Police helicopters fly overhead, sirens wail and the man is led away. The dance track kicks in, Philly-esque strings soaring as the clip shows various outdoor acts taking place, including two longshoremen kissing atop a high-rise crane and two men in the back of a pickup truck. Next the grimy toilets of the opening scenes are transformed into a shiny disco as the urinals become coated with mirrors like a glitter ball. A clutch of fake female police officers rip open their shirts to take part in a dance routine with George Michael, resplendent in a police uniform and mirrored shades, every bit the Village People extra.

'Outside' was just one of the non-album tracks included on *Ladies & Gentlemen*. Stevie Wonder's 'As' with Mary J. Blige, 'Desafinado' with Astrud Gilberto and 'Too Funky' were just some of the extras that bulked the collection up to an impressive 29 tracks over two CDs. The first disc was designated 'for the heart', while the second disc, containing the more danceable songs, was titled 'for the feet'.

To tie in with this greatest hits release, Michael agreed to do the media rounds. His appearances were also masterminded to continue the rehabilitation of his image. On 9 November he appeared on the long-running and highly rated *Late Show* with David Letterman, filmed at the Ed Sullivan Theater in New York City. Michael was the first guest of the night and his host was clearly not up to speed with the singer's recent past. First he was confused as to whether Michael had been on the show before. 'Well excuse me, you should know, shouldn't you?' asked Michael. 'Is this your first time on the show?' Then he thought the Los Angeles toilet incident had been a year ago, rather than seven months. Finally he asked Michael to sing, which wasn't in the programme.

But there was only one topic that Letterman really wanted to talk about – Will Rogers Park. When he asked directly what had happened, Michael replied, 'This is the nicest way I can put it. I will put it this way and I don't want to be graphic and nasty. He played a game called I show you mine and you show me yours, then I will take you down to the police station. Actually the police report says that he was trying to simulate urination. Now excuse me, how do you simulate urination and make no noise? If you tried to simulate urination doing that with your hands you would get wee all over the shop! Don't try it at home, folks. Actually, try it at home. You are safe there!'

Through the first half of 1999 George Michael kept his own counsel. In October he made a brief appearance at the Net Aid concert, organised to raise money for refugees, but he spent most of his time working on an album of cover versions with producer Phil Ramone, who had produced everyone from Bob Dylan to Rod Stewart, Frank Sinatra to Madonna. The album, *Songs From The Last Century*, was released in December. A mix of old and new standards, it drew lukewarm reviews but went to number two in the UK chart, backing up Michael's assertion that reviews never affected his sales figures. The lead-off track, 'Brother Can You Spare A Dime', had originated in the 1932 musical *New Americana*, though Bing Crosby had been famous for singing it. The George Michael version was cool and jazzy, which suited his voice, and a similar style was employed on the Police's 'Roxanne', which was all brushed drums and upright bass. This track had a video prepared for it. Opening with the message, 'This video was filmed in the red light district of Amsterdam. None of the people featured are actors. We thank them for their spirit and goodwill', the clip shows a group of prostitutes walking around in their underwear outside a townhouse on a city street. At the end of the film we're told that the black prostitute identified as 'Roxanne' has since retired from the business.

'My Baby Just Cares For Me' was presented as a big band swing number, but it didn't quite work and his vocal style didn't fit. On the other hand, Roberta Flack's 'The First Time Ever I Saw Your Face' could have been written specifically for Michael. 'I Remember You' was recently done better by Björk, but the big band 'Secret Love' was a success. Overall the album was a mixed bag that didn't test Michael's abilities enough to satisfy.

As the twenty-first century dawned, George Michael hadn't written an album of new material for four years. He was in a happy relationship, *Ladies & Gentlemen* was still selling well and *Songs From The Last Century* hadn't been out for long. There was no real pressure yet, but he was having trouble writing new songs.

Publicly 2000 was a quiet year for Michael. In April he performed alongside Garth Brooks and Melissa Etheridge at Equality Rocks, a gay and lesbian rights fundraiser in Washington DC.

One way in which he did make the news headlines was at an auction. In October the piano on which John Lennon had written 'Imagine' was being sold. This wasn't the white grand piano made famous by the video clip of the song set at Lennon's home in Tittenhurst Park, but the upright which could be seen during the sessions in the film *Gimme Some Truth*. The bidding opened at £500,000 and George Michael, via phone, was not the only celebrity bidder; Noel Gallagher and Robbie Williams were also in the running. After they dropped out at the £1 million mark, Michael eventually placed the final bid of £1.45 million, making it the most expensive musical instrument in history. But Michael didn't hide it away. As well as later using it to compose songs, he shipped it to the USA in 2006 as part of an anti-war exhibition being staged by Kenny Goss, the first time the piano had been taken outside the UK. 'We decided to do it in Dallas, because what better place is there to reiterate how important peace is?' said Goss. 'Dallas is George Bush's home. It's a great place to remind people how important it is to find peace.'

Through 2001 Michael continued trying to write. He'd go to the studio, work a little, then go home, usually without having made much progress. He was following this routine in September when, on the 11th, he watched on a TV at the studio as the World Trade Center came crashing down. '[My producer] ran in and said, "You're not going to believe what you're about to see". When I saw it, it was just after the first plane had hit, so it just looked like a tragic accident. Then the second plane hit and everybody in the studio realised it was deliberate and started to freak out. Within an hour, apart from being as terrified as everybody else, I was just totally freaked out that what I had been writing about was happening in front of my eyes.' He was moved to tears as the TV images grew worse and worse. He'd been working on a new song that addressed the mess that the world found itself in as the new century began, called 'Shoot The Dog'. 'I cried simply because it was such a shocking, sickening attack on humanity, you know, beyond any callous acts that you could ever remember. It was just the worst thing to even conceive of doing something as evil as that. But I felt confused because I'd written this song for a reason, but now the reason was very puzzling. I certainly didn't want to look opportunistic, so I sat on the song and didn't know what to do with it.'

It would be a further six months before he showed his fans he'd started to break through his writer's block with the release of 'Freeek!' in March 2002. Concerning futuristic sex, in a blend of dirty urban beats, this heavy bump 'n' grind single was nothing like Michael had ever written before. Was this going to be the new direction on his next album or merely an experiment? If it was the latter, it was an expensive one. He reportedly wrote a cheque for £1 million for the video, half of that being spent on the computerised visual effects. This price tag outdid even the costs of the videos for 'Fastlove' (£250,000) and 'Outside' (£500,000). In a *Blade Runner*-esque cityscape employing effects similar to those featured in the Spice Girls' 1997 'Spice Up Your Life' video, Michael wears a number of giant rubber outfits while a host of weird sexual encounters take place in front of the viewer. The fetish outfits in 'Freeek!' were Michael's take on the commercialisation of extreme sexual imagery. This made him angry, he said, hence the full-on song.

The *Sunday Express* 2002 Rich List revealed that Sir Paul McCartney was Britain's first 'pop billionaire', supposedly worth £1.1 billion, with George Michael ranked in the top ten and said to be worth a whopping £210 million. With that kind of money in the bank he could be forgiven for not worrying too much about future earnings; he might feel that he had the financial freedom to do and, importantly, say what he thought. Though in the past he'd supported causes such as the families of striking miners, famine in Africa and gay rights, he'd never spoken to the press directly. Instead he'd let his music do the talking, quietly making financial contributions where he saw fit. Now for the first time Michael started speaking out on political issues.

By the end of 2002, more than a decade after the first Gulf War, the situation in Iraq was becoming a cause for concern to the USA, the world's last remaining superpower. United Nations inspectors had been playing a game of cat and mouse with Saddam Hussein while they looked for his weapons of mass destruction. It was becoming clear that Tony Blair and George W. Bush were set on a course of war, and in March 2003 the second Gulf War began with the invasion of Iraq by a western coalition. George Michael had spent the months leading up to the war talking to as many press outlets as he could about the situation, taking part in heavyweight political discussions like the BBC's *Hardtalk* with Tim Sebastian, as well as speaking to Sir David Frost and appearing on everybody's favourite teatime television show, *Richard & Judy*. And in May 2002 he'd finally released the song he'd been working on about 9/11, 'Shoot The Dog'. But he had reckoned without the backlash that he would experience for speaking out on the war, both for his views and for the fact that he'd dared to air them.

The 'Shoot The Dog' video seemed to cause offence to some. A cartoon produced by the people behind *2DTV*, the clip lampoons both the US government and Tony Blair's sycophancy towards it. The opening scene shows George W. in the Oval Office being lectured by one of his generals using a sock puppet, while Blair himself is the 'dog' in question; to the refrain of 'good puppy, good puppy', Bush throws a ball for Blair to fetch on the White House lawn. The cartoon isn't without a dose of self-deprecating humour. Michael enters the scene from a gents' toilet with a shuttlecock down his trousers before joining Bush and his general in a cheesy dance routine. He also appears as a Homer Simpson clone – in fact he appears as the whole Simpson family, complete at one point with towering Marge Simpson hair. He later rides a missile into the Blairs' bedroom where he encounters Cherie in bed, while Tony attaches an outboard motor to a map of the British Isles and floats it across to America.

'I simply wanted to write a song that said to everybody, "People, let's be aware of this situation and understand that there's some very pissed-off people out there and that America – and us, for that matter – need to start to listen to them a little",' he said. 'I see politics in very human terms. In other words, even though there is a lot of complication and complexity to politics, what it really boils down to is human reaction between different factions, at least when you're talking about the possibility of war.

'I just hope that this record helps in a tiny way to consolidate the idea that we don't automatically do as we're told in terms of our relationship with America. This is the most political thing I've ever done and it's a massive and totally unnecessary risk for me. I don't know how it will go down, particularly in America. But it's important to me that I should be free to express myself. This is the first time I've really had the guts to go for something knowing I might get critically savaged for it. There's always been this nagging worry of people saying, "Look, mate, you're a rich pampered pop star – what the fuck do you know about it?" But now I feel confident enough to just go for it. And I should have a right to say these things without being ripped to pieces.'

He was correct on all counts. He obviously did have the right to air these views, and millions of people agreed with him. But he was also battered by the press and criticised for speaking out as a pop star, even by other pop stars. Noel Gallagher was one of those to question Michael's outspoken attitude. He was also right about the US reaction. The final nail had been hammered into the coffin of his American career, even though he always maintained a hard core of about a million US fans. 'I was perfectly aware of the repercussions, but I have had a non-career in the US for so long it didn't matter. I think they see me as a communist fag over there,' he said.

As 'Shoot The Dog' was released, Michael gave an interview to Piers Morgan at the *Mirror*. 'I know this is dangerous territory,' he said. He admitted that he'd spent years discussing such issues over dinner tables but only now could he give his ideas more public expression. 'I really feel this is such a serious time for us all that being silent is not an option. I was moping around the house, smoking spliffs, drinking too much and watching a load of serious late-night television like *Question Time* and *Newsnight* because I couldn't sleep. And I noticed a lot of stuff about the growing fear of a war between the secular world and the fundamentalist world. It was something I'd never really thought about but the more I learned, the more fearful I became that it might happen, and that Britain might be caught right in the middle of it. Tony Blair was being seen as America's strongest ally at a point when the Middle East was feeling increasingly bullied by the West, and America in particular, and when many developing countries were getting their hands on some serious weapons of destruction. I very rarely agree with anything I read in the tabloids but I did agree with a lot of your stuff. If we just storm in there now there'll be a disaster that will destroy any chance of stability in that region for a very, very long time.'

Elsewhere he was given an hour on MTV and took part in a debate with Conservative Party leader Iain Duncan Smith on BBC Radio Five Live. Ultimately, as the war went ahead, Michael stopped watching the news programmes and reading the papers. In 2006 he said, 'As the years go by Mr Blair is making ['Shoot the Dog'] a word perfect protest song.'

The battering Michael took over his anti-war stance pushed him close to the edge. Even his closest advisors feared that he might have brought his commercial career to an end. 'It was so stupid not to expect what I got, not just on a political level but on the level of "listen, these people don't like you, they find it hard enough taking it coming from a pop star let alone one they think is too snotty to talk to them in general". I knew that a lot of these papers were centre-left and actually agreed with me but they were still jumping up and down on me. So I did start to take that personally.' Suffering from a media backlash and without a new album for the last seven years, he was going to have to make one heck of a comeback.

TEN

SURVIVOR

2003–2007

sur·vi·vor

1 a person or thing that survives.

2 Law. the one of two or more designated persons, as joint tenants or others having a joint interest, who outlives the other or others.

3 a person who continues to function or prosper in spite of opposition, hardship, or setbacks.

'I've suffered this kind of wishful thinking from the press, the subtext to it is, "Well, he was all right before he came out and now he lives this depraved gay life and he's miserable and fat, right?"'

George Michael

'[Honesty] is my problem. That in itself creates more PR these days because everyone for the past 20 years has been giving pat answers to pat questions. Because there's this battle going on between left and right, the past and the future, and some people are trying to kick liberalism out of the door. Some of the ideas that I grew up with as being completely ordinary, and if you were an intelligent person it shouldn't be a question, are now questioned again. The fact that I'm a gay man, and the fact that politically, I'm not afraid to risk my career in terms of speaking my mind, that makes me stand out like a sore thumb.'

George Michael

More than 15 years after its release the *Faith* album was still revered by music critics. In 2003 the album was listed as one of *Rolling Stone*'s 'Greatest Albums of All Time' and the song 'Faith' was included in VH1's *100 Best Songs of the Past 25 Years*. But the hip-swinging days of the late Eighties seemed long past when, in March 2003, George Michael made his first live appearance on *Top of the Pops* for 17 years. Last time, in 1986, he had performed Wham!'s 'Edge Of Heaven'. Now, introduced by the comedian and writer Ben Elton with 'He's a true genius of rock and pop, he's funky, he's thought provoking', he was performing Don McLean's protest song 'The Grave', written by the American years before to highlight his stance against the Vietnam war.

Michael was informed by the BBC that they wouldn't allow him to wear a T-shirt printed with the slogan 'No War Blair Out'. An official BBC statement read: 'We are not giving George Michael a platform to air his political views, we are giving viewers the fantastic opportunity to see an international star perform on *Top of the Pops* for the first time in 17 years.' Someone at the Beeb was missing the point – Michael was only appearing on the show so that he could make a political point. The backing singers also wore the T-shirts and because they didn't have a change of clothes they were edited out of the broadcast. Despite the clothing snub Michael gave a powerful performance, wearing tinted glasses and perched on a stool. The acoustic and Spanish guitars sounded beautiful against the string section while the singer told the story of a young man's terror at finding himself on a battlefield.

Michael certainly didn't need any more money. The BBC TV show *Liquid Assets* claimed he was worth £95 million in 2003, adding that his charitable donations had topped £5 million. In 2001 he'd bought a sixteenth-century country house. Located an hour from London, it had previously featured in a painting by Turner. The beamed ceilings, the Aga and the library filled with antique books were a long way from the urban chic of his recent videos. Outside there were extensive gardens and a large pool house where he could relax with Kenny and their two golden labradors; when asked what his most treasured possession was, Goss had replied, 'My dogs, Meg and Abby, and, of course, George.'

Michael spent much of 2003 at George Martin's AIR Studios working on his next album, but progress was slow. Work had been advancing on and off since 1999 but he still had a long way to go. The first fruits of this labour were evident when the comeback single, 'Amazing', was released in March 2004. It showed that Michael still had the magic touch when it came to fusing dance beats with soft rock and a slice of white-boy soul. The single hit number four in the UK; in the US it topped the *Billboard* dance chart but made no impression on the main chart positions.

The video was simple but effective. Michael is filmed sitting in a room of fresh-faced young people. Everyone wears white and the walls and seating are also white. Then someone puts on a holographic video of Michael dressed in jeans, jacket and shades and playing a guitar, reminiscent of the *Faith* look. Accompanied by a small band dressed in black, he plays the song via the life-sized 3D transmission while everyone has a good time.

The long-awaited album finally arrived. Aptly named *Patience*, it went straight to number one in the UK, knocking Norah Jones from the top spot. In the 14 years between 1990 and 2004 Michael had only released one album of new material, partly because of the court case with Sony. Now, in a one-off deal, *Patience* appeared on Sony! After securing the payoff from Virgin enabling him to leave Sony, he had now agreed to release his next album with his original label after just one album, *Older*, had been issued on Virgin.

After such a long absence the singer knew that he had a lot of ground to make up. He agreed to promote the album through interviews again. 'I really thought I would never be able to do this again,' he said. 'I have gone through so much to get to this album. I have worked through so much depression, fear and anxiety. My life has been like a really bad soap opera for the past 10 years. Everything was going my way. And I was happily marching into the history books, but then it all just fell apart.' He explained that he'd gone to work at the studios every day but the music just wouldn't come out. He'd invariably return home no further forward. He just couldn't create like he could before, and this situation had lasted for the best part of three years. The turning point was reached when he moved back into a house he'd lived in some time before. His mother used to visit the house to clean it and he'd previously written a lot of music there. It was the place that he most closely associated with her during his adulthood. This simple change of scenery did the trick and the songs started flowing again.

'There is something about the vocals on this album that's a lot more confident, more certain,' he said. 'Even though I love *Songs From The Last Century* and *Older*, there's an energy level to this record that I haven't had since before all this shit started, before I met and lost Anselmo and my mother died. If you think about the energy of "Freedom" on *Listen Without Prejudice*, I don't think I had that energy to give again until last year. Which is why "Amazing" reminds me of Wham! more than anything I've done. The work I've done over the last 12 years might have a certain intensity or depth, but nothing has had the energy of the earlier work. I think it's come with the relief of feeling good again.'

To push the album as much as possible Michael went back to the rounds of promotional duties that he'd walked away from almost 15 years earlier. He appeared on TV shows, gave radio interviews and even made personal appearances and shop signings. He hated doing it, but it worked. The album topped the charts and he was in the news again for the right reasons. As part of the promo work, he returned to the *Parkinson* show for the first time since the one-hour special in 1998, appearing alongside actor Bill Nighy and impressionist Jon Culshaw. The singer, heavily bearded, quickly found himself talking about his sexuality, explaining what a positive experience his coming out had been. Of the eight-year gap between albums of new material he said that even though he'd been 'on form' during his last appearance in 1998, the Los Angeles toilet incident had been a subconscious distraction from the grief he was still going through; once the fuss over his arrest had subsided, he had found himself on a downward spiral. While he didn't have trust in organised religion he did have beliefs, and his spirituality had been damaged to such an extent that writer's block had taken over. Moving on, he talked about his support for the idea of higher taxation for the rich, and said that he would like to set up a website where people could download his music for free. After all, he said, I don't need any more money.

In 2004 Michael agreed to let a camera crew follow him around while he carried out some of his promotional duties for *Patience*. Part way through the filming Michael became unhappy with the way things were going. In a move characteristic of the control-freak side of his nature, he bought the unfinished film from the production company and completed the job himself, the way he wanted.

If any other megastar had made such a move you'd expect the finished product to be a fawning portrait of a tortured artist. With George Michael, however, the film became an intimate look at his life, his childhood and the much publicised ups and downs of recent years. The final cut, titled *A Different Story*, was sold to fans at Michael's 2006 concerts. He gave plenty of airtime to his detractors; for example, Noel Gallagher is seen saying 'This is the guy who hid who he actually was from the public for 20 years, and now all of a sudden he's got something to say about the way of the world. I find it fucking laughable!' We also see him meeting up with a follicly challenged Andrew Ridgeley to discuss the Wham! days. In a poignant moment, Michael is asked whose life he would have preferred. He indicates that it would have been Ridgeley's.

Much of *Patience*, including the title track, had been written on the 'John Lennon piano', an instrument which was a constant source of inspiration for Michael. The album covered a lot of ground, some said too much – sexual excesses with 'Freeek', family matters, boyfriends, the war in Iraq and much more. Trimming it down by a song or two might have been a good idea. At 70 minutes you need a lot of time to take it all in. And some of it isn't easy listening at first; some of the writing is supremely personal. 'My Mother Had A Brother' tackles his uncle's suicide. 'When I was 17 my mum sat me down and told me about her brother who killed himself on the day I was born,' he explained. 'She told me she thought he was probably gay and couldn't cope with the family's situation. So I feel this song is a nice message for my uncle to know that life is so much better now, and if in some way I am his reincarnation to tell him how happy I am and that I share my life openly with a man.'

'Round Here' deals with both his family's past and his own childhood, name-checking early musical heroes like the Specials, The Jam and The Beat, whose 'music fell like rain from the streets'. The CD booklet carried a picture for each song on the disc, and for 'Round Here' there is an image of George and his sisters playing as children. 'Amazing' shows two gold rings with 'amore' etched into them, while 'American Angel' unsurprisingly has a picture of Kenny Goss. He also finds room for a song about Anselmo Feleppa, 'Please Send Me Someone'. The production work is sparklingly clean, perhaps too much so. A rough edge here and there might have given the music a more natural feel.

George Michael continued his dancefloor and club mix success with the June release of the infectious 'Flawless (Go To The City)'. The single came out in a host of different mixes including the 'Shapeshifters Remix', 'Hot Fridge Vocal Mix', 'Jack 'n Rory Vocal Mix' and the 'Boxer Mix'. The video of a hotel room populated by numerous people who had stayed there at various times and were all going about their business at once, unaware of the others' presence, was nominated for a Grammy in February 2005. 'Round Here' completed the single releases for 2004.

In June 2005 Michael tested the internet market by issuing a download-only single. 'John And Elvis Are Dead', a contemplative song about someone waking from a 30-year coma, touches on religion and the fragility of life. The video was soaked in pop culture images, from the 1969 Moon landings and images of the Vietnam war to Phil Daniels in *Quadrophenia* and clips of The Jam, Blondie and Nelson Mandela – not to mention Lennon and Presley, as mentioned in the title.

In February 2006 Michael hit the news for all the wrong reasons again. Bumping into parked cars, falling asleep at the wheel, being photographed late at night on Hampstead Heath – he did it all.

'If I've had any type of traffic altercation, if I've hit their car in any way, people see me and they start to grin because they think, well, I can bump this up a bit!' he said. 'The poor people whose parked cars kind of slammed into each other this week, they've all been told that they're welcome to use a hire car and I don't suppose they're getting Nissan Micras.' Michael explained that he was leaving a friend's house early one morning. Having parked on a steep hill he accidentally bumped into a car which ran into a second one. He drove off and asked someone else to return and get the owners' details. The press reported that he'd 'done a runner';

in fact he just wanted to avoid a situation on a public street where newspaper photographers would have been alerted, and what in reality was a very minor incident would have been spread all over the news. 'By the time I'd sent somebody to get details of what I thought was one incident, the *Daily Mail* were already there and from that point on it just escalated and escalated. I had people calling my house, people frantically trying to find out whether I was in hospital or not. And I'd literally had a parking accident.'

He poured more fuel on the press fire when he was arrested by the police after being found asleep at the wheel of his car while waiting at a set of traffic lights. 'I was at the lights at Hyde Park Corner,' he laughingly told Michael Parkinson. 'I don't know if you've ever been at the lights at Hyde Park Corner but it's quite easy to fall asleep. I don't know how long it happened for, I guess it was momentary. But I was at the lights, foot on the brake and I must have nodded off like that. I was woken up by a policeman banging on the window, and of course they had to check out whether I was fit to drive. I might not have been out of control but I was asleep! They breathalysed me, I was fine. The ambulance driver who checked me out there and then said I was fine but one of the arresting officers wanted to make sure. So you know they're doing their job, but the fact that it's then going to turn into an international incident doesn't really bother the policeman concerned. So they took me . . . it was nothing really but again it became a massive drama.'

While making sure his side of the story was told loud and clear on the chat shows, Michael was quizzed about his relationship with Kenny Goss. As one of the UK's most famous gay men, with a known long-term partner, it was inevitable that he would be asked whether he was planning to get married. 'I think we'll formalise it for sure, because I think from a legal point of view it's essential to have the same safeguards that straight couples have,' he said. 'We've been together for ten years, I think we're entitled to that.

I must admit I want a slightly better than 50 per cent chance of success! So I don't think I'm going to emulate [Elton John's] marriage in that sense. I don't think there'll be a ceremony, we'll probably do it on our tenth anniversary. I think we'll just do the formal legal thing and then we'll have a party. But no one's going to be getting into a dress. Neither of us have the body for it!'

George Michael certainly seems to have something of a self-destructive streak. Why else would he constantly tempt a sometimes vicious press pack with the kind of stories that would have ended the careers of lesser men? Hiding his sexuality for years; coming out, literally, in a public toilet; speaking out against the Iraq war; scraping his car and falling asleep at the wheel; they all mounted up in the minds of the press. Then, in July 2006, he was snapped cruising by the ever-reliable *News of the World*.

As usual the press were quick to twist the knife. The headline in the *News of the World* proclaimed 'GEORGE'S SEX SHAME', the paper explaining that its 'investigators' had 'caught the singer red-handed and red-faced as he emerged from the bushes after cavorting with a pot-bellied, 58-year-old, jobless van driver'. Why the paper thought it was in the public interest for its reporters to be lurking around Hampstead Heath in the early hours waiting for a possible scoop is anyone's guess. But this time they got 'lucky', going so far as to track down Michael's alleged partner for the evening in Brighton and pay for his side of the story, which was reproduced in graphic detail.

When confronted at the scene Michael had been understandably upset, supposedly shouting at the photographer, 'Are you gay? No? Then fuck off! This is my culture! I'm not doing anything illegal. The police don't even come up here any more. I'm a free man, I can do whatever I want. I'm not harming anyone.' A so-called friend was also quoted (anonymously) as saying, 'We're really concerned. It's long been known he's a heavy cannabis user but we're beginning to fear the pot may have affected his mind. He's lost his judgment.

He must seek professional help or things could end very badly for him.' This unconfirmed quote was probably included simply to justify the newspaper's angle that he was losing his mind because of drugs. 'Ultimately they're not life- changing events and the press would like them to be career changing events,' he said. 'I'm not the only one that's being treated like this. You know everyone is being treated like this, they just seem to like playing this game with me.'

Michael spoke to ITN's Nina Hussein about his 'cruising', but he was upset by her line of questioning and lost his temper. As she wasn't a member of the gay community, he asked, what did she know about the risks? 'Even with my therapist, who I'd started seeing when I found out Anselmo was positive in 1991 and I still see today, I talked about everything with him. But I couldn't talk about the cruising because it was so stupid,' Michael admitted. 'He's an amazing man and he's helped to change my life. But one of the best things about LA [the park incident in 1998] happening is that I talked to him about that and it stopped it being so covert and compulsive. And fun, if I'm being honest. The compulsion to do something stupid was what kept me doing it. I would tend to do it when I was feeling bad about something. I would tend to do it as a form of self-punishment. I don't do that any more. I wish to God I could get that excited about it! Don't knock a bit of guilt. Catholics have the best sex on earth, I'm told.'

The fallout from these reports was that Kenny had called off their wedding, at least according to 'a source' at the *Daily Mail*. 'Gay Lover Tells George: The Wedding's Off', read the headline on 25 July. As ever George was quick to put the record straight. This time he called *Richard & Judy* so that he could talk about it live on air. 'The truth is, the *News of the World* knows I've got no issue with cruising, I've talked about it many times,' he said. 'So they have to make me look like the gay Wayne Rooney! Much as I don't want be ageist or fattist, it's dark up there, but it's not that dark!' By this point he had husband-and-wife hosts Richard Madeley and

Judy Finnegan in fits of laughter. This didn't sound like a man on the verge of some kind of breakdown.

'I've no idea who that guy was,' he continued. 'I don't even think the people at Fleet Street think the words "shame" and "depravity" are real. There can't be any shame in a situation unless the person is ashamed, and I'm certainly not that. I think it's a very sad thing for young gay people growing up, that words like "depravity" are available to Rupert Murdoch when he wants to have a go at a gay person. I think that should change, I really genuinely do. But from my own point of view, I just don't want people to think my life is troubled, when it's not. And I think I should be able to be what I am to young gay people, which is a man that's managed to succeed in the industry for 25 years. You know, I've just had the fastest-selling tour of perhaps all time in Britain. And I'm not allowed to be that to young gay people, I have to be somehow troubled.'

The wedding, he said, hadn't been called off. They'd simply decided to delay it to avoid the inevitable media circus: 'We didn't have our wedding because we knew at this point in time, with me just about to go on tour, with all the rubbish I've had to put up with the last six months, we wouldn't get a nice, private, small wedding; which is what I want. I didn't want a big, lavish wedding. I wanted something small and quiet. But I don't even think we'd get away with that. There'd be intrusion. So we postponed it on that basis.

'There's never any question of taking anyone for a drink or for dinner,' he explained about his more casual encounters. 'There have to be some boundaries somewhere. And those are ours.' (That is, his and Goss'.) 'There's never any question of spending the evening with someone. It's just sex. I get puzzled by gay men who do lie and cheat one another. OK, with Kenny and I it was harder at the beginning. But I think that was more the fact we didn't have any experience. I think it's a wasted opportunity not to be directly honest with one person in your life. Kenny is the one person in my life I can be absolutely honest about absolutely everything with. And you have an opportunity to do that as a gay man that I'm not sure you do as a straight man. Men understand each other better than men and women do.'

In 2004 there had been a very public falling out between Michael and Elton John; John hadn't been too kind about *Patience* on its release and was widely reported to have said, 'George is in a strange place. There appears to be a deep-rooted unhappiness in his life. He needs to get out more.' Such comments seemed especially curious because Michael was donating his US royalties from the album to the Elton John AIDS Foundation. Michael decided to reply through the press, writing an open letter to *Heat* magazine to give his side of the story:

> Elton John knows very little about George Michael and that's a fact. Contrary to the public's impression, we have spoken rarely in the last 10 years and what would probably surprise most people is that we have never discussed my private life. Ever. Sadly, I was always aware that Elton's circle of friends was the busiest rumour mill in town and that respect for my private life was not exactly guaranteed. So, we never became genuinely close, which is very sad. And to this day, most of what Elton thinks he knows about my life is pretty much limited to the gossip he hears on the 'gay grapevine' which is, as you can imagine, lovely stuff. Other than that, he knows I don't like to tour, I smoke too much pot and my albums still have a habit of going to Number One. In other words, he knows as much as most of my fans. What he doesn't know is I have rarely been as happy and confident as I am today, thanks to my partner Kenny and the continued support of my fans. If I stay at home too much, if anything it is because I am too contented right now. I have travelled the world many times and at 41, I think I have earned the right to a quiet life, which I truly love, and maybe Elton just can't relate to that. He makes millions playing those old classics

day in and day out, whereas my drive and passion is still about the future and the songs I have yet to write for the public.

Now, in September 2006, it was reported that their disagreement had been resolved. Since their very public dispute the two had made up due to the peacemaking efforts of, of all people, celebrity chef Gordon Ramsay. Michael invited John to his house where Ramsay cooked them a meal, after which they were left to patch things up.

July 2006 had seen the release of 'An Easier Affair', one of the new tracks recorded for the multiple CD 'best of' compilation about to be issued in celebration of George Michael's 25 years in the music business. A double DVD and – it was announced – a tour would also be based around this milestone.

'It's amazing,' said Michael. 'I think I had a clue that things would last, probably from about two or three years into it, but I would never have dreamed of anything like this as a child. I saw as far as *Top of the Pops*, and didn't really see beyond that. I thought about being a star and never thought about the possibility of being in that position for 25 years. Because in 1980 so few people were in that position, whereas there are quite a few of us now. Just the numbers, just being able to round it off to a quarter of a century, feels like an achievement to me. And it feels like the right number to put on what I think of as my real mainstream commercial career. Because I definitely want things to go off in another direction after this. I want to explore things differently.'

The announcement of a tour had taken most people by surprise, especially after the singer's troubled news headlines and the lack of a new album. It was his first tour of any kind since the Cover to Cover dates 15 years before, and the first tour on which he would sing his own material for 18 years, since the Faith tour in 1988. Now, secure in his relationship with Kenny and having served his grieving time for his mother and lover, he felt that it was time to play shows again.

But he wasn't quite ready to jump into a worldwide year-long jaunt. 'The tour is going to be all over Europe. To be honest I'm still a bit nervous about a world tour, so I thought what I'd do was a European tour which allows me to come home if I need to,' he admitted. 'It's about fifty dates over the course of about three months. I always said I'd never do it again. But I have a feeling I'm going to enjoy it this time and actually it's an alternative to the career I have now. In other words, if I can establish a live rapport with an audience again I might not have to worry about releasing singles and putting myself in the way of the media the whole time.

'I think any real artist has that doubt. I don't think you can keep going for 25 years if you're not full of self-doubt. What would motivate you? You have to keep proving yourself. Now, in terms of making records and writing songs, I don't feel a need to prove myself any more. But I do feel a need to prove that I'm still alive and well.'

On 15 September, the opening night of the 25Live tour in Barcelona was packed with 18,000 fans and masses of the world's press. There was intense anticipation. After such a long absence from the stage, could George Michael still pull it off? The answer was a resounding yes.

'I must have been crapping myself really, but it didn't feel like that,' he explained. 'When I'm ready to go onstage, something else takes over. It's not fear, it's another frame of mind. The fear was all in the anticipation, I think, months before. Until halfway through the rehearsals I was truly, truly scared. Once I realised my voice was going to be great, that it sounded the same way it did before, then from that point on I started to relax. And after three or four shows, it's just been a breeze.'

Musically and visually it was a spectacular production. Dressed in a figure-hugging shiny grey suit, Michael looked a little heavier, his beard and temples speckled with grey. But he was 43 years old now. Either side of the stage were large video screens and a three-tiered scaffolding arrangement which held the large band and backing singers. Running down from high behind the stage, across the floor and over the lip into the audience was a massive state-of-the-art video screen, in front of which Michael performed and over which he walked during the course of the lengthy show. This screen pulsed and shone with colour and sparkle as well as showing photos, movie clips and cartoons. Opening night ran for almost two and a half hours and included over 20 songs, but then Michael had a lot of material he'd never toured with before. 'Flawless' got the place up and dancing, and was quickly followed by 'Fastlove', accompanied on the gigantic screen by a giant mirror ball. But the set piece that understandably grabbed the headlines took place during 'Shoot The Dog'. The screen showed the cartoon video clip as the song was performed, before a giant inflatable George W. Bush emerged from an opening in the screen. The plastic president stood with a glass in one hand and a cigar in the other for a minute or so before Michael strode purposefully up to him, took hold of the front of his trousers and ripped them open, to hoots of delight from the crowd. In doing so he caused a second inflatable to burst out, this one a bulldog wearing a Union flag waistcoat and simulating oral sex on Bush. Alongside the video's less than flattering depiction of British Prime Minister Tony Blair, there could be little doubt who the dog was supposed to be.

There were other highlights during the show. For 'Father Figure', six backing singers stepped forward to provide a glorious vocal arrangement of the old Wham! song. During 'Too Funky'

40-foot images of the supermodels from the video were shown, while 'Faith', 'I'm Your Man', 'Careless Whisper' and 'Outside' all brought the house down as the show progressed. The show ended with 'Freedom! '90' as cinema-style credits rolled up the screen. People left the arena thinking, why hasn't he been doing that for the last 18 years?

The tour ended back in the UK with shows in Manchester, Glasgow, Birmingham and two residencies in London, at Earls Court and Wembley Arena. Issued to tie in with the UK dates, the compilation *Twenty Five* became Michael's eighth UK number one album ahead of a deluge of 'best of' collections. Along with Jamiroquai's *High Times* collection, the Sugababes' *Singles Collection* and Girls Aloud's *The Sound of* . . . the top four were all compilations. Who said new music was dead?

'Just looking at people having such a good time, with the world we live in today, I look at that and I get this incredible reaction every night when I go out on stage. People go away really having had a good night. And you understand somehow as you get older how much of a privilege it is to be able to do that; to be able to change many people's evening into a great evening. I don't think I appreciated that when I was younger, so I really have this time. But apart from that I think I've just realised that I must have been a very lonely man. That's all I can think of because this hasn't been frightening or difficult at all. This has actually been a kind of worry-free experience. Kenny and I have had a great time . . . the whole thing's been really pleasant, so I have no doubt I'll be up for doing it again quite soon.'

George Michael's final musical act of 2006 was an emotional one. On 20 December he played a special free concert for NHS workers at the Roundhouse in London as a thank you to the staff who had nursed his mother during her final months. Members of NHS staff were entered into a draw, the 2,000 lucky winners getting free tickets: it was by far the smallest venue that he'd played in for many years. Comedian Catherine Tate opened the proceedings in full costume as her Irish nurse character, while Michael introduced the show, saying, 'Tonight is all about my mother. This room is full of heroes. Society calls what you do a vocation, and that means you don't fucking get paid properly. This evening is me saying thank you to you. Thank you for everything you do; some people appreciate it. Now if we can only get the government to do the same thing.' The show was another greatest hits set and brought the house down, especially when fake snow fell from the rafters during the appropriately seasonal 'Last Christmas'.

During the autumn, George Michael featured in more TV shows. Channel 5 screened the infamous 'profile' *Careless Whiskers*, marketed around the co-operation by Michael's former confidant Andros Georgiou. On a more substantial note, Michael allowed Melvyn Bragg and the *South Bank Show* crew to film his tour preparations at AIR Studios in August. At the start of the broadcast a message appeared on screen for several seconds: 'George Michael wishes to inform viewers that he has never tested positive for drink or drugs whilst driving.' Though he'd grown afraid of living in the eyestorm as he'd done in the Eighties, he didn't want to grow old and regret not touring one more time. He needed to get back to George Michael being about music. The media perception of him was that he was a man on the brink. What better way of demonstrating that he was alive and well than getting out there in person and showing people?

The show nevertheless caused another newspaper storm. 'I should learn to shut my mouth,' he quipped on the show, but he obviously wasn't taking his own advice. He openly talked during the programme about how much marijuana he smoked, and he was filmed smoking a joint. 'If I'd drunk as much as I've smoked

I'd look like Keith Richards,' he added. 'This stuff keeps me sane and happy.' The next day it was all over the newspapers. While the *Guardian* pointed out that he had been filmed smoking in Madrid, and that in Spain smoking cannabis was legal, a spokesman for mental health charity Rethink commented, 'As a huge international star any public comments will draw enormous attention. His comments are stupid and naive. Cannabis is not a risk-free drug. For a significant minority of people it is a trigger for developing a severe long-term mental illness like schizophrenia.'

Michael ended the year with a triumphant and very lucrative gig in Moscow on New Year's Eve. Russian billionaire Vladimir Potanin paid a staggering £1.7 million for a 75-minute greatest hits performance, the *Daily Mail* calculating this to be a salary of £23,823 per minute. Michael then flew straight back to London on a private jet.

At the end of the 2006 tour, Michael had been so happy about the decision to tour again that he wanted more. 'I thought, you know what, bite the bullet and do it. I don't remember it being inspired by anything in particular. I remember just thinking to myself, sitting here on my little bouncy ball that I use to keep my back adjusted, and having this understanding about the fear of regrets. I've always planned for the future in a strange kind of way, and don't live in the moment, because I'm always terrified of regret. And it occurred to me that I was going to regret not playing before a certain age at least. I don't remember why that kind of epiphany actually came to me, but as soon as it did it seemed very clear that what I should do is plan to take it on again. I wasn't sure at that point that I wanted to do it at this level, but I can't think of anything that will stop me taking it to stadiums now. It was quite a revelation.'

In the new year the news of a stadium tour brought fresh joy to millions of European fans, with Wembley Stadium being the centrepiece of his UK dates. The new dates would start at the Aarhus Stadium in Denmark on 18 May and proceed to five British stadia and then France, Italy, Belgium, Germany, Denmark, Slovakia, the Czech Republic, Sweden, Holland and Hungary. Confounding the popular press, he was emerging stronger than he had been in years.

In early 2007 the spectre of police action still hovered over Michael. At the tail end of the previous year he had been charged by the Metropolitan Police with being 'unfit to drive' after falling asleep at the wheel of his car, and was cautioned at the same time for possessing cannabis. The BBC revealed that he would be appearing at Brent Magistrates' Court on 11 January 2007 to answer the charge. In March 2007 a preliminary court case was heard, at which Michael's defence team pointed out that it was difficult to arrange a trial date because of his upcoming tour commitments. They also sought to argue that the prosecution should be thrown out due to an 'abuse of process', as no blood sample had been taken from him at the scene of the incident. The judge said, 'He is playing Wembley on 9 June, isn't he? So he is in the area anyway. I'm going to treat him as being at work and he may have to take a day off work.' And an additional charge was added, that of being in charge of a motor vehicle while being unfit to drive through drugs.

In another twist to the story, the sentencing hearing was scheduled for Friday 8 June, just one day before the momentous Wembley gig was due to take place. Advance reports indicated that such a case could carry a custodial sentence – something that would not only scupper the Wembley gig, but the rest of the summer stadium tour. Fans needn't have worried though. Judge Katherine Marshall explained that she had considered both jail and a curfew order, both of which would have been disastrous. Finally she decided that 100 hours of community service and a two-year driving ban would be sufficient punishment. Michael emerged from the Brent Magistrates' Court in north London looking happy and relieved. He read a short statement to the massed ranks of the press in which he said he accepted full responsibility for his actions before adding that he was off to do the biggest show of his life.

Despite some changeable weather leading up to the weekend, 9 June was warm and dry for the first pop concert at the new Wembley Stadium. The show was seen as such an important event that Channel 4 carried live coverage of part of the show built around an interview with Chris Evans and some archival footage. The gig proved that the George Michael stage show could comfortably transfer from large arenas to stadia with ease. A couple more monstrous video screens were added and a catwalk that led out from the stage into the audience in a large semi-circle helped to make the quieter moments more intimate. It was another greatest hits set with the songs being carefully chosen for live TV broadcast in light of the previous day's news, including 'Outside' (for which the singer donned a US police uniform) and 'Freedom! '90'. There were inflatables including a Statue of Liberty with Tony Blair's face and a missile instead of the torch.

PART THREE

•

2007–Present

ELEVEN

RETURN

2007–2008

re•turn

1 come, or go, back to a place or person.

2 give, put, or send (something) back to a place or person.

3 a profit from an investment.

'I remember realising [with] this wave of clarity how much I was going to regret not going out there and singing to people after my 20s. I thought, "Another ten years and you won't be able to stand unassisted. But for the moment, you can get out there and still do a really good show." And I just had this overwhelming sense of urgency.'

George Michael

'I just chose to come back. The truth is, the things that used to annoy me because I'd lost them in America are actually not things I chase any more. And I'm much less angry than I was. Really I was just angry about losing my partner and losing my mother. But I was very angry at the kind of rejection, and those feelings of anger are completely gone.'

George Michael

After the Wembley show, George Michael was fined for overrunning his allotted time slot by 13 minutes. As the fine was based on a tariff of £10,000 per minute, his encore cost him a grand total of £130,000. In the overall budget for the tour that was not a vast amount of money, with the tour bringing in hundreds of millions through ticket sales and an estimated £20 million for two Wembley shows alone. Norwich, Manchester, Glasgow and Plymouth were visited before the tour headed back to continental Europe and then finished in the UK in Belfast on 4 August.

The summer 2007 stadium tour could be seen as nothing but a great success, and George took time during the autumn to plan his next moves. After such a long break from touring it had been thrilling to get back on the road for such an extended time, but he wanted more. In the meantime he kept up his profile by appearing in a number of TV shows before Christmas.

In *The Catherine Tate Show* he came up against the comedian's rampant Irish nurse character 'Bernie' as she prepared for her hospital ward's Christmas karaoke party. George played himself and appeared from a screened-off bed, asking Bernie to keep the noise down when she started singing Wham! songs. Her reaction to his arrival? 'Jay-sus wept!' Later he joined her on the hospital's stage to duet in the Pogues' 'Fairytale of New York' in his striped pyjamas, all played out to raucous cheers from the studio audience.

George also appeared as himself in Ricky Gervais' *Extras Christmas Special* in a skit where he wasn't shy about poking fun at his own recent past. Gervais and another man are sitting on a park bench when Michael appears, saying he's on a break from community service and looking for 'some action'. He further explains how he got caught by the police: 'Sting called the fucking council because he's a fucking do-gooder.' When Gervais won a British Comedy Award in 2008 he missed the event but submitted a video to play when the trophy was collected. In it, he's shown in bed with George in a scene reminiscent of *Morecambe and Wise*. Gervais does his piece to camera while George, sitting up next to him in a string vest, reads a tabloid newspaper.

A final quartet of TV appearances came about when George appeared in four episodes of US crime show *Eli Stone* alongside Jonny Lee Miller. When Miller's character has a brain aneurysm, he starts to imagine George as his guardian angel. Each episode's title was also the title of a George Michael song throughout the first season. The episodes featuring George Michael aired on ABC in 2008.

In March 2008 the announcement came that many had been expecting. George would be taking his 25Live show to North America. Starting in California in mid-June the tour would last 22 dates and travel from coast to coast, including three shows in Canada. A week later the *25* compilation was released in North America as a two CD set covering 29 songs. Wham! and his solo years filled out the bulk of the material while new songs and tracks not on his solo albums were added in the form of 'Feeling Good', 'Too Funky', 'Outside', 'As' with Mary J. Blige, 'An Easier Affair', 'Heal the Pain' with Paul McCartney, 'Don't Let the Sun Go Down on Me' with Elton John and 'This Is Not Real Love' with Mutya Buena. The collection reached number 12 on the *Billboard 200*.

With the album in the charts and the tour tickets on sale, Michael set off on a publicity campaign like he hadn't done for many years. On 21 May he appeared on *American Idol* to sing 'Praying for Time'. In the show the final 12 contestants sang a medley of George Michael songs before the man himself took to the stage and, despite suffering with a cold, delivered a lesson in understated vocal power.

His honesty about why he was suddenly doing interviews was plain to see; he said he was doing them because he had never been in a situation where he needed to sell tickets: 'Of course I've waited until you guys [North America] are right in the middle of a recession to come back with a very expensive ticket, because it's a very expensive show. I'm there to absolutely acknowledge there are a million people in America that carried on seeking out my music even though it wasn't on the radio. On the one hand the industry rejected me at a certain point in America. And that was very much a directed thing; I don't think that the industry had much choice, really. But it's a combination of rejection, because you have the radio rejection and not selling albums the way I do in Europe, and yet you've got a million people who buy my stuff, even though they're not hearing it on the radio. That is really special to me.'

Those same fans came out in strong numbers to support the tour. At the opening night in San Diego, Michael thanked lawmakers for legalising gay marriage in California and put on a show similar to the ones witnessed earlier in Europe. The North American dates opened with 'Waiting (Reprise)', 'Fastlove' and 'I'm Your Man', with the first half ending with 'Too Funky' and 'Star People '97' rather than 'Shoot the Dog', which had occupied that place in the set around the world. In fact this latter song was dropped from the North American dates completely. 'Faith' got things rocking to start the second half and the usual encores of 'Careless Whisper' and 'Freedom! '90' closed the show.

At the Inglewood Forum in Los Angeles on 25 June, Bo Derek took to the stage with a birthday cake for George on his 45th birthday. *Entertainment News* caught up with the tour that night, writing, 'By halfway through the evening, Michael had the full house dancing and singing along without the need for a phalanx of dancers and production numbers with myriad costume changes. The staging certainly was impressive, full of dazzle, sparkle and rainbow hues of lighting coupled with vivid video images.

'Yet despite all the flash and glitz, the music always came first, the arrangements big but tasteful and even sometimes surprisingly understated for the more subtle songs.'

As in Europe, the tour continued to get great reviews across the States. The *Twin Cities Pioneer Press* reported on the St Paul show of 7 July, saying 'despite his occasional tendency to overindulge in vocal theatrics — appearing on the *American Idol* finale must have rubbed off on him — Michael proved to be a terrific entertainer, displaying none of the rancour he's very publicly expressed toward show business. He's also savvy at sequencing, slipping his numerous ballads (including a magnificent "A Different Corner" and a gospel-themed "One More Try") between the also numerous calls to the dance floor.

'The proceedings rarely dragged, thanks to the high-tech, eye-popping stage and Michael's obvious enthusiasm.'

One lukewarm review came via the *New York Times* which highlighted a speech George gave from the stage about his legal battles with Sony. They reported that he said, 'Artists were losing all control as the biggies got bigger, and I didn't think it was fair that I was on roughly a 30-year deal for £500. Somehow I lost that battle.

'Basically I went from being just as successful in America as I was in the rest of the world to having a fantastic career in Europe and almost no career here. That was not because Americans don't like my music. [no one would] play it to you.'

While in New York, Michael was featured in a two-part interview for *Good Morning America* discussing his understanding of women ('I grew up with two sisters, I used to date them!'), not touring ('I have two titanium rods in my back due to back problems') and Kenny Goss ('Someone to hold you when you see no point in anything, hopping around on one leg waiting for somewhere to put the other one and I felt like that for a good eight years').

By the last night of the tour, in Miami, the singer was suffering with a cold and was no doubt tired from the hectic schedule. The *Miami Herald*'s take on the show was that the audience were longing for the 1980s and George Michael, for one night at least, helped recreate them. 'He was greeted with the veneration accorded to the second coming of the disco Christ,' they reported. 'All of modern popular culture was there in a glorious, gay-Elvis kind of way, from the gospel-tinged "One More Try" with Michael in the middle of a praise circle formed by a phalanx of African-American back-up singers, to "Outside", his response to the tabloids.

'The concert was an evening with a true pro, an entertainer who understands that we all want our stars to suffer before redeeming themselves in pageantry and comebacks.'

After the last US dates in Florida at the beginning of August, Michael flew home to recharge before the final push with 'The Final' show in London. Sales were so strong that two 'final' shows were sold out at London's Earls Court, and 'The Final' became 'The Finals'. Actually, they weren't final shows at all as he played in Copenhagen as well, five days later ('The Final One'). At Earls Court, Michael told the near-hysterical crowd that he had practised over 100 times for the show; the polish was there for all to see. The *Independent* wrote, "Upbeat songs were mixed with slower numbers such as "Father Figure", which showed off his still pitch-perfect voice, even if perching on a stool left him looking like a middle-aged member of Westlife.' And that is exactly where George Michael was. He'd been around the block and more, he could still pop and rock with the best of them, and his catalogue was impeccable but he was a middle-aged man, and not afraid of getting old. His millions of fans loved him for it.

'I had no idea what a positive experience it was going to be to go out there again,' Michael said, looking back at the tour. 'I was just absolutely blown away. It was a totally different feeling than the feelings I had about playing live when I was younger. I'm so privileged to be able to stand there and have the ability to make all those people smile — and Jesus, they smile. It's a great show. I've never seen an audience have a better time. It's really the most remarkable thing I've ever seen, people's response to this show. And after two years of it, I think my entire mood about everything has been lightened.'

Unfortunately, especially given the positive vibes given off by the tour, George was soon in trouble with the law once again. This time it was another charge of drug possession. He had been spotted loitering around the underground toilets on Hampstead Heath and a park attendant called the police. When the officers arrived shortly afterwards, they found the singer in the toilet block and a search found him to be in possession of both class A (crack cocaine) and class C (cannabis) drugs.

The *Daily Telegraph* quoted a Metropolitan Police spokesman who said, 'I can confirm that a 45-year-old man was arrested on September 19 on suspicion of possession of drugs in the Hampstead Heath area. He was taken to a north London police station where he received a caution for possession of class A and class C drugs.' When he reached the station, Michael was upset as he realised that a charge might put a stop to a forthcoming AIDS benefit that he was going to attend in the US.

It was widely felt, and reported, that Michael had been fortunate to be given only a caution rather than a more formal charge. The decision on whether to proceed with a caution rests with the inspector in charge at the station; while that officer can take legal advice, it is their say that is final. In this case the fact that he had relatively small amounts of the drugs, showed his remorse and obviously could not contest the finding of the drugs meant he could be dealt with more leniently. However, Keith Matthewman QC, a retired judge, was quoted as saying, 'I cannot understand how or why someone in his position, and with his previous record, could be let off with a caution. It gives the wrong impression to young people who are thinking about drugs or are actually addicted. I find the decision appalling.'

Former Flying Squad Commander John O'Connor was quoted by the *Telegraph*: 'He should have been prosecuted. What does he have to do to be dealt with properly?' It was also pointed out that a drug addict and mother had been sentenced at Reading Crown Court just a week earlier to five days in jail for possession of a similar amount of crack cocaine. 'I want to apologise to my fans for screwing up again, and to promise them I'll sort myself out,' said Michael in a statement. 'And to say sorry to everybody else, just for boring them,' he added.

Having avoided a prison sentence, George ended the year in a flurry of activity. He flew out to play a show in Abu Dhabi as part of their National Day celebrations. The show was rapturously received in front of 30,000 fans at the Zayed Sports City. Then he surprised everyone by issuing a new composition, 'December Song', as a free download from his website. If 2008 had been quite a rush, how would he top that? It would be a two-year period he never forgot, for all the wrong reasons.

TWELVE

INCARCERATION

2009–2011

in•car•cer•a•tion

1 the act of incarcerating, or putting in prison or another enclosure.

'By the time I went to court, I knew this wasn't going to happen again. I knew I was going to lose my licence. I was assured I wasn't going to prison but I thought I was, and it was much easier to take because I felt it was deserved. This was a hugely shameful thing to have done repeatedly, so karmically I felt like I had a bill to pay. I went to prison, I paid my bill. Remarkably enough – I know people must think it was a really horrific experience – it's so much easier to take any form of punishment if you believe you actually deserve it, and I did.'

George Michael

After two years of touring and promoting, George Michael was not seen or heard of much during the first half of 2009. During this period he and Kenny Goss broke up, though George didn't announce this in public until 2011. In fact when asked, he denied it. In August 2009, just after his driving ban had expired and only eleven months after his caution for drug possession, Michael was once again in police custody. Driving on the A34 near to Newbury, Berkshire, at one in the morning, he hit the back of a seven-ton lorry. The driver of the lorry told the *Sun*, 'When he got out he couldn't walk straight. I was driving at 45 mph in the inside lane when I saw a car come speeding up behind me, its lights on full beam. It must have been doing about 100 mph and was weaving all over the place as if it was overtaking and undertaking. It smashed into the back of my cab and I felt a hell of a thump. His car went spinning across the outside lane and into the central barrier before bouncing back into my cab. He then hit the barrier again.'

George's recollection of the incident was very different from the lorry driver's. 'He came into my lane,' the singer told the *Guardian*. 'I had nowhere to go and ended up being battered between him and the central reservation, and I have to say it's fucking amazing that I'm alive.'

Michael was taken to Lodden Valley police station for questioning on suspicion of being under the influence of drink or drugs, but was released after five hours without charge. Michael denied being drunk in a statement soon afterwards. 'Neither of us was charged because we were both stone-cold sober,' he said. 'We both think the other is to blame so this is just an insurance fight. I don't want my fans or my family worried by what they are reading all over again.' Unfortunately this would be far from the last motoring incident and fans and family would have to read it all over again before too long.

In the lead-up to Christmas 2009 a DVD of the 25Live tour was being promoted. *Live in London* was a two-disc set; the first disc featured 23 tracks from the Earls Court shows filmed in August 2008, while the second disc included bonus featurettes and three further songs. George gave an in-depth interview to the *Guardian*

newspaper around this time and spoke at length about his drug history. 'I probably do about seven or eight [spliffs] a day now,' he explained (having previously admitted to smoking as many as 25 a day). He went on to talk about his police record. 'For all the doctored pictures, every single breathalyser test I've taken in my life has read 0.0, and I've never failed a sobriety test,' he said. 'I always preface this with, "I deserved to lose my licence, I *needed* to lose my licence." I had a problem with sleeping pills for about a year and a half, and I fucked up really badly. I got in the car twice when I'd forgotten I'd already downed something to try to get me to sleep. It doesn't matter that it wasn't deliberate – ultimately, I did it a second time, and I could have killed somebody. But the fact remains I was never accused of driving under the influence. I got done for exhaustion and sleeping pills.'

The *Live in London* DVD sold over 50,000 copies and went to number three in the UK Music Video Charts. Alongside this a new CD single, 'December Song (I Dreamed of Christmas)' was commercially issued for the first time, backed with 'Jingle (A Musical Interlude)', 'Edith & The Kingpin' (live at Abbey Road), 'Praying for Time' (live at Abbey Road) and the video to the title track. The single peaked at number 14 in the UK and made the Top 30 of various European charts (Belgium #26, Netherlands #18).

In early 2010 George seemed to be over the bumps of having too much time on his hands between tours and in February he flew to Australia for his first shows in the country for 22 years. The three-concert mini-tour, imaginatively titled, 'George Michael Live in Australia', played to a combined audience in excess of 100,000 and collected almost US$15 million in ticket sales at the shows in Perth, Sydney and Melbourne. With no further shows planned during the year, Michael took some time to relax down under before heading home for the British summer.

✧

London's Gay Pride festival parade took place on Saturday 3 July and Mayor Boris Johnson took the chance to lead the festivities in a photo-op at the front of the procession with the Gay Liberation Front who were celebrating their 40th anniversary. The parade began in Baker Street and worked its way through to Trafalgar Square. George Michael attended with friends and the event went well.

Michael started the drive home from the event in the early hours of 4 July, went to one of his London homes and then decided to drive to another. He never completed the journey, as he drove his car up a kerb and into a branch of Snappy Snaps photography services at the corner of Hampstead High Street and Willoughby Road. Michael's 4 x 4 left a dent in the yellow shopfront. Michael was found slumped over the steering wheel and was arrested at the scene before being bailed pending further enquiries. The crash site soon became a mini-tourist attraction. One humorous fan wrote "wham" on the outside of the shop where the car had impacted.

The court case that followed proved to be one too many for George Michael. On 12 August he was charged with possession of cannabis and proceedings began on 24 August at Highbury Corner Magistrate's Court.

During the case for the prosecution, the court heard that when the police arrived, Michael failed to notice they were there and tried to get his car into gear. When an officer banged on Michael's car window the singer was 'spaced out', 'sweating and breathing heavily.' Michael managed to give his name but when told he had been in an accident he replied, 'No I didn't. I didn't crash into anything.'

During his police interview, Michael had admitted smoking a 'small quantity' of cannabis the previous evening, and that he had also taken a prescribed sedative to help him sleep. He said that he had decided to drive between his homes in Highgate and Hampstead and had forgotten that he had taken the sedative. After being taken to Hampstead police station, the singer had failed a 'fit to drive' test. He had not been drinking, but a blood test showed chemicals linked to cannabis in his system. The prosecution put forward that '[Michael] could not remember the route he took or crashing his car. He just remembers the police officer knocking at his window.' The defence team revealed that the day after the crash Michael had started a 14-day detox programme and had begun drug counselling sessions several times a week. Sentencing was delayed for three weeks, but Michael was warned he could face jail.

The media circus descended on the same court on 14 September to find out George's fate. His barrister asked that mitigating factors should be taken into account. He explained that his client felt 'profound shame and horror' after the crash. 'He recognises his action of driving had the effect of causing other road users to be in danger and that stark fact caused him to be greatly ashamed,' he said. The barrister also added that Michael had started writing again, 'His creativity, so long hampered by his drug dependence, is re-emerging.'

In sentencing, district judge John Perkins told Michael that on the night he had taken a 'dangerous and unpredictable mix' of drugs and cannabis. He explained that he had taken into account Michael attending rehab after the accident, his remorse and his charity work. 'Your record is of concern. It shows cautions for possession of cannabis twice in 2006, a conviction at Brent Magistrates in 2007 when you were disqualified from driving for two years for your first offence of driving whilst unfit, and again a caution for possession both of class A and class C drugs in September 2008. Despite the resources at your command, it does not appear that you took proper steps to deal with what's clearly an addiction to cannabis. That's a mistake which puts you and, on this occasion, the public at risk,' said Perkins. 'I accept entirely that you have shown remorse for the offence, that you are ashamed of it, that you admitted it.'

The judge passed down a sentence of eight weeks in prison, a fine of £1,250 (plus costs) and a ban from driving to last five years. In response, Michael merely sighed and was led away while Kenny Goss at the back of the court put his head in his hands.

Nick Freeman, a defence lawyer who has represented many celebrities and sports personalities, criticised the sentence. 'This is a man in the public eye who clearly has problems,' he said. 'What good will this kind of sentence do? He obviously needs help. Locking him up will achieve nothing. It is obvious that he is being made an example of. An immediate jail term is a terrible outcome for him. The government tell us that short-term sentences don't work, so why has one been given in a case like this where treatment is clearly the best solution?'

Michael was immediately taken to Pentonville Prison, a Victorian-era establishment in Islington, North London. He was far from the first celebrity to be locked up there. Oscar Wilde had served time there in 1895 and, in more recent times, George Best, Boy George, Pete Doherty and Hugh Cornwell of the Stranglers had all been incarcerated there.

Stories of George's time in prison soon began to leak out. After his first night in Pentonville, the *Express* reported that inmates cheered as he was led into the cell block before being taken away to a high-security wing. Reporters were quick to ask questions of prisoners released the following day, and visitors going to see other inmates for any scrap of information. All kinds of snippets were reported. 'He couldn't get his shampoo open', 'He hasn't come out of his cell yet', 'He's been crying in the dinner hall'.

As might be expected, many of the inmates found it humorous that a celebrity was in their midst and they sang versions of George's songs to him, 'Freedom' being a favourite. During his first 48 hours in prison, Michael was only allowed a single three-minute phone call, which he used to speak to Kenny Goss. The *Sun* quoted an inmate as saying, 'When he went to use a payphone in the communal area he was hunched over it – distraught and in tears. He was whispering and very emotional.'

The cell that Michael had been given was nicknamed The Ritz by other prisoners. The *Daily Mirror* spoke to another inmate who explained, 'It's the best cell in the whole prison. It has duvets, cushions, even its own digital TV box. He's being treated like a king and has guards swarming all over him. The last thing they want is for something to happen to him. Pentonville is really tough and some people can't cope with being locked up.'

The singer's lawyers were soon preparing a legal bid to gain bail, but when the authorities agreed to move him to a Grade C prison they dropped their arguments. He was transferred to Highpoint Prison in Suffolk where a further 1,000 convicts were housed. It was the same prison where 'Moors Murderer' Myra Hindley was held until her death.

Shortly before his release from Highpoint on 11 October, Michael put out a statement to counteract some of the more outrageous press stories about his time in prison:

> Much as I would prefer to rise above the usual rubbish that I'm reading day after day about my time here in prison, I think it's only fair to my fans, family and friends to respond in some way even though I will be home soon.
>
> So please believe me when I tell you that in the last three weeks, there have been no tears, no anxiety, no bullying – in fact, not so much as a sleepless night for me. On the contrary, I've been treated with kindness by fellow inmates and prison staff alike and, as far as I can tell, have received no special treatment of any kind whatsoever, unless, of course, some of the guys here are letting me win at the pool table.
>
> Most of my days have been spent reading thousands of letters and post cards of incredible support from people around the world. I

promise to repay their kindness with new music as soon as I possibly can.

When he was released, it was via a rear service entrance and earlier than the normal release time of 10 am so he could get away without being hounded by the press. After making a short statement outside his London home, it would be five months before Michael spoke in public about his time in prison.

'Well, it was Pentonville,' he said. 'It wasn't a weekend break, put it that way. What did I think? Well, I didn't feel sorry for myself. I thought, "Oh my God, this place is absolutely filthy", because it was Pentonville. I just thought, "You get your head down." Those stories of me crying are rubbish. They wish that was me, but that's not me.' As for Highpoint, he explained that the last night was great as he signed autographs for every single staff member and inmate, often on prison stationery.

Michael's first musical release after leaving prison came in March 2011 when he issued a cover of New Order's 'True Faith' in aid of the Comic Relief charity. This slowed-down version, with Michael's vocals put through an electronic device, failed to gather great reviews and the single just scraped into the Top 30. For once his take on a cover version had failed to match the original.

He also filmed a segment to be shown for the charity with James Corden's Smithy character. This would become the blueprint for Corden's later, wildly successful, Carpool Karaoke. 'My original idea was to pick George Michael up from prison in a car,' explained Corden. 'And then we realised, "Maybe we'll lose the prison, but what if there's still some fun for me and George to be in the car and we'll sing some Wham! songs?"'

The scene starts with Corden telling Michael he can't attend Comic Relief. When the singer asks why, Corden replies, 'Because you're a joke, George! It's embarrassing! I can't walk into Comic

Relief with you. Comic Relief is about helping people like you! Don't put your sad face on. We'll just listen to some music.' Corden then tunes the radio until Wham!'s 'I'm Your Man' comes on and he starts singing along until George loses his bad mood and joins in too.

Another George Michael TV 'appearance' around this time was far more bizarre. Channel 5's weekday chat show *The Wright Stuff* was discussing a newspaper report that George and Kenny Goss had split up. In a strange twist, George then called the show and was put on air to dispute the story. 'It is complete bullshit about myself and Kenny breaking up,' he said. 'Don't believe this story. We've had our problems, but he's never had a problem with my lifestyle. I love Kenny very much.'

While talking on *The Wright Stuff*, Michael told the presenter that he'd watched the show every morning while in prison. He was also known to binge on episodes of *Coronation Street*, and this gave rise to a popular myth that had him spending his days watching TV, rolling joints and taking an occasional cruise up to Hampstead Heath. While some of this might be vaguely accurate, his days when not on tour were quickly filled up. Whenever he parked his car outside his London home he would usually find some fans waiting for him. It was an open secret where he lived and he'd take time to sign autographs and pose for selfies. He had dogs which he would walk, and he'd often spot paparazzi hanging around for some kind of scoop. In 2009 he spoke to the *Guardian* about an average day in his life: 'I normally get up about 10 am, my PA will bring me a Starbucks, I'll have a look at my emails,' he said. 'Then, if I'm in the mood, I'll come up to the office in Highgate, do some work, writing, backing tracks or whatever. Come home. Kenny will be here, the dogs are here. Maybe eat locally, hang out.' After the trauma of prison, it hadn't taken George long to fall back into a seemingly stable home life. For such a megastar it was a surprisingly low-key life, but one he felt most comfortable in. A glass of wine in front of the fire with his partner was more appealing than showing up at the latest film premiere. Despite this domesticity, he always managed to find his way back into the tabloids.

THIRTEEN

ALIVE

2011–2013

a•live

1 having life, living, existing, not dead or lifeless.

2 living.

3 in a state of action, active.

4 full of energy and spirit.

'I've got to tell you that I'm shitting myself here.'

George Michael

George Michael's next, and ultimately final, tour was unlike any tour he'd previously undertaken. Expanding on the jazzy roots he had explored on *Songs from the Last Century* (more than half a dozen of the songs from that album would be sung on the tour), Michael took his usual touring band and supplemented it with symphony orchestras from across the continent.

It was with bated-breath that the audience, with a wide selection of media from around Europe present, watched Michael take to the stage on 22 August at Prague's State Opera House. 'Welcome to a very different evening with George Michael,' he said. Later he added, 'I've got to tell you, I'm shitting myself.' He needn't have worried. The mix of material and the singular strength of his voice carried away any doubts about this being a posh karaoke show. Michael was at ease chatting between songs (explaining that he and Kenny Goss had split up in 2009, getting emotional when discussing the late Amy Winehouse and telling a story about nodding off on the phone while chatting to Rufus Wainwright, to name but three stories) and the audience lapped up the arrangements of the songs. The opening night saw him joined by the Czech National Symphonic Orchestra, and it was strange to see that ensemble, in this venue, backing Michael on New Order's 'True Faith'. Rufus Wainwright's 'Going to a Town', the Police's 'Roxanne' and Rihanna's 'Russian Roulette' only added to the eclecticism of the show. Later in the evening, George introduced 'Where I Hope You Are' as a song for Kenny Goss. A highlight of the show came with the string-heavy arrangement of 'A Different Corner', while an encore medley including 'I'm Your Man' and 'Freedom! '90' led to a lengthy standing ovation which the *Guardian* reported as 'entirely deserved'.

The tour made its way across Europe and after 34 shows in 12 countries it was back in London for four nights at the Royal Albert Hall. The second of these shows was cancelled because Michael had a viral infection, his heart rate was elevated and his temperature was high, but he was well enough to play the next two nights. 'I cancelled that show but didn't get myself checked out,' he explained later. 'I took it for granted that I'd just fought off flu. I went and played for another three weeks in Europe. And then one afternoon I was having lunch and suddenly felt really odd and said to everyone that I needed to go and lay down for half an hour on my own. And that's the last thing I remember for five weeks. It was three weeks of them trying to save my life and two weeks awake.'

It was ten shows later, and after travelling to Vienna from Germany, that Michael felt ill. Hours before his show in Vienna on 21 November, the singer was taken to the city's AKH hospital when he complained of chest pains. After a couple of days he seemed to be responding to treatment, but then his condition worsened due to pneumonia. His health fell to such a dangerous level that it was only revealed much later. 'There are no other health issues with regards to the patient other than the underlying pneumonic disorder, and no further measures had to be taken,' said a hospital statement to cut off any rumours about drugs at the time. 'Mr Michael is receiving precisely the same treatment as any ordinary patient in Austria would receive at the hospital for this disease.'

The rest of the tour was cancelled and, while no one was saying it in public, there were concerns that this was more serious than was being let on. As the days turned to weeks, little news was forthcoming, but then rumours of his discharge led to it being announced he was suddenly home in London. A couple of days before Christmas, he was well enough to meet the press outside his home.

It was a brief, but emotional press conference which detailed just how serious his condition had been and what he'd been through. Dressed in a heavy winter coat and scarf and understandably looking frail in front of a large Christmas tree, George said, 'They spent three weeks keeping me alive basically. I don't want to take you through all of it because some of it I want to protect my family from, and I'm sure I'll get it all written down, but it was basically by far the worst month of my life. I'm incredibly, incredibly fortunate to be here and incredibly fortunate to have picked up this bug where I did, because apparently the hospital in Austria that they rushed me to was absolutely the best place in the world I could have been, to deal with pneumonia. So I have to believe that somebody thinks I've still got some work to do here. I spent the last ten days since I woke up literally thanking people for saving my life, which is something I've never had to do before, and I don't want to have to do it again. I really, really, really, really, from the bottom of my heart, thank everybody who sent messages, and everyone in that IC unit that made sure that I'm still here today. I really can't say any more as I'm still getting over the tracheotomy. I'm not supposed to speak for very long at a time. I feel amazing. I'm very weak, but I feel amazing.'

The cancelled concerts were originally rescheduled for April and May 2012, but as his recovery eventually took longer than expected they were put back to September. George's first public appearance of 2012 came in February, when he surprisingly showed up to present Adele with the Best British Album award at the Brits ceremony at London's O2 Arena. He was given a standing ovation.

Over the summer he gave some interviews and talked in detail about the previous autumn's drama in Austria. It emerged that he'd been in a coma and under intensive care treatment and when he finally came to he had developed a West Country accent. 'They were worried I had this condition where people wake from comas speaking French or some other language,' he said. 'Mine was two days of this vague Bristolian accent and they were afraid I'd have it for life. There's nothing wrong with a West Country accent – but it's a bit weird when you're from North London.'

As the Foreign Accent Syndrome faded, he had other issues to face. 'I literally had to learn to walk again and weird stuff, because when they keep you sedated for that long your muscles literally atrophy at an incredible rate. And I just woke up like this feeble old man. I think maybe the reason I find it still a little bit upsetting to talk about is because it was so random. When something like that happens in such a random fashion, I think it takes a while to think that life is safe again.'

These anxieties would stay with Michael for some time, though now at least he had a new love to turn to for support. Fadi Fawaz was a Lebanese-born Australian hairdresser and photographer. The pair had met, depending on who you believe, in either 2011 or early 2012 and were now an item.

George's major appearance over the summer came at the closing ceremony for the London 2012 Olympic Games. The ceremony was billed as a Symphony of British Music and featured Annie Lennox, Take That, the Spice Girls and Ray Davies, among others. Michael sang 'Freedom! '90' and then the new song 'White Light', written after his illness in Vienna. The singing of a new song was claimed by some as being unnecessary promotion, but Michael was unrepentant. 'It was my one chance on TV to thank you all for your loyalty and prayers, and I took it,' he wrote on Twitter. 'And I don't regret it.' With 80,000 people in the stadium and more than 20 million watching on TV, he certainly reached a large audience and that no doubt helped the song chart across Europe and reach number 15 in the UK.

The *Symphonica* tour re-started where it had abruptly halted, with two shows in Vienna. George made sure 1,000 tickets were given to the doctors and staff of the AKH hospital. The September and October shows went well, with no obvious ill-effects of his illness hampering George's on stage presence. His voice sounded as good, if not better, than ever.

However, in private he was still suffering from anxiety and the fall-out from such a serious health scare, which as he said, was so random and unexpected. In 2017 Fadi Fawaz revealed through Twitter that during 2013 he had supported George through two 'tough' months at an Australian rehab clinic. The Sanctuary at Byron Bay, New South Wales, was reportedly a £37,000-a-week facility which treated the singer for anxiety.

In May 2013 George made the headlines again; he just couldn't help himself. This time it was one of the most bizarre stories he'd been associated with. He fell out of the passenger seat of a moving car on the M1 motorway while travelling at around 70 miles per hour. Amazingly, he suffered only relatively minor injuries. It seems he was checking to make sure his door was closed properly and must not have had his seat belt on as the door opened and he fell into rush-hour traffic. Miraculously, no following cars hit him.

The motorway was closed for 60 minutes during rush hour as both ambulances and air ambulances attended the scene. Michael had an injury to the back of his head and was stabilised before being air-lifted to hospital. 'That,' said George Michael, 'was just a very, very unlucky accident. But I've put it behind me, thank goodness. I've purposely decided not to dwell on what happened.'

FOURTEEN

REDEMPTION

2014–2015

re•demp•tion

1 an act of redeeming or atoning for a fault or mistake.

2 deliverance (from sin, salvation), rescue.

3 atonement for guilt.

4 repurchase, as of something sold.

'This is about the voice – this part of my career is about the voice. On a subconscious level [taking ill in Vienna] was very frightening and I'll probably never feel quite as safe again. But oh my God, I was just so grateful to come out alive. It felt very honest to be doing a tour like Symphonica. I like to challenge myself – to improve as a vocalist. And believe me, singing with an orchestra is one way to do it.'

George Michael

George Michael's first album in ten years. When spelled out simply like that it was quite shocking. Was it really that long? Since *Patience* in 2004 so much had happened in his personal life (Kenny / Fadi, major illness), his public life (police incidents and prison) and his musical life (two major tours).

The new release, *Symphonica*, was the culmination of the ambitious tour that had been broken up by the health scare in Austria and the complete return to touring after such a serious illness. While *Symphonica* only reached number 60 on the US *Billboard* chart (the tour never did reach North America), it did much better in Europe. It was a number one album in the UK, Poland, Ireland and Croatia and made the Top 10 in both Belgian charts (Wallonia and Flanders), while narrowly missing the top by reaching number two in Denmark, Netherlands and Italy.

Described as a live album, George Michael's vocals were recorded at the Royal Albert Hall show, while the string arrangements were added from studio recordings at AIR in London and Legacy in New York. Six original George Michael songs were supplemented with a host of cover versions ranging from dusty old-time classics to Terence Trent D'Arby.

The collection was produced by Phil Ramone, who had a client list almost like no other. Aged in his late 70s by the time he worked on *Symphonica* he had produced the likes of Bob Dylan, Stevie Wonder, Frank Sinatra, Billy Joel, Ray Charles, B.B. King, Barbra Streisand, Paul Simon and Dusty Springfield, to name just a few.

Michael was clearly in awe of the producer. 'The first track I ever sang for Phil was the Police's "Roxanne",' he recalled. 'I thought to myself, "Christ, this had better be good!" After I'd finished, he was so complimentary. It was one of the greatest moments of my life.'

Unfortunately, having worked on *Symphonica*, Ramone took ill and died on 30 March 2013, a year before the album was actually released. George Michael dedicated the album to Ramone, writing in the liner notes, '. . . he was one of the greatest men I have ever met. I will always be grateful.'

Reviews of *Symphonica* were generally good if not great. 'Competently organised and confidently delivered, it's an engaging set, but ultimately, like all live albums, essentially a souvenir,' said the *Independent*; 'the reliance on cover versions rather than the opportunity to unveil new material, as is customary, does nothing to scotch rumours that the singer has finally hung up his microphone for good.'

Rolling Stone awarded 3 out of 5 stars, and the *Guardian* did the same, saying 'Michael glides through the songs like a pop swan, foregrounding his elegance as a balladeer. Really, the album is all about technique – his and the orchestra's. To be fair, he can croon the stuffing out of the most well-worn covers, but it's at the expense of spontaneity.'

One of the longest reviews came in *Vogue*, which asked Kate Moss to turn her hand to music criticism. 'George's ability to communicate as a performer and make you feel part of a journey is a rare gift,' she wrote. 'It's an ability that defines the musical greats and, for me, it also defines what makes *Symphonica* such a beautiful album.' Moss also wrote of her long-standing friendship with Michael: 'When I was growing up, I'd dance to "Everything She Wants", and I still play it all the time. We danced to it at his house after the London Olympics, when he performed at the closing ceremony. He was doing all the George Michael moves! When I was about 12, I tried to get tickets for Wham! The Final, their last gig. I was on the phone for hours and hours, but I still didn't get one. I was so upset that I just cried. So when I was dancing with George to "Everything She Wants", with him doing all his moves, it made up for all those years of disappointment.'

To tie-in with the album, a one-hour film from the tour was issued for TV broadcast. *George Michael at the Palais Garnier, Paris* had been recorded on 9 September 2012. With the opera house being such a prestigious venue, Michael had had to pull some strings in order to be allowed to perform there in the first place. Michael became the first contemporary artist to be allowed to play there. 'It was a very great honour,' said Michael, whose friendship with former French First Lady Carla Bruni tipped the balance. 'I had lunch with her at the Presidential Palace,' he explained. 'Every other pop singer who has asked to play there has been refused.' He also donated all proceeds from the show to France's largest AIDS charity, Sidaction.

Amidst this rush of activity, it emerged that Michael was also working on songs for a new album which he hoped to release in 2015. He told *Ham & High*, 'This will be a pretty upbeat collection I think, and some of them are dance tracks. A lot of my hits kind of tap you on the shoulder and say, "Right, listen to me a few times and you'll get it." The ones that I've written for this album, though, are more like, "Well here we are – bang!" I'll be interested to know which of the tracks the public thinks will be the potential classics.'

Things were going well, but as the public had grown used to expecting, it wasn't long before another drama was unfolding for the tabloid press. In late May 2014 Michael obliged the hungry masses with another little drama for them to cover in detail. On 22 May someone called an ambulance to George's home at 8 am after a 'mystery collapse'. Two ambulance crews were dispatched and after treating the singer in his house for four hours they decided to take him into hospital where he spent several days before being allowed home.

An initial statement said he'd gone in for 'routine tests' but after a slew of newspaper coverage another statement read: 'In response to newspaper reports today we can confirm George was admitted to hospital on 22nd May. He was discharged last weekend and is well and resting. He is very much looking forward to the release of his new single in July. Given the personal nature of this matter there will be no further comment.'

Co-writer David Austin spoke outside the singer's house to say that worries about George's health were 'ridiculous'. 'He's not ill,' he said. 'He's been mixing his record over the weekend he's perfectly fine. We've been working down at Air Studios round the corner in Hampstead, that's where we do all the recordings. He's been mixing his demo tape over the weekend.'

After this incident George dropped out of public view; it would be over a year until he was in the headlines again, and they weren't the sort of headlines he would have wanted. In a 'world exclusive', the *Sun* ran with the attention-grabbing headline: 'George is a Crack Addict' on 11 July 2015. The 'story' had come from Jackie Georgiou, the wife of Andros, a second-cousin to George Michael. The article stated that George Michael was 'still being treated by the £190,000-a-month Kusnacht Practice'. Jackie was quoted talking about George smoking crack, collapsing at parties and more. She also claimed that some family members had travelled to Switzerland for George's birthday but had found that he was still drinking. 'Everyone said he's not the same. The spark has gone,' Jackie was quoted as saying. 'He is not himself after his drug use. And I know he was still drinking after a year in rehab.' Andros and George had been close when young, but it's unclear what relationship they had at the time of the Jackie revelations.

Days later the *Daily Mail* reported that Michael had checked himself into 'an exclusive addiction clinic in Switzerland' having been spotted at a Zurich restaurant. The *Mail* also passed on that German newspaper *Bild* had claimed that Michael had been at the centre 'for months'. Anonymous neighbours from London spoke of not seeing George at home during 2015 and that someone came to walk his dogs for him. A follow-up article in the *Mail* stated, 'sources in Zurich say he has been through a long-term rehab programme. They say he is now taking a break, but is expected to return to complete it in a clinic soon. He is said to have already had three months of treatment at the Kusnacht Practice, near Zurich. It costs an astonishing £200,000 a month and is reputedly the most exclusive establishment of its kind in the world.' The Kusnacht clinic was indeed exclusive and has no more than two or three patients under its care at any one time, each with their own chef.

The Michael camp responded to the newspaper allegations with a statement which raised more questions than it answered. 'We do not comment on private and confidential matters, such as anything related to previous medical treatment George may or may not have received – and we also expect you to respect his rights of privacy in such matters. However, we can say that contrary to some of the reports in the Press, George has not just entered rehab but is spending time in Europe. He is well and enjoying an extended break, as the recent photographs in a national newspaper clearly illustrate.'

They also responded directly to the Jackie Andros story by saying, 'We refer to reports that have appeared in today's newspapers concerning George Michael. Whilst it is our general policy not to comment on private matters, we would in this instance note that these highly inaccurate stories have been apparently provided to the press by the wife of a very distant family member, neither of whom has had any dealings with him for many many years.

'It is therefore unsurprising that they are so incorrect. Beyond this we have no further comment to make as the matter is now in the hands of Mr Michael's lawyers.'

George also commented on *Twitter*, saying, 'To my lovelies, do not believe this rubbish in the papers today by someone I don't know anymore and haven't seen for nearly 18 years.'

Whatever the exact truth, George had certainly been lying low away from home for many months, he had not followed up on the relative success of the *Symphonica* album and tour, and the new album seemed as far away as ever.

FIFTEEN

MEMORIAL

2016–2017

Mem•or•ial

1 something designed to preserve the memory of a person, event.

2 a written statement of facts.

'I've achieved what every artist wants, which is that some of their work will outlive them.'

George Michael

Not many facts are known about the final year of George Michael's life. The few that have emerged were concerned with relatively mundane things, such as a dispute over a neighbouring house being demolished and turned into flats with an underground car park. When the proposals were submitted to Camden Council, George Michael's lawyers opposed the application: 'The development will have a negative impact on the character of the local community. The proposal's size and much increased footprint together with the loss of trees and green space sets an undesirable precedent for future development which will have an adverse impact on the area and is out of keeping with surrounding improvements to local buildings. It will be visually overbearing.

The underground car parking is excessive as the property clearly already benefits from off street parking facilities.' Michael's large back garden of Japanese trees, steam room and swimming pool was a sanctuary he was protective of, having previously said that his house could be like a prison. 'Mind you, if you're going to live in a prison, it might as well be a good one,' he quipped.

There was no news of new material, a tour or any public appearances. The *Daily Mail* claimed that Michael had flown back to the AKH hospital in Vienna on a private jet in November 2016. Fadi Fawaz, his father and George were said to have travelled together. The *Daily Mirror* said Fawaz explained the trip was to 'sell an item', but the *Mail* named Dr Zielinski and Dr Staudinger as two doctors who saw Michael on the trip.

As late as November 2016 the *Sun* was reporting that George was once again close to Kenny Goss. An unnamed 'close friend' was quoted as saying, 'George and Kenny are back spending time together again and it's an exciting time for those of us who have been so worried over the last few years. There have been some really dark periods for George, especially during the time apart from Kenny. When he was with him, there always seemed to be something keeping him on the straight and narrow. It was never straightforward but Kenny is the love of his life and is really good for him, so this is very good news.' Yet again, even when George Michael was doing and saying nothing the press were looking for stories. Their appetite for George Michael seemingly knew no bounds.

The *Sun* published photos taken by an Italian fan on 9 December outside a London studio which showed George inside, smiling and looking somewhat slimmer than he had in a photo reported to have been taken at an Oxfordshire restaurant in September. The studio photos were purported to be the last ever published of the singer.

In the days leading up to Christmas, George was at home in London. Nile Rodgers (of Chic) said he'd visited Michael at his

London home on 23 December, but later that day George and Fadi travelled to the singer's Goring-on-Thames home in Oxfordshire. While George kept a low profile, a number of visitors were seen coming and going, along with a delivery of flowers, another from a supermarket and a worker mending an external light.

Christmas Eve 2016 fell on a Saturday and on that day Fadi was photographed coming and going at the Goring house; a photographer was stationed outside. It was the day of the annual torchlight procession through the village, and George had been spotted watching it from his window. In 2015 he had attended the midnight church service in the village, but this year he wasn't there.

The next day, Christmas morning, Fadi arrived to wake George as the two were planning a Christmas Day meal together. Fadi let himself in, went to George's bedroom to see if he was awake yet but found the singer unresponsive. He had died sometime during the night. Fawaz called 999, a call that was later leaked to the press.

South Central Ambulance arrived at the house at 1.42 pm and the police arrived soon afterwards. Fadi released a statement, 'We were supposed to be going for Christmas lunch. I went round there to wake him up and he was just gone, lying peacefully in bed. We don't know what happened yet. Everything had been very complicated recently, but George was looking forward to Christmas, and so was I.' On Twitter, he added, 'It's a xmas I will never forget finding your partner dead peacefully in bed first thing in the morning. I will never stop missing you xx'. There were conflicting accounts of where Fawaz had been before Christmas. One report said he'd spent the weekend at George's house, another source claimed he said he'd slept in his car on Christmas Eve.

With Christmas falling on a Sunday, and Boxing Day being a bank holiday, it was Tuesday 27 December before the newspapers carried news of George's death. All the UK dailies had front-page coverage, with some of the tabloids including pull-out tribute sections. Most carried photos of Fadi leaving the house on Christmas Eve.

Fans had started travelling to George's Highgate house and his Oxfordshire home almost as soon as the news broke late on Christmas night. By the end of Boxing Day there were masses of floral tributes, cards and photos at both addresses. The tributes in London would continue for weeks and swamp the area outside the house.

George's post-mortem was carried out on Thursday 29 December. Thames Valley police said, 'The cause of death is inconclusive and further tests will now be carried out. The results of these tests are unlikely to be known for several weeks. Thames Valley police will prepare a file for the Oxfordshire coroner. Michael's death is still being treated as unexplained but not suspicious.'

As expected, the tributes to George Michael came in from around the globe, from the world of music and far beyond. 'He was a major part of my life and I loved him very, very much,' said Kenny Goss. 'The beautiful memories and music he brought to the world will always be an important part of my life and those who also loved and admired him.'

George's publicist released a statement which read: 'The family and close friends of George have been touched beyond words by the incredible outpouring of love for him in the hours and days since his death. For someone whose life was ultimately about his music and the love he had for his family and friends, his fans and the world at large, there could be no more fitting tribute than the many, many kind words that have been said and the numerous plays his records have received. Contrary to some reports, there were no suspicious circumstances surrounding his death, and from the bottom of our hearts we thank those who, rightly, have chosen to celebrate his life and legacy at this most distressing of times.'

In the week following the singer's death his music was celebrated and there was a massive surge in sales of his albums and singles. By the Friday charts, six of his albums were back in the Top 100. The greatest hits collection, *Ladies and Gentlemen*, bounced up to number 8 (the first time in the Top 10 for 17 years) and 'Last Christmas' went to number 7 in the singles chart (the first time it had been in the Top 10 for 31 years). Streaming of George's music on Spotify went up more than 3,000 per cent while the iTunes Chart showed four albums in its Top 10.

As with many of the other musicians and performers who had died during 2016, questions were asked about the possibility of any unreleased music being issued. Fadi Fawaz posted a link on Twitter to a previously unreleased song called 'This Kind of Love'. The song is believed to be from an album that Michael recorded, and then shelved, in 1991. Fawaz removed the link when lawyers for the family protested. Andrew Ridgeley commented on Twitter that 'GM controlled all his output. I, nor anyone else have the right to transgress that principle.' Andros Georgiou also said he had a collection of unreleased songs written and sung by George.

Fadi Fawaz got into further difficulties with Twitter after a message stated that Michael had previously tried to commit suicide – though he said that his account had been hacked. Fadi's older brother Daniel was quoted in the *Mirror*, 'It is so bad what's happened to my brother and what they are saying. I have heard a lot in the last few weeks. But it will all come out in the end. Until then I can't say anything about this.'

At the 2017 Grammy Award ceremony on 12 February, Adele paid tribute to George Michael with an orchestral version of 'Fastlove'. However, part way through the song she stopped. 'I fucked up, I can't do it again like last year,' she said, visibly upset. 'I'm sorry, I can't mess this up for him.' The crowd applauded as she re-started a flawless rendition at the second attempt.

At the time of his death there were plans to issue a new documentary which George himself had narrated, titled *Freedom*, and also a re-issue of his 1990 album *Listen Without Prejudice*. His hope that some of his work would endure after his death would certainly be borne out.

George Michael had been blessed with a set of principles instilled by his mother and a sense of autonomy embedded from the battle of wills with his father when he was a teenager. He found it hard to live with these traits as a media figure. 'It's almost like I'm the same about my relationship with the media as I am with my music. When you look back on my career, I don't want it, musically or in terms of ethics, to be a bumpy ride. I want to be consistent. I want to be able to say that I stood up for myself as an individual and as a gay man – as a musician, the way I did against Sony. I want these things to be remembered consistently.

'That's my trouble actually. I think you can't be selective with truth and honesty so I always go that bit further than my generation does and get myself into trouble. But that's my own dysfunction. If there's a hard way to do it, do it the hard way. That's me as well.'

EPILOGUE

TRIBUTES

Stories of George Michael's generous nature began circulating as soon as news of his death was announced. TV presenter Richard Osman told how Michael had phoned the offices of *Deal or No Deal* to anonymously pay for IVF treatment that a contestant was seeking to win money for. He once tipped a student barmaid £5,000 because she was in debt. Another woman who had been on the TV show *This Morning* to discuss her problems in trying to have a child had her IVF treatment paid for by Michael. He was well known to have supported AIDS charities and supported the homeless. Here are just a few of the many tributes given to this extraordinary man.

'Heartbroken at the loss of my beloved friend Yog. Me, his loved ones, his friends, the world of music, the world at large. 4ever loved. A x x'

Andrew Ridgeley

'George Michael was one of the true British soul greats. A lot of us owe him an unpayable debt. Bye George x x'

Mark Ronson

'He was so loved and I hope he knew it because the sadness today is beyond words. Devastating. What a beautiful voice he had and his music will live on as a testament to his talent. I can't believe he is gone.'

Boy George

'I am in deep shock. I have lost a beloved friend – the kindest, most generous soul and a brilliant artist.'

Sir Elton John

'Having worked with him on a number of occasions, his great talent always shone through and his self-deprecating sense of humour made the experience even more pleasurable.'

Sir Paul McCartney

'I've loved George Michael for as long as I can remember. He was an absolute inspiration. Always ahead of his time.'

James Corden

'This year has cruelly taken so many fine people way too young. And George? That gentle boy? All that beautiful talent? Can't begin to compute this. RIP George. Sing with Freddie. And the Angels.'

Brian May

BIBLIOGRAPHY

Books

30 Years of NME Album Charts, Boxtree, London, 1993

Blythe, Daniel, *The Encyclopaedia of Classic 80's Pop*, Allison & Busby, London, 2002

Crampton, Luke and Rees, Dafydd, *Rock & Pop, Year by Year*, Dorling Kindersley, London, 2003

Crampton, Luke, *Wham! The Official Biography*, Virgin, London, 1986

Dessau, Bruce, *George Michael: The Making of a Superstar*, Pan, London, 1991

Dodd, Peter, et al, *Albums of the 80s*, Igloo, Kettering, 2004

Ellis, Lucy and Sutherland, Bryony, *The Complete Guide to the Music of George Michael & Wham!*, Omnibus Press, London, 1998

Erlewine, Michael, et al, *All Music Guide*, Miller Freeman Books, San Francisco, 1997

Gambaccini, Paul, et al, *British Hit Albums*, Guinness, London, 1994

Gambaccini, Paul, et al, *British Hit Singles*, Guinness, London, 1995

Goodall, Nigel, *In his Own Words: George Michael*, Omnibus Press, London, 1995

Kercher, John, *Wham! Special*, Grandreams Ltd, London, 1985

Mercer, Derek, *The 20th Century Day-by-Day*, Dorling Kindersley, London, 1999

Michael, George and Parsons, Tony, *Bare*, Penguin, London, 1991

Middles, Mick, *George Michael Freedom*, Chameleon, London, 1997

Napier-Bell, Simon, *I'm Coming to Take you to Lunch*, Ebury Press, London, 2006

Reynolds, Simon, *Rip it Up and Start Again*, Faber, London, 2005

Wapshott, Nicholas and Tim, *Older: The Unauthorized Biography of George Michael*, Sidgwick & Jackson, London, 1998

Yapp, Nick, *Getty Images 1980s*, Konemann, London, 2001

Periodicals and related articles on George Michael

John Aizlewood, *Q*, December 1998
John Aizlewood, *Q*, June 1999
Nick Allen, *Daily Telegraph*, 22 September 2008
Martin Bagot, *Daily Mirror*, 8 January 2017
Lynden Barber, *Melody Maker*, 1983
Jess Bell, *Daily Star*, 16 January 2017
Mark Brown, *The Guardian*, 21 October 2006
Tom Bryant, *Daily Mirror*, 27 December 2016
Alex Canfor-Dumas, *Daily Mail*, 19 March 2014
Mark Cunningham, *Sound On Sound*, 1997
Andy Davis, *Record Collector*, January 1998
Adrian Deevoy, *Q*, June 1988
Adrian Deevoy, *Q*, October 1990
Adrian Deevoy, *Q*, February 1992
Paul Du Noyer, *Q*, June 1996
A J Delafield, *Ham & High*, 5 June 2014
Paul Elliott, *Q*, December 2006
Josie Ensor, *Daily Telegraph*, 17 May 2013
Helen FitzGerald, *Melody Maker*, 28 July 1984
Rosanna Greenstreet, *The Guardian*, 11 March 2006
Rosanna Greenstreet, *The Guardian*, 9 August 2014
Allan Hall and Alsion Boshoff, *Daily Mail*, 21 June 2015
Simon Hattenstone, *The Guardian*, 9 December 2005
Simon Hattenstone, *The Guardian*, 5 December 2009
Chris Irvine, *Daily Telegraph*, 15 August 2009
Andrew Jameson, *Daily Star*, 18 January 2017
Sarah Knapton, *Daily Telegraph*, 21 September 2008
Paul Kelbie, *Independent*, 18 April 2006
Tom Kelly, *Daily Mail*, 15 September 2010
Jerry Lawton and Tom Savage, *Daily Star*, 16 October 2010
Josh Layton, *The Mirror*, 29 May 2014
Eleanor Levy, *Record Mirror*, 20 June 1987
Samantha Maine, *NME*, 12 February 2017
Shiv Malik, *The Guardian*, 17 May 2013
Clemmie Moodie, Vanessa Allen and Emily Kent Smith, *Daily Mail*, 27 December 2016
Piers Morgan, *Daily Mirror*, July 2002

Kate Moss, *Vogue*, 17 March 2014
Alex Mostrous and Sathnam Sanghera, *The Times*, 27 December 2016
Nick Parker, Neil Syson, Jonathan Reilly and Patrick Gysin, *The Sun*, 27 December 2017
Tony Parsons, *The Face*, August 1985
Tony Parsons, *The Face*, November 1987
Oliver Pritchard, *Daily Star*, 6 February 2017
Mark Reynolds, *Daily Express*, 27 December 2016
Matthew Rolston, *Rolling Stone*, 28 January 1988
Alice Ross, *The Guardian*, 26 December 2016
Pete Samson, *The Sun*, 11 July 2015
Patrick Sawyer, Lexi Finnigan and Lydia Willgress, *Daily Telegraph*, 27 December 2016
Jason Solomans, *Daily Express*, 31 March 1997
Richard Spillett, *Daily Mail*, 16 June 2015
Steve Sutherland, *Melody Maker*, July 5 1986
The Express, 16 September 2010
Adrian Thrills, *New Musical Express*, 19 June 1982
Adrian Thrills, *New Musical Express*, 18 September 1982
Alexandra Topping, *The Guardian*, 14 September 2010
Judy Wieder, *The Advocate*, 30 April 2000
Jon Wilde, *GQ*, December 1998
Unattributed, *Daily Telegraph*, 3 October 2010
Unattributed, *The Guardian*, 6 March 2011
Unattributed, *The Guardian*, 3 November 2015
Unattributed, *The Guardian*, 30 November 2011
Unattributed, *Daily Telegraph*, 23 December 2011

Websites

www.yogworld.com
www.georgemichael.com

General music articles

Associated Press, Billboard, City Lights, Los Angeles Times, Mojo, New York Times, Select, Sounds, Vox, Uncut

CHART POSITIONS

Wham!

	Australia	Canada	Germany	UK	USA
Wham Rap!	9	–	17	8	–
Young Guns (Go For It!)	4	3	20	3	–
Bad Boys	9	19	12	2	60
Club Tropicana	60	–	13	4	13
Club Fantastic Megamix	–	–	56	15	–
Wake Me Up Before You Go-Go	1	1	2	1	1
Freedom	3	5	3	1	1
Last Christmas	3	–	7	2	–
Everything She Wants	7	2	8	2	1
I'm Your Man	3	4	7	1	3
The Edge Of Heaven	2	5	4	1	9
Where Did Your Heart Go?	–	52	–	–	50

George Michael Solo

	Australia	Canada	Germany	UK	USA
Careless Whisper	1	–	3	1	1
A Different Corner	4	3	7	1	7
I Knew You Were Waiting	1	9	5	1	1
I Want Your Sex	2	2	3	3	2
Faith	1	1	5	2	7
Father Figure	5	3	18	2	1
One More Try	34	2	22	8	1
Monkey	11	6	24	13	1
Kissing A Fool	66	7	44	18	5
Praying For Time	15	1	19	6	1
Waiting For That Day	44	15	–	23	27
Freedom! '90	17	2	41	28	8
Heal The Pain	–	–	–	31	–

	Australia	Canada	Germany	UK	USA
Cowboys And Angels	–	–	–	45	–
Soul Free	91	–	–	–	–
Don't Let The Sun Go Down On Me	3	1	4	1	1
Too Funky	4	3	12	4	10
Five Live	–	–	8	1	–
Jesus To A Child	1	7	12	1	7
Fastlove	1	5	25	1	8
Spinning The Wheel	15	–	67	2	–
Older	–	–	–	3	–
Star People	–	–	64	2	–
You Have Been Loved	–	–	–	2	–
Outside	–	–	30	2	–
As	–	–	38	4	–
If I Told You That	–	–	62	9	–
Freeek!	–	–	7	7	–
Shoot The Dog	–	–	44	12	–
Amazing	–	–	19	4	–
Flawless (Go To The City)	–	–	54	8	–
Round Here	–	–	–	32	–
An Easier Affair	–	–	44	13	–
This Is Not Real Love	–	–	–	15	–
Heal The Pain	–	–	–	–	–
December Song	–	–	37	14	–
True Faith	–	–	27	–	.
White Light	88	–	21	15	–
Let Her Down Easy	–	–	–	53	–

DISCOGRAPHY

Wham! Albums

Fantastic

Innervision	IVL 25328	UK	LP	July 1983
Innervision	40–25328	UK	Cassette	July 1983
Innervision	CDEPC 25328	UK	CD	July 1983
Epic	450090-2	UK	CD	1998

Bad Boys/A Ray Of Sunshine/Love Machine/Wham Rap! (Enjoy What You Do?)/Club Tropicana/Nothing Looks The Same In The Light/Come On!/Young Guns (Go For It!)

Make It Big

Epic	EPC 86311	UK	LP	October 1984
Epic	40-86311	UK	Cassette	October 1984
Epic	CDEPC 86311	UK	CD	October 1984
Epic	465576-2	UK	CD	1998

Wake Me Up Before You Go-Go/Everything She Wants/Heartbeat/Like A Baby/Freedom/If You Were There/Credit Card Baby/Careless Whisper

The Final

Epic	EPC 88681	UK	LP	July 1986
Epic	EPC 88681	UK	2 × LP*	July 1986
Epic	40-88681	UK	Cassette	July 1986
Epic	CD 88681	UK	CD	July 1986
Epic	WHAM2	UK	2 × LP**	1987
Epic	088681-2	UK	CD	1999

Wham Rap! (Enjoy What You Do?)/Young Guns (Go For It!)/Bad Boys; Club Tropicana/Wake Me Up Before You Go-Go/Careless Whisper/Freedom/Last Christmas (Pudding Mix)/Everything She Wants (Remix)/I'm Your Man/A Different Corner/Battlestations/Where Did Your Heart Go?/The Edge Of Heaven

* = Track listing for double LP/Wham Rap! (Enjoy What You Do?) (12" Version)/Young Guns (Go For It!) (12" Version)/Bad Boys (12" Version)/Club Tropicana/Wake Me Up Before You Go-Go/Careless Whisper (12" Version)/Freedom/Last Christmas (12" Version)/Everything She Wants (12" Version)/I'm Your Man (Extended Stimulation)/Blue (Armed With Love)/A Different Corner/Battlestations/Where Did Your Heart Go?/The Edge Of Heaven

** = Limited edition boxed set in gold vinyl with T-shirt, calendar, notebook and pencil

---

Music From The Edge Of Heaven

Columbia	40585-S1	USA	LP	July 1986
Columbia	C 40585	USA	Cassette	July 1986
Columbia	CK 40285	USA	CD	July 1986

The Edge Of Heaven/Battlestations/I'm Your Man (Extended Simulation)/Wham Rap '86/A Different Corner/Blue (Live In China)/Where Did Your Heart Go?/Last Christmas (Pudding Mix)

If You Were There: The Best Of Wham!

Epic	489020-2	UK	CD	December 1997

If You Were There/I'm Your Man/Everything She Wants/Club Tropicana/Wake Me Up Before You Go-Go/Like A Baby/Freedom/Edge Of Heaven/Wham Rap! (Enjoy What You Do?)/Young Guns/Last Christmas/Where Did Your Heart Go/Everything She Wants (1997 Mix)/I'm Your Man (1996 Mix)

Solo Albums

Faith

Epic	631 522 1	UK	LP	November 1987
Epic	631 522 4	UK	Cassette	November 1987
Epic	460000 2	UK	CD*	November 1987
Epic	460000 9	UK	CD**	December 1987

Faith/Father Figure/I Want Your Sex (Parts I & II)/One More Try/Hard Day/Hand To Mouth/Look At Your Hands/Monkey/Kissing A Fool/Hard Day (Shep Pettibone Remix)/A Last Request (I Want Your Sex Part III)

* = With three extra tracks

** = Picture disc with three extra tracks

Listen Without Prejudice Vol. 1

Epic	467 295 1	UK	LP	September 1990
Epic	467 295 4	UK	Cassette	September 1990
Epic	467 295 2	UK	CD	September 1990
Epic	467 295 9	UK	CD*	September 1990

Praying For Time/Freedom! '90/They Won't Go When I Go/Something To Save/Cowboys And Angels/Waiting For That Day/Mother's Pride/Heal The Pain/Soul Free/Waiting (Reprise)

* = Picture disc

Older

Virgin	V 2802	UK	LP	May 1996
Virgin	TCV 2802	UK	Cassette	May 1996
Virgin	CDV 2802	UK	CD*	May 1996
Virgin	CDVX 2802	UK	CD**	November 1997

Jesus To A Child/Fastlove/Older/Spinning The Wheel/It Doesn't Really Matter/ The Strangest Thing/To Be Forgiven/Move On/Star People/You Have Been Loved/Free

* = Picture disc

** = With bonus disc: Fastlove (Part II)/Spinning The Wheel (Forthright Mix)/Star People '97 (Radio Version)/The Strangest Thing '97 (Radio Version)/You Know That I Want To/Safe

---

Ladies & Gentlemen: The Best Of George Michael

Epic	749 170 2	UK	2 × CD	November 1998

CD1: Jesus To A Child/Father Figure/Careless Whisper/Don't Let The Sun Go Down On Me/You Have Been Loved/Kissing A Fool/I Can't Make You Love Me/Heal The Pain/Moment With You/Desafinado/Cowboys And Angels/Praying For Time/One More Try/Different Corner

CD2: Outside/As/Fastlove/Too Funky/Freedom! '90/Star People '97/Killer/Papa Was A Rollin' Stone/I Want Your Sex/Strangest Thing '97/Fantasy/Spinning The Wheel/Waiting For The Day/I Knew You Were Waiting (For Me)/Faith/Somebody To Love

---

Songs From The Last Century

Virgin	8 48741-2	UK	CD	December 1999

Brother Can You Spare A Dime?/Roxanne/You've Changed/My Baby Just Cares For Me/The First Time Ever I Saw Your Face/Miss Sarajevo/I Remember You/Secret Love/Wild Is The Wind/Where Or When/It's All Right With Me

---

Patience

Aegean	515402-2	UK	CD	March 2004

Patience/Amazing/John And Elvis Are Dead/Cars And Trains/Round Here/Shoot The Dog/My Mother Had A Brother/Flawless (Go To The City)/American Angel/Precious Box/Please Send Me Someone (Anselmo's Song)/Freeek! '04/Through/Patience Pt. 2

Twenty Five

Sony	700900-2	UK	2 × CD	November 2006
Sony	700901-2	UK	3 × CD*	November 2006

CD1: Everything She Wants/Wake Me Up Before You Go-Go/Freedom/Faith/Too Funky/Fastlove/Freedom! '90/Spinning The Wheel/Outside/As/Freeek!/Shoot The Dog/Amazing/Flawless (Radio Edit)/An Easier Affair

CD2: Careless Whisper/Last Christmas/A Different Corner/Father Figure/One More Try/Praying For Time/Heal The Pain (with Paul McCartney)/Don't Let The Sun Go Down On Me (with Elton John)/Jesus To A Child/Older/Round Here/You Have Been Loved/John And Elvis Are Dead/This Is Not Real Love (with Mutya)

* = **CD3:** Understand/Precious Box/Roxanne/Fantasy/Cars And Trains/Patience/You Know That I Want To/My Mother Had A Brother/If You Were There/Safe/American Angel/My Baby Just Cares For Me/Brother Can You Spare A Dime? (with Pavarotti & Friends)/Please Send Me Someone (Anselmo's Song)/Through

Symphonica

Virgin	3769932	UK	CD	March 2014

Through/My Baby Just Cares for Me/A Different Corner/Praying for Time/Let Her Down Easy/The First Time Ever I Saw Your Face/Feeling Good/John and Elvis Are Dead/One More Try/Cowboys and Angels/Idol/Brother Can You Spare a Dime?/ Wild Is the Wind/You've Changed

Wham! Singles

Wham Rap! (Enjoy What You Do?)

w/Wham Rap! (Club Remix)

Innervision	IVLA 2442	UK	7"	June 1982

Wham Rap! (Social Mix) / Wham Rap! (Unsocial Mix)

Innervision	IVLA 13 2442	UK	12″	June 1982

Wham Rap! (Special U.S. Remix Part 1) / Wham Rap! (Special US Remix Part 2)

Innervision	IVL A 2442	UK	7″	January 1983

Wham Rap! (Special U.S. Remix) / Wham Rap! (Special Club Remix)

Innervision	IVL A 13 2442	UK	12″	January 1983

Young Guns (Go For It!)

w / Going For It

Innervision	IVL A 2776	UK	7″	September 1982

Young Guns (Go For It) (12″ Version) / Going For It

Innervision	IVL A 13 2776	UK	12	September 1982

Bad Boys

w / Bad Boys (Instrumental)

Innervision	A 3143	UK	7″	May 1983
Innervision	WA 3143	UK	7*	May 1983

* = picture disc

Bad Boys (12″ Mix) / Bad Boys (Instrumental)

Innervision	TA 3143	UK	12	May 1983

Club Tropicana

w / Blue (Armed With Love)

Innervision	A 3613	UK	7″	July 1983

w / Blue (Armed With Love) / Club Tropicana (Instrumental)

Innervision	TA 3613	UK	12″	July 1983

Club Fantastic Megamix

w/A Ray Of Sunshine (Instrumental Mix)

Innervision	A 3586	UK	7"	November 1983

w/A Ray Of Sunshine (Instrumental Mix)

Innervision	TA 3586	UK	12"	November 1983

Wake Me Up Before You Go-Go

w/Wake Me Up Before You Go-Go (Instrumental)

Epic	A 4440	UK	7"	May 1984

w/A Ray Of Sunshine (Recorded for 'The Tube')/
Wake Me Up Before You Go-Go (Instrumental)

Epic	TA 4440	UK	12"	May 1984

Freedom

w/Freedom (Instrumental)

Epic	A 4743	UK	7"	October 1984

Freedom (Long Mix)/Freedom (Instrumental)

Epic	TA 4743	UK	12"	October 1984

Last Christmas

w/Everything She Wants

Epic	A 4949	UK	7"	December 1984

Last Christmas (Pudding Mix) w/Everything She Wants

Epic	TA 4949	UK	12"	December 1984

w/Blue (Armed With Love) (Live In China)

Epic	WHAM 1	UK	7"	December 1985

Last Christmas (Pudding Mix) w/Blue (Armed With Love)
(Live In China)/Everything She Wants (Remix)

Epic	WHAM T1	UK	12"	December 1985

Everything She Wants

Everything She Wants (Remix) w/Last Christmas

Epic	QA 4949	UK	7″	December 1984

Everything She Wants (Remix) w/Last Christmas (Pudding Mix)

Epic	QTA 4949	UK	12″	December 1984

I'm Your Man

w/Do It Right

Epic	A 6716	UK	7″	November 1985
Epic	TA40 6716	UK	Cassette	November 1985

I'm Your Man (Extended Simulation)/Do It Right/I'm Your Man (a cappella)

Epic	TA 6716	UK	12″	November 1985
Epic	WTA 6716	UK	12″*	November 1985

* = Picture disc

Edge Of Heaven

w/Wham Rap '86

Epic	A FIN 1	UK	7″	June 1986

w/Wham Rap '86/Battlestations/Where Did Your Heart Go?

Epic	FIN 1	UK	7″*	June 1986

w/Battlestations/Where Did Your Heart Go?/Wham Rap '86

Epic	FIN T1	UK	12″	June 1986

* = Limited edition double pack

Solo Singles

Careless Whisper

w/Careless Whisper (Instrumental)

Epic	A 4603	UK	7″	August 1984

w/Careless Whisper (Instrumental)/Careless Whisper (Ext. Version)

Epic	TA 4603	UK	12″	August 1984
Epic	WA 4603	UK	12″*	August 1984

* = Picture disc

w/Careless Whisper (Instrumental)/Careless Whisper (Wexler Version)

Epic	QTA 4603	UK	12″	August 1984

A Different Corner

w/A Different Corner (Instrumental)

Epic	A 7033	UK	7″	March 1986
Epic	GTA 7033	UK	12″*	March 1986

* = Gatefold sleeve

I Want Your Sex

w/Rhythm 1 Lust mix/Rhythm 2 Brass In Love mix

Epic	LUST 1	UK	7″	June 1987

w/Monogamy Mix: Rhythm 1 Lust, Rhythm 2 Brass In Love, Rhythm 3 A Last Request/Hard Day

Epic	LUST C1	UK	Cassette	June 1987
Epic	LUST T1	UK	12″	June 1987
Epic	LUST QT1	UK	12″*	June 1987

* = Picture disc

w/Monogamy Mix: Rhythm 1 Lust, Rhythm 2 Brass In Love, Rhythm 3 A Last Request

Epic	CDLUST 1	UK	CD gatefold	June 1987

Faith

w/Hand To Mouth

Epic	EMU 3	UK	7″	October 1987

w/Faith (Instrumental)/Hand To Mouth

Epic	EMU C3	UK	Cassette	October 1987
Epic	EMU T3	UK	12"	October 1987
Epic	EMU P3	UK	12"*	November 1987

* = Picture disc

w/Hand To Mouth/Hard Day (Remix)

Epic	CDEMU 3	UK	CD	October 1988

Father Figure

w/Love's In Need of Love Today

Epic	EMU 4	UK	7"*	December 1987
Epic	EMU P4	UK	7"**	December 1987

* = Initial copies with calendar
** = Square picture disc

w/Love's In Need of Love Today/Father Figure (Instrumental)

Epic	EMU T4	UK	12"	December 1987
Epic	CDEMU 4	UK	CD	January 1988

One More Try

w/Look at Your Hands

Epic	EMU 5	UK	7"	April 1988
Epic	EMU B5	UK	7"*	April 1988
Epic	EMU T5	UK	12"	April 1988
Epic	651 5322	UK	3" CD	April 1988
Epic	CD EMU 5	UK	5" CD	April 1988

* = With free badge

Monkey

w/Monkey (a cappella)

Epic	EMU 6	UK	7"	June 1988
Epic	EMU G6	UK	7"*	June 1988

* = Gatefold sleeve

w/Monkey (a cappella)/(Extended version)/(Extra Beats)

Epic	EMU T6	UK	12″	June 1988
Epic	CD EMU 6	UK	CD	June 1988

Kissing A Fool

w/Instrumental mix

Epic	EMU 7	UK	7″	November 1988

w/Instrumental mix/A Last Request

Epic	EMU T7	UK	12″	November 1988
Epic	CD EMU 7	UK	CD	November 1988

Praying For Time

w/If You Were My Woman

Epic	GEO 1	UK	7″	August 1990
Epic	GEO M 1	UK	Cassette	August 1990
Epic	GEO T1	UK	12″	August 1990
Epic	CDGEO 1	UK	CD	August 1990

w/If You Were My Woman/Waiting (reprise)

Epic	GEOC 1	UK	CD (numbered)	August 1990

Waiting For That Day

w/Fantasy

Epic	GEO 2	UK	7″	October 1990
Epic	GEO M2	UK	Cassette	October 1990
Epic	GEO T2	UK	12″	October 1990

w/Fantasy/Father Figure/Kissing A Fool

Epic	CDGEO 2	UK	CD	October 1990
Epic	GEO C2	UK	CD*	October 1990

* = Picture disc

Freedom! '90

w/Freedom (Back To Reality Mix)

Epic	GEO 3	UK	7"	December 1990
Epic	GEO M3	UK	Cassette	December 1990

w/Freedom (Back To Reality Mix)/Mother's Pride

Epic	GEO T3	UK	12"	December 1990
Epic	GEO C3	UK	CD	December 1990

Heal The Pain

w/Soul Free

Epic	656 647 7	UK	7"	February 1991
Epic	656 647 4	UK	Cassette	February 1991
Epic	656 647 6	UK	12"	February 1991
Epic	656 647 2	UK	CD	February 1991

w/Soul Free/Hand To Mouth

Epic	656 647 5	UK	CD*	February 1991

* = Gatefold sleeve

Cowboys And Angels

w/Something To Save

Epic	656 774 7	UK	7"	March 1991
Epic	656 774 4	UK	Cassette	March 1991
Epic	656 774 6	UK	12"	March 1991
Epic	656 774 2	UK	CD	March 1991

Too Funky

w/Crazyman Dance

Epic	658 058 7	UK	7"	June 1992
Epic	658 058 4	UK	Cassette	June 1992

w/Crazyman Dance/Too Funky (Extended)

Epic	658 058 2	UK	CD*	June 1992

* = Picture disc

Too Funky (Extended) w/Crazyman Dance

Epic	658 058 6	UK	12"	June 1992

Jesus To A Child

w/One More Try (Live Gospel Version)/Older (Instrumental Version)

Virgin	VSC 1571	UK	Cassette	January 1996
Virgin	VSCDG 1571	UK	CD	January 1996

w/Freedom '93 (Live Version)/One More Try (Live Gospel Version)/Older (Instrumental Version)

Virgin	VSCDX 1571	UK	CD	January 1996

Fastlove

Fastlove (Part I)/I'm Your Man

Virgin	VSC 1579	UK	Cassette	April 1996

Fastlove (Part I)/I'm Your Man/Fastlove (Part II Fully Extended Mix)

Virgin	VSCDG 1579	UK	CD	April 1996

Fastlove (Part II Fully Extended Mix)/I'm Your Man/Fastlove (Part I)

Virgin	VST 1579	UK	12"	April 1996

Spinning The Wheel

Spinning The Wheel (Radio Edit) w/You Know That I Want To/Safe/Spinning The Wheel (Forthright Edit)

Virgin	VSC 1595	UK	Cassette	August 1996
Virgin	VSCDG 1595	UK	CD	August 1996

Spinning The Wheel (Forthright Club Mix) w/Fastlove (Forthright Edit)/Spinning The Wheel (Jon Douglas Remix)

Virgin	VST 1595	UK	12"	August 1996
Virgin	VSCDX 1595	UK	CD	August 1996

Older

Older (Radio Edit)/I Can't Make You Love Me/Desafinado (with Astrud Gilberto)/The Strangest Thing (live)

Virgin	VSC 1626	UK	Cassette	January 1997
Virgin	VSCDG 1626	UK	CD	January 1997

Star People '97

Star People '97 (Radio Edit) w/Everything She Wants (Unplugged)/Star People (Unplugged)/Star People (Forthright Edit)

Virgin	VSC 1641	UK	Cassette	April 1997

w/Everything She Wants (Unplugged)/Star People (Unplugged)

Virgin	VSCDG 1641	UK	CD	April 1997

The Dance Mixes: Galaxy Mix/Forthright Club Mix/Galaxy Dub Mix/Forthright Edit

Virgin	VSCDX 1641	UK	CD	April 1997

You Have Been Loved

w/The Strangest Thing '97 (Radio Mix)/Father Figure (Unplugged)/Praying For Time (Unplugged)

Virgin	VSCDG 1663	UK	CD	September 1997

The Strangest Thing '97 (Loop Ratz Mix)/The Strangest Thing '97 (Radio Mix)/You Have Been Loved

Virgin	VSCDX 1663	UK	CD	September 1997

Outside

w/Fantasy 98/Outside (Jon Douglas Remix)

Epic	666562-2	UK	CD	December 1998

The Mixes: Garage Mix/House Mix/K-Gee's Cut

Epic	666562-5	UK	CD	December 1998

As

w/A Different Corner (Live At Parkinson)/As (Full Crew Mix)

Epic	666870-2	UK	CD	March 1999

The Mixes: Original/Full Crew Mix/CJ Mackintosh Remix

Epic	667012-5	UK	CD	March 1999

As (Original Version) w/As (Full Crew Mix)

Epic	666870-6	UK	12"	March 1999

Freeek!

w/The Long And Winding Road

Polydor	5706974	UK	Cassette	March 2002

w/Freeek! (The Scumfrogs Mix)/Freeek! (Moogymen Mix)

Polydor	5706812	UK	CD	March 2002

w/Freeek! (Max Reich Mix)/The Long And Winding Road

Polydor	5706822	UK	CD	March 2002

Shoot The Dog

Explicit Album Version/Moogymen Mix/Alex Kid Shoot The Club Remix/CD-ROM Video

Polydor	5709242	UK	CD	August 2002

w/Freeek!

Polydor	5709839	UK	DVD	August 2002

Amazing

w/Freeek! '04

Sony	6747262	UK	CD	March 2004

w/Amazing (Jack 'n' Rory Vocal Mix)/Amazing (Full Intention Club Mix)

Sony	6747265	UK	CD	March 2004

Flawless (Go To The City)

w/Please Send Me Someone (Anselmo's Song)

Sony	6750681	UK	CD	June 2004

The Mixes: Album Version/Jack 'n' Rory Vocal Mix/Shapeshifters Remix/Boxer Mix/The Sharp Boys Hot Fridge Vocal Mix

Sony	6750682	UK	CD	June 2004

The Mixes: Shapeshifters Remix/The Sharp Boys Hot Fridge Vocal Mix/Jack 'n' Rory Vocal Mix/Boxer Mix

Sony	6750686	UK	12"	June 2004

Round Here

w/Patience/Round Here (CD-Rom Video)

Sony	6754702	UK	CD	November 2004

John And Elvis Are Dead

Sony	–	UK	Download only	2005

An Easier Affair

w/Brother Can You Spare A Dime (Live)

Aegean	82876869462	UK	CD	July 2006

This Is Not Real Love

This Is Not Real Love (Main Mix) / Edith & The Kingpin (Live at Abbey Road)

Sony	88697019792	UK	CD	October 2006

This Is Not Real Love (Main Mix) / Everything She Wants (Remix) / I'm Your Man (Extended Stimulation Mix)

Sony	88697020702	UK	CD	October 2006
Sony	88697019791	UK	12"	October 2006

December Song (I Dreamed of Christmas)

December Song (I Dreamed of Christmas) / Jingle (A Musical Interlude) / Edith & the Kingpin / Praying for Time / December Song (I Dreamed of Christmas) (Video)

Island	–	UK	CD	December 2009

True Faith

True Faith / True Faith (instrumental)

Aegean	–	UK	CD	March 2011

White Light

White Light / Song to the Siren / White Light (Voodoo Sonics Remix) / White Light (Kinky Roland Remix)

Aegean	–	UK	CD	August 2012

VIDEOGRAPHY

Wham!

Wham! The Video

CBS Fox	3048-50	UK	Video	1984

Wham Rap!/Club Tropicana/Wake Me Up Before You Go-Go/Careless Whisper/Last Christmas

Wham! 85

CBS Fox	3075-50	UK	Video	1985

Everything She Wants (Extended Version)/Freedom (Extended Version)/I'm Your Man (Extended Version)

Wham! The Final

CBS Fox	3846-50	UK	Video	1986

The Edge Of Heaven/A Different Corner/Where Did Your Heart Go?

Wham! In China: Foreign Skies

CBS Fox	7142-40	UK	Video	1986

Bad Boys/Club Tropicana/Blue/Wake Me Up Before You Go-Go/Ray Of Sunshine/Young Guns (Go For It)/Careless Whisper/Everything She Wants/Like A Baby/If You Were There/Runaway/Love Machine

Wham! The Best Of

Sony	200777-2	UK	Video	December 1997
Sony	200777-9	UK	DVD	2000

Wham Rap!/Club Tropicana/Wake Me Up Before You Go-Go/Last Christmas/The Edge Of Heaven/Where Did Your Heart Go?/I'm Your Man/Everything She Wants/Freedom

George Michael

I Want Your Sex

CBS Fox	5199-50	UK	Video single	June 1987

Faith

CMV	49000-2	UK	Video	November 1988

I Want Your Sex (Uncensored Version)/Faith/Father Figure/One More Try/Monkey/Kissing A Fool/Interview Footage

The South Bank Show

CMV	49063-2	UK	Video	November 1990

Ladies & Gentlemen: The Best Of George Michael

Sony	200850 2	UK	Video	November 1998
Sony	200850 9	UK	DVD	November 1998

Outside/Fastlove/Spinning The Wheel/Freedom! '90/Killer/Papa Was A Rollin' Stone/Too Funky/Faith/I Want Your Sex/Jesus To A Child/Waltz Away Dreaming (with Tony Bourke)/Father Figure/Don't Let The Sun Go Down On Me (with Elton John)/Kissing A Fool/I Knew You Were Waiting For Me (with Aretha Franklin)/Somebody To Love (with Queen)/Monkey/One More Try/Star People '97/I Can't Make You Love Me/A Different Corner/You Have Been Loved/Careless Whisper

Twenty Five

Sony	701978-9	UK	2 × DVD	November 2006

DVD1: Club Tropicana/Wake Me Up Before You Go-Go/Freedom/Last Christmas/Everything She Wants/I'm Your Man/The Edge Of Heaven/Careless Whisper/A Different Corner/I Knew You Were Waiting (For Me) (with Aretha Franklin)/I Want Your Sex/Faith/Father Figure/One More Try/Monkey/Kissing A Fool/Freedom! '90/Don't Let The Sun Go Down On Me (with Elton John)/Too Funky

DVD2: Fastlove/Jesus To A Child/Spinning The Wheel/Older/Outside/As (with Mary J. Blige)/Freeek!/Amazing/John And Elvis Are Dead/Flawless (Go To The City)/Shoot The Dog/Roxanne/An Easier Affair/If I Told You That (with Whitney Houston)/Waltz Away Dreaming/Somebody To Love/I Can't Make You Love Me/Star People '97/You Have Been Loved/Killer/Papa Was A Rollin' Stone/Round Here

---

Live in London

Sony	–	UK	DVD / Blu Ray	December 2009

Waiting (Reprise)/Fastlove/I'm Your Man/Flawless (Go to the City)/Father Figure/You Have Been Loved/An Easier Affair/Everything She Wants/One More Try/A Different Corner/Too Funky/Shoot the Dog/John and Elvis Are Dead/Faith/Spinning the Wheel/Feeling Good/Roxanne/My Mother Had a Brother/Amazing/Fantasy/Outside/Careless Whisper/Freedom! '90

COLLABORATIONS

Elton John

Wrap Her Up

w / Restless (Live)

Rocket	EJS 10	UK	7"	November 1985
Rocket	EJSP 10	UK	7"*	November 1985

* = Picture disc

w / Restless (Live) / Nikita (feat. George Michael) / The Man Who Never Died

Rocket	EJS 10/9	UK	7"*	November 1985

* = Double pack in PVC wallet

w / Too Low For Zero (Live)

Rocket	EJSC 10	UK	7"*	November 1985

* = Fold-out box sleeve

Wrap Her Up (Extended Remix) / Restless (Live)

Rocket	EJS 1012	UK	12"	November 1985

Wrap Her Up (Extended Remix) / Restless (Live) / Nikita (feat. George Michael) / Cold As Christmas

Rocket	EJS 1012	UK	12"*	November 1985

* = Double pack in PVC wallet

Don't Let The Sun Go Down On Me

w / I Believe (When I Fall In Love It Will Be Forever) (Live)

Epic	657 646-7	UK	7"	November 1991
Epic	657 646-4	UK	Cassette	November 1991

Don't Let The Sun Go Down On Me

w/I Believe (When I Fall In Love It Will Be Forever) (Live)/Last Christmas (Wham!)

Epic	657 646-5	UK	12"*	November 1991

* = Fold-out poster sleeve

w/I Believe (When I Fall In Love It Will Be Forever) (Live)/If You Were My Woman/Fantasy

Epic	657 646-2	UK	CD	November 1991

Two Rooms

Mercury	845 749-2	UK	CD	October 1991

Includes 'Tonight (Live)'

Aretha Franklin

I Knew You Were Waiting (For Me)

w/I Knew You Were Waiting (For Me) (Instrumental)

Epic	DUET 2	UK	7"	January 1987

(Extended Remix) w/ I Knew You Were Waiting (For Me) (Percappella)/I Knew You Were Waiting (For Me) (Edited Remix)

Epic	DUET T2	UK	12"	January 1987

Boogie Box High

Jive Talkin'

w/Rhythm Talkin' (Part 1)

Hardback	BOSS 4	UK	7"	July 1987

w/Jive Talkin' (Fever Pitch Mix)/Rhythm Talkin' (Part 1)

Hardback	BOSS 4	UK	12"	July 1987

Queen

Five Live EP

Parlophone	R 6340	UK	7"	April 1993
Parlophone	TCR 6340	UK	Cassette	April 1993
Parlophone	CDRS 6340	UK	CD	April 1993

Somebody To Love / Killer / Papa Was A Rollin' Stone / These Are The Days Of Our Lives / Calling You

Parlophone	12R 6340	UK	12"	April 1993

Killer / Papa Was A Rollin' Stone (PM Dawn Remix) / Papa Was A Rollin' Stone (PM Dawn Remix Instrumental)

Parlophone	CDR 6340	UK	CD*	April 1993

Killer / Papa Was A Rollin' Stone (PM Dawn Remix) / Somebody To Love / These Are The Days Of Our Lives
* = Picture disc

Deon Estus

Heaven Help Me

w/ It's A Party

Mika	MIKA 2	UK	7"	April 1989
Mika	MIKAG 2	UK	7"*	April 1989

* = Poster sleeve

w/ It's a Party / Love Can't Wait

Mika	MIKAZ 2	UK	12"	April 1989

w/ It's a Party / Love Can't Wait / Me Or The Rumours (Instrumental)

Mika	871 539-2	UK	CD	April 1989

Toby Bourke

Waltz Away Dreaming

w/Things I Said Tonight (Live Demo Version)

Aegean	AEC 01	UK	Cassette	May 1997
Aegean	AECD 01	UK	CD	May 1997

Whitney Houston

If I Told You That

w/If I Told You That (Johnny Douglas Mix)/Fine (Album Version)

Arista	176628 2	UK	CD	2000

THANKS AND ACKNOWLEDGEMENTS

Having finally got the kids to bed just before 11 pm on Christmas night, I sat down and turned on the TV to see the late-night news. Like everyone else I was well aware that 2016 had seen what seemed to be an unprecedented number of celebrity deaths, but that still didn't prepare me for the shock of the headlines that night. George Michael dead at the age of 53. Within half an hour I'd had an email from a TV station in Moscow asking for a Skype interview. I politely declined.

Once the natural shock had worn off I thought a lot about George Michael's life and career over the next few days; indeed it was hard not to with all the TV coverage, newspaper headlines and internet saturation. It came as no surprise to find that people wanted to know his story, nor that the original version of this book, which had been mostly written in 2006, was in need of an update.

I'd like to thank Carolyn, Milan and Cece for their support and Alice at Piatkus for the original commission. For this updated volume my gratitude goes to Jillian Young, Kate Hibbert, Andy Hine and all at Piatkus / Little, Brown who helped get it into your hands. Finally, this book would never have been possible without the use of the Allcock office!

Rob Jovanovic
February 2017

PICTURE CREDITS

Every effort has been made to identify and acknowledge the copyright holders. Any errors or omissions will be rectified in future editions provided that written notification is made to the publishers.

Page 1 top Frank Hopkinson
Page 1 bottom © Dave Hogan/Getty Images
Page 2 top left © Silverhub/REX/Shutterstock
Page 2 top right © Dave Hogan/Getty Images
Page 2 bottom © GRANT/AP/REX/Shutterstock
Page 3 top © Fiona Hanson/PA Archive/PA Images
Page 3 bottom © Duncan Raban/EMPICS Entertainment
Page 4 © REX/Shutterstock
Page 5 top left © Andrew Shawaf/Getty Images
Page 5 top right © KMazur/Getty images
Page 5 bottom right © Robichon/EPA/REX/Shutterstock
Page 5 bottom left © Dave Benett/Getty Images
Page 6 top left © Chapman/REX/Shutterstock
Page 6 top right © Richard Young/REX/Shutterstock
Page 6 bottom © Ken McKay/REX/Shutterstock
Page 7 top © Andy Rain/EPA/REX/Shutterstock
Page 7 bottom left © Newspix/REX/Shutterstock
Page 7 bottom right © NIVIERE/SIPA/REX/Shutterstock
Page 8 top © Jack Taylor/Stringer/Getty Images
Page 8 bottom © Geoffrey Swain/REX/Shutterstock

INDEX